Library of
Davidson College

Graded Problems in Computer Science

Andrew D. McGettrick
University of Strathclyde
Glasgow, Scotland

Peter D. Smith
California State University
Northridge, California, U.S.A.

ADDISON-WESLEY PUBLISHING COMPANY
London · Reading, Massachusetts · Menlo Park, California · Amsterdam
Don Mills, Ontario · Manila · Singapore · Sydney · Tokyo

To Peter James and
Peter, Bobby, Kate and Andrew

©1983 Addison-Wesley Publishers Limited

All rights reserved. No part of this publication may be reproduced, stored in a retrieval system, or transmitted in any form or by any means, electronic, mechanical, photocopying, recording or otherwise, without prior written permission of the publisher.

Set by the author in elite-12 using NROFF, the UNIX text-processing system, at the University of Strathclyde, Glasgow.

Cover design by Alan Rudge.
Printed in Finland by Werner Söderström Osakeyhtiö, Member of Finnprint.

British Library Cataloguing in Publication Data
Graded problems in computer science
McGettrick, Andrew D.
 1. Electronic data processing – Problems, exercises, etc.
 I. Title II. Smith, P.D.
 001.6'4   QA76

ISBN 0-201-13787-9

Library of Congress Cataloging in Publication Data
McGettrick, Andrew D., 1944-
  Graded problems in computer science.

  Bibliography: p.
  Includes index.
  1. Electronic digital computers–Programming–Problems, exercises, etc.   I. Smith, P.D. (Peter DeCost),
1941–   . II. Title.
QA76.6.M3987   1983   001.64'076   82-11671
ISBN 0-201-13787-9

ABCDEF 89876543

Chapter 6 Records and structures — 162

- 6.1 Simple records — 162
- 6.2 Type declarations and operators — 164
- 6.3 Variants or unions — 166
- 6.4 Simple linked storage — 168
- 6.5 More complex data structures — 172
- 6.6 Miscellaneous exercises — 175

Chapter 7 Modules and packages — 189

- 7.1 Groups of items — 190
- 7.2 Simple packages — 191
- 7.3 Encapsulating data types — 192
- 7.4 Own variables and the use of globals — 194
- 7.5 Abstract data types — 199
- 7.6 Note on generics — 200
- 7.7 Miscellaneous exercises — 201

Chapter 8 More advanced programming — 207

- 8.1 Stepwise refinement — 207
- 8.2 Divide-and-conquer revisited — 208
- 8.3 Backtracking — 212
- 8.4 Recursive descent — 215
- 8.5 Pattern matching — 221
- 8.6 Miscellaneous exercises — 225

Chapter 9 Files — 242

- 9.1 Serial files — 243
- 9.2 Jackson design method — 245
- 9.3 External sorting — 251
- 9.4 Sequential files — 252
- 9.5 Direct access files — 254
- 9.6 Indexed sequential files — 258
- 9.7 Miscellaneous exercises — 261

Chapter 10 Interactive programming — 279

- 10.1 Simple interaction — 279
- 10.2 Computer-assisted learning — 281
- 10.3 Simulation — 284
- 10.4 Game playing — 287
- 10.5 Miscellaneous exercises — 288

References and suggestions for further reading — 305

Index — 308

Contents

Preface vii

Chapter 1 Straight line programs 1

    1.1 The nature of programming languages 1
    1.2 Abstraction 2
    1.3 Simple programs 4
    1.4 Specification and testing 6
    1.5 Miscellaneous exercises 8

Chapter 2 Conditionals 15

    2.1 Conditional statements 15
    2.2 Case statements 17
    2.3 Remarks about testing 19
    2.4 Miscellaneous exercises 19

Chapter 3 Loops 26

    3.1 Repeating a process several times 26
    3.2 Control variables 32
    3.3 While loops and iteration 38
    3.4 Other variations 41
    3.5 Nested loops 44
    3.6 Miscellaneous exercises 48

Chapter 4 Subprograms 73

    4.1 Functions 74
    4.2 Subroutines or procedures 79
    4.3 Simple recursion 82
    4.4 Divide-and-conquer 84
    4.5 Stepwise refinement 86
    4.6 Miscellaneous exercises 89

Chapter 5 Arrays 95

    5.1 Scanning arrays 96
    5.2 Frequency counts 102
    5.3 String processing 105
    5.4 Sorting and related topics 108
    5.5 Multi-dimensional arrays 113
    5.6 Miscellaneous exercises 117

Preface

The proper teaching of programming is a topic which is of concern to all who are involved with computing. Yet both introductory and advanced programming courses tend to suffer from certain rather severe deficiencies.

It frequently happens that the teaching of a programming language and the teaching of programming itself are so intertwined that they become confused. The reason for this is, of course, perfectly understandable: to write programs that have to be executed it is necessary to use some programming language. Another criticism that can be levelled at many courses and indeed many texts is that they are designed in such a way that they incorporate clever tricks which show the abilities of the teacher to good effect but which can be confusing and offputting to the learner.

Our motivation for writing this book was to produce a set of carefully graded programming exercises which gradually increase in difficulty and complexity. Within each chapter the earlier exercises should be of such a standard that everyone should be able to solve them. It is hoped that the later exercises will tax even the better students. The problems and the treatment are suitable for all those involved in their first two years of computing. We would like to think that the text would naturally accompany any first and many second courses on programming. Only such knowledge as is commonly assumed in first year college or university courses is assumed in this book.

This book is basically about programming. We have tried to make the material independent of any particular programming language. Each chapter and each section contain explanations about how to write programs but only informal descriptions of programs are provided. Throughout we have tried to adhere to (what would normally be regarded as) the elements of good programming practice. Since the difficulty, the complexity and the size of programs increase as more programming language constructs emerge, it becomes desirable to introduce exercises which might be viewed as student projects. Yet it is sensible to do this only when programmers have at their disposal the means of properly structuring their programs. Although they are not identified as such, exercises which could be regarded as projects start to appear after the introduction of subprograms such as procedures and functions.

In preparing the material for this book one important matter had to be given careful consideration. People may learn to program either in a batch environment or in an interactive environment; the latter is increasing in popularity with the introduction of relatively cheap microprocessors. Should interactive programs be included? Should the examples we provide be suitable for both environments? To cover as wide a spectrum of interest as possible we introduced a special chapter on interaction (which can be omitted if the environment so dictates); the examples in the remaining chapters can be run in both interactive and batch environments.

Unfortunately it has been necessary to limit the number of topics and the number of areas of programming that could be covered in the book. There is little or no mention of problems involving interrupts, parallel processing, graphics, and so on. Even the more interesting aspects of compiling techniques, operating systems and general systems software have had to be omitted. We hope that the few examples that do exist whet the appetite of the interested reader.

Finally we are aware of the duty to record our debt of gratitude to those who have helped in the preparation of the book. This is extremely difficult since similar questions and problems have occurred in several places; the origins of most problems are by no means clear. Therefore lest we unwittingly cause offence, we shall refrain from mentioning any names. However, special mention should be made of the help provided by Dr. Robin Hunter and Mr.Ray Welland and other colleagues at the University of Strathclyde in Glasgow and California State University at Northridge.

October 1982   A.D.McG. and P.D.S.

1 | Straight line programs

This book is about programming. Its aim is to provide a set of programming problems which cover a wide spectrum of interest and are carefully graded in difficulty. Within each section the earlier problems should be within the grasp of everyone. The more difficult problems should challenge even the more gifted.

It is intended that this text should be used in conjunction with a book or course on some programming language. It is not intended that all the resulting programs should be entered into a computer and executed. Indeed such a practice should be discouraged. Certainly it is necessary to try to execute some of the programs but only a relatively small proportion, perhaps 5 to 10 per cent. The aim is to provide practice in thinking, not typing!

1.1 The nature of programming languages

To focus attention on programming as opposed to programming languages we have decided to make the contents of this book as language independent as possible. Yet it is important to comment on the sorts of programming language facilities we assume at each stage. Fortunately there is a set of commonly used languages which includes (in alphabetical order) Ada, Algol 60, Algol W, Algol 68, Basic, Cobol, Fortran 66, Fortran 77, Pascal and PL/I. These tend to have similar facilities for simple programming and so it is possible to make some progress.

Programming languages will typically have statements, instructions or facilities whereby it is possible to

*introduce identifiers which can be used to denote variables and possibly constants of a particular kind (and perhaps within some range)

* remember or store within variables certain values or the results of calculations

* perform calculations such as the evaluation of arithmetic or logical expressions

* read information from input files or a reader and send information to output files, a visual display unit or a printer

The more common programming languages all possess such facilities.

Typically simple variables and, if they are present, constants can only be of certain specified types such as integers, reals, characters, Booleans and possibly enumeration types. Where appropriate, declarations are usually used to introduce variables, constants, etc. and associate with them a type (and perhaps range).

The kind of arithmetic calculation commonly allowed includes the addition, subtraction, multiplication and division of integers and reals. There is usually also some means of finding the quotient and remainder when two integers are divided and a means of raising a number to a power. Apart from these there are usually standard functions or equivalent facilities for finding square roots (of non-negative numbers), absolute values and signs, and for applying trigonometric functions, logarithmic functions, exponential functions and so on.

The input of information is generally controlled by READ, INPUT or GET statements and the output by WRITE, OUTPUT or PUT statements or the equivalent.

1.2 Abstraction

When a programmer has to write a program for even a very simple task there are usually various decisions he will have to take. He will be given a problem phrased in terms of familiar concepts such as mortgage rates, account numbers, salaries, number of hours worked, names, addresses, dates of birth, examination marks, train times and so on. One of the important tasks a programmer has is to represent each such item by a corresponding object in a program in the programming language. This object will typically be represented by the identifier of a variable of a particular type. How should the programmer select the identifier and type?

In choosing identifiers a programmer should have regard to the way in which the corresponding variable is to be used in the program. The identifier should be easy to remember and it should remind the programmer of the role it is to play and the item it represents in the eventual program. Long identifiers are more descriptive but are cumbersome and adversely affect the speed of thought and the speed at which the program can be written - a consideration which tends to encourage the most important property of correctness. On the other hand, short identifiers are easy to manipulate but are less descriptive. Usually some compromise is possible. At any point in a program the number of concepts under consideration should be severely limited in the interests of simplicity - the number of concepts is usually closely related to the number of variables. There is therefore usually little need for long identifiers. Note that the rules of the programming language itself, in the case of for example BASIC or FORTRAN, may force the programmer to adopt certain conventions.

In deciding on the precise representation of some item within a program a programmer must be able to focus attention on the relevant aspects of that item. He must be able to abstract the relevant qualities. In some cases this is straightforward. If for example the problem specification refers to measurements of some kind then it is natural to expect that these might be represented as real numbers held in real variables or perhaps as integers held in integer variables. Consider however a bank account number. Should this be treated as an integer or as a string of characters? The answer comes from observing the kinds of operation which the programming language will permit on integers and strings of characters. Typically

*integers can be added, subtracted, multiplied, divided and so on, as well as read, printed and compared

*strings of characters can be read and printed and

examined in limited kinds of ways, usually comparison of two strings is easy.

Other characteristics which might be important are the amount of space taken by a representation (integers are normally more compact), and any size limitations (integers are typically less than about ten decimal digits). It is not usually desirable or sensible to add or multiply account numbers. For this reason it is usually most appropriate to represent an account number as a string of characters. Note that the decision has been based both on the type, on properties such as range limitations and storage requirements and on the operations which can be performed on that type. Illegal operations (for example attempts to multiply account numbers held as character strings) will normally be detected and a message output to the programmer - no attempt will be made to perform them.
Note the crucial role played by types. Illegal operations can be detected and highlighted by a compiler so that the programmer can correct them. A somewhat similar role is played by ranges when they appear. But generally errors caused by range violation appear when a program is actually being executed. A programmer must strongly resist the temptation to alter ranges merely to accommodate particular values. Usually these errors are a symptom of some more fundamental error perhaps caused by a misunderstanding of some kind; this more fundamental error is what should be remedied.

1.3 Simple programs

For most simple programs of the kind we shall encounter in this chapter the structure of the program is straightforward:

   *introduce identifiers, initialise, etc.
   *read in information
   *perform calculations
   *print out results

Programs such as these are called straight line

programs; execution proceeds from the start and progresses step by step to the end of the program. No concept of branching, repetition or looping is present.

Example 1.3.1 Circumference and area of a circle

Given as data the radius of a circle, write a program which prints out the circumference and area of that circle. The program might take the following form

```
introduce the constant PI = 3.14159265
introduce identifiers R, CIRCUM, AREA
read value and store in R
evaluate 2 x PI x R and store the result in CIRCUM
evaluate PI x R² and store the result in AREA
print CIRCUM and AREA
```

The notation we have used here is informal but has the merit of being independent of any particular programming language. The task of translating the above into a particular programming language ought to be completely straightforward.

In the example above we have used capital letters for the identifiers of variables and will continue to do so but from now on we will omit references to the introduction of identifiers; the appearance of an identifier in an example should convey sufficient information.

Some advice should be given about the nature of input and output. Let us concentrate for the moment on output. Really the programmer ought to ask: for whom or for what purpose is the program being written? There are two situations worth mentioning.

If output is for human consumption and for reading then the output should be self explanatory and should usually contain, in some form, information about the input data it processed. This usually means that there should be text describing or explaining the significance of the various pieces of information in the output. This is the usual position with elementary programming and our examples will tend to reflect this view.

Sometimes programs provide output which has merely to be read and absorbed by another program. In this case explanatory text is often unnecessary and even wasteful.

6 GRADED PROBLEMS

All that is necessary is a set of results in stark form. However, we do stress that this is not the usual situation in real life or in this book.

1.4 Specification and testing

Associated with every problem there is usually an informal description of that problem. From this the programmer must extract a more formal program specification - an exact interpretation of what his program must accomplish. It is vital that such descriptions should be clear, unambiguous and accurate. Further it should be free of any mention of the particular variables, constants, etc. in the program. The format of the data should be clearly defined as should the nature of the resulting output. In particular the range of values with which the program deals should be clearly defined. In producing specifications of programs a programmer should pay particular attention to the use of words such as positive, negative, non-negative, and so on; he should be careful about including units of measurement where necessary; where numeric data should be supplied to a particular accuracy, this should be specified; and so on.

There is a difficulty associated with specifications and this arises from the nature of high-level programming languages. Programs written in Ada, Fortran, Pascal, etc. are intended to be portable in the sense that a program which runs on one machine should run with little or no extra effort on another machine of a different type. Now the range of numbers that can be handled may vary from machine to machine; consequently the specification details may also vary.

To overcome the need to give different specifications for different machines it is customary to write specifications in a way that is independent of particular machine limitations. A reader should then understand that if a program is run, and there are no storage violations or whatever, the result will be as predicted in the specification.

We illustrate a typical specification by describing

the form of the input and the nature of the output expected in Example 1.3.1.

> input: one non-negative number which may be presented either as an integer or as a real number possibly preceded by a + sign; the number will be assumed to represent units of some kind.

> output: two signed real numbers separated by a space. The input will be interpreted as the radius of a circle; the first number produced represents the circumference of the circle (in the assumed units) and the second represents its area (in square units). Both results are accurate to 8 decimal places.

Note that the statement of what output is produced assumes that the input is in the expected form. Should the input violate these rules, the specification says nothing whatsoever about the behaviour of the program. Basically the above can be understood by a client who can immediately determine how to use the program and can learn its effect; running the program should cause him no surprise.

We have seen that the program specification is extracted from the initial problem specification. From this it should also be clear that the final program should work for certain sets of input. Indeed sets of data to test the eventual program can be derived at the same time as the formal program specification is derived − before the program is even written. The testing stage involves running the program with certain kinds of data in an attempt to discover whether the program does what was intended. The choosing of test data is not always straightforward. For the kinds of program discussed in this chapter, tests should include typical sets of data but also peculiar or unlikely situations. In particular boundary conditions should always be tested, e.g. if an integer represents an age (at most 100) then tests should include typical ages that include both the ages 0 and 100.

It is important to be aware of the fact that there are severe limitations to the process of program testing. Tests are not a guarantee that a program is accurate;

they indicate the presence of errors, not their absence. Another activity, program proving or program verification, will demonstrate the latter. A study of this topic is beyond the scope of this book although many of its lessons are incorporated in a great deal of the material that is provided.

1.5 Miscellaneous exercises

In the exercises below the programmer should initially supply detailed program specifications for all the resulting programs. Appropriate testing should also be undertaken.

1 Code the solution of example 1.3.1 in a programming language of your choice.

2 Design and run a program to convert a measurement in metres and centimetres into centimetres.

3 Write a program to read three numbers and output them in reverse order.

4 Write a program which inputs a temperature in degrees Centigrade and outputs the corresponding temperature on the Fahrenheit scale.

5 Write a program which calculates the value of sin(x) where x is expressed in degrees. The data is just the value of x.

6 A rational number is usually written in the form P/Q where P and Q are integers. Write a program which reads a rational number in the form of the pair of integers corresponding to P and Q and outputs the equivalent real number.

7 At the beginning of a journey the reading on a car's odometer is S kilometres and the fuel tank is full. After the journey the reading is F kilometres and it

takes L litres to fill the tank.
Write a program which reads values of S,F, and L and outputs the rate of fuel consumption rounded to the nearest integer followed by the actual rate correct to four decimal places.

8 Write a program which reads a positive integer N and outputs the sum of the first N integers.

9 Write a program which reads a positive integer N and outputs the sum of the first N squares, that is 1+4+......+NxN.

10 Show how to convert automatically from centimetres into metres and centimetres by writing a suitable program.

11 In the "old days" in Britain measurements used to be expressed in yards, feet and inches (12 inches = 1 foot, 3 feet = 1 yard). Show how to convert from inches into yards, feet and inches.

12 A local council levies rates on a house as follows. The total liability is made up of a water tax and a dwelling house tax. These are computed by multiplying the surveyed rateable value of the property (R) by the water rate (W) and the house rate (H) respectively. Householders are given a choice of two methods of payment:

    (i) 10 monthly payments
    (ii) 2 six-monthly payments

In the latter case, a discount of 5% is given.
Write a program which reads R, W and H and outputs an annotated Rates Notice.

13 If an amount of money A earns R% interest over a period of P years then at the end of that time the sum will be

$$T = A \times ((100 + R) / 100)^P$$

Write a program which inputs A, R and P and outputs T.

10 GRADED PROBLEMS

14 An object falls to the ground from a height h in time t given by

$$t = (2h/g)^{0.5}$$

where g is the gravitational constant (= 9.81 metres/sec^2).

(a) Write a program which computes the time it would take an apple to hit Newton on the head assuming he was 1.37 metres high (when sitting) and the apple was on a branch 6.7 metres high.

(b) At the time of writing, a typical computer takes a microsecond to obey an instruction. Write a program which outputs the number of instructions that it can obey during the time it takes for an egg to drop to the floor from a table 1 metre high.

15 In order to pay off in N years a mortgage of \$P on which interest is charged at an annual rate of R% and computed annually, \$A must be repaid every year where

$$A = \frac{P \times (1 + r)^N \times r}{(1 + r)^N - 1}$$

and r = R/100. Write a program which reads P,N and R and outputs A.

16 Write a program which inputs 3 quantities T,N,R and outputs the monthly repayments on a loan of \$T over a period of N years at a fixed interest rate of R% when the interest is computed only once (at the beginning of the loan period).

17 A room is B metres wide, L metres long and H metres high. It has a door (B1 metres wide and H1 metres high) in one wall and a window (B2 metres wide and H2 metres high) in another. Wallpaper is available in rolls M metres long and F metres wide. Write a program which reads values for B, L, H, B1, H1, B2, H2, M and F and calculates how many rolls of wallpaper would be needed to paper the walls assuming no waste.

18 A magnetic tape has the following characteristics

   Length of tape   = 1000 metres
   Recording density   = 800 bytes per centimetre
   Reading speed   = 250 centimetres per
                           second
   Gap between records   = 25 millimetres
   Time taken to start tape moving or to stop it
                         = 10 milliseconds

   (a) Write a program which outputs
      (i) the amount of information that can be stored on the tape when the record size is 1000 bytes;
      (ii) the time taken to read the entire tape, given that the tape has to be stopped between each record.
   (b) Write a program which reads as data the five characteristics of the tape together with the record size and outputs the number of books the size of the Bible (approximately 5 million characters) that can be stored on it.

19 A farmer has a field B metres wide, L metres long. The field yields C cubic metres of grain per hectare (1 hectare = 10000 square metres). The farmer has a number of cylindrical grain silos, R metres in radius, H metres in height in which he stores the harvest. Write a program which reads B,L,C,R,H and outputs
      (i) the number of completely filled silos
      (ii) the height of grain in any unfilled silo

20 Write a program which inputs a time as a number of seconds after midnight and outputs it as hours:minutes:seconds. For example if the input were 50000 the output should be

            13 : 53 : 20

21 Convert a measurement in metres and centimetres into yards, feet and inches; convert to the nearest inch (1 metre = 39.45 inches).

12 GRADED PROBLEMS

22 Write a program which inputs 3 numbers representing the lengths of the sides of a triangle and outputs the area of the triangle.

23 Write a program which reads in a date (after 1582) expressed as

       day, month, year

and calculates the day of the week using Zeller's congruence

$$d = ([2.6M-0.2]+D+Y+[Y/4]+[C/4]-2C) \text{ modulo } 7$$

where:
 D is the day of the month, 0 = Sunday, 1 = Monday, ... , 6 = Saturday;

 M is the month number, March = 1, .. December = 10 and January and February are months 11 and 12 of the previous year;

 C is the century;

 Y is the year within the century;

 (thus for 25th February 1960, D=25, M=12, C=19, Y=60)

 and $[x]$ is the largest integer not greater than x.

24 Write a program which reads the coordinates of the vertices of a triangle and outputs the area of the triangle.

25 An automatic cash register is told the cost of a customer's purchases and then the amount of money handed over by the customer. It responds by indicating the number of notes of denomination 10, 5, 1 and the number of coins of value 0.50, 0.20, 0.10, 0.05, 0.02 and 0.01 to be returned to the customer. Indicate the nature of the program that controls the cash register; ensure that as few notes and coins as possible are returned.

26 Write a program to read an equation in the form of a string such as

$$7x = 42$$

and output its solution as a real number.

27 Write a program to read an equation in the form of a string such as

$$5x^2 - 8x + 3$$

and a value of the variable (x) and output the value of the polynomial.

28 Write a program which integrates expressions of the form x^n expressed in some suitable notation. Assume that the power is some arbitrary integer (not -1).

29 Write a program which calculates the distance of an arbitrary point from an arbitrary line. The data should consist of some suitable representation of the point and of the line.

30 Write a program which reads in 2 numbers and outputs the value of the larger. (You will probably need a function which gives you the absolute value of its parameter.)

31 Extend the program above to output the largest of 3 numbers read.

32 Write a program which computes the length of the shortest path between two points on the surface of the earth. No tunnels are allowed, hence the path must lie on the surface of the globe. Each point is represented as a pair of numbers giving latitude and longitude in degrees. Assume the earth is spherical and has a radius of 6372 km.

33 The integers 0,1,2,3,... can be arranged on a 2-dimensional plane in the form of a rectangular spiral. Thus

14 GRADED PROBLEMS

```
16 ← 15 ← 14 ← 13 ← 12
 ↓                     ↑
    4 ← 3 ← 2         11
    ↓       ↑          ↑
    5   0 → 1         10
    ↓                  ↑
    6 → 7 → 8 →  9
```

Assuming that the initial 0 is stored at position (0,0)
(a) write a program which inputs integers I and J and outputs the value of the number at location (I,J) on the plane,
(b) write a program which inputs a positive integer N and outputs the co-ordinates of the point at which N may be found.

2 | Conditionals

The programs of the previous chapter basically involved reading (which was sometimes absent), calculation and printing. Further there was no deviation of any kind from the strict sequencing of the statements; execution started at the beginning of the program and progressed statement by statement through to the end.

An increase in computing power can be obtained if a programmer is able to perform tests of various kinds and then, depending on the result of such tests, cause one part of a program or another to be executed. These tests may take the form of checks to ensure that data is in a valid format or they may be more fundamental.

Programming languages usually provide a variety of facilities for performing tests. Typically there are conditional and/or case statements. We look at these in turn.

2.1 Conditional statements

One form of conditional statement is the if ... then ... statement. Typically this will take the form

```
If test is true then
   perform some action;
end if.
```

Here the test is performed and, if it is true, the action enclosed by the 'then' and the 'end if' is executed.

The tests themselves will typically take the form of comparisons between values, for example

   (a) if N is greater than 0 then ...

   (b) if CH is a letter then ...

(c) if X is in the range A to B then ...

Different programming languages will have their own way of expressing such tests. In general, a logical or Boolean expression will be available. In particular it is likely that the execution of an action can be made conditional upon two or more tests succeeding; in another situation it can be made conditional on either of two or more tests succeeding. Comparisons will be possible between numbers, and perhaps between characters and strings. The possibilities are extensive.

The if ... then ... construction is curious in one respect. It is not symmetrical in that it causes an action to be performed in one case (namely when the test is true) but not in the other case. As such it tends to be used for dealing with exceptional cases. Let us illustrate with an example.

Example 2.1.1 Absolute value

Design a program which reads an integer N and produces its absolute value. If N is positive we merely produce N; if N is negative we remove the sign and produce effectively - N.

The following illustrates a possible program.

```
Read an integer and store it in N.
Store N in ABSOLUTE VALUE.
If N is negative then
   change the sign of ABSOLUTE VALUE;
end if.
Print N and ABSOLUTE VALUE in an appropriate
manner.
```

Another typical conditional command is the if... then ... otherwise ... form of construct. Typically this takes the form

```
If test is true then
   perform action_one;
otherwise
   perform action_two;
end if.
```

If the test is true the action between the 'then' and the 'otherwise' is executed; if this is not so, the action between the 'otherwise' and the 'end if' is performed.

Example 2.1.2 Finding the maximum

Write a program to find the larger of two real numbers supplied as data.

```
Read two values and store them in X and Y
If X is greater than Y then
   store X in LARGER;
otherwise
   store Y in LARGER;
end if.
Print out message that LARGER is the bigger
   of X and Y.
```

Before looking at some examples which use the conditionals described above we note a lack of symmetry about the if... then... otherwise... form of construction. Only one test is present though there are two sets of alternative actions. There is a form of conditional (Dijkstra's guarded command) which is more symmetrical but this tends not to exist in the present collection of more popular programming languages.

2.2 Case statements

When several alternative courses of action exist within a particular problem, the conditional constructions of section 2.1 tend to become rather unwieldy, even confusing. Another form of construction - we refer to this as the case statement - tends to be more useful and permits a decomposition into several instances which can be dealt with separately in a natural and clear manner.

The nature of case statements tends to vary considerably from one programming language to another. In some cases switches are an alternative construction. However we shall envisage a situation where there exists

18 GRADED PROBLEMS

a statement of the form

```
Case
    test 1:  action if test 1 is true;
    test 2:  action if test 2 is true;
           ...
    test n:  action if test n is true;
end case.
```

We imagine that the various tests are mutually exclusive, i.e. no two of them can be true simultaneously. When one test is true the corresponding action is then executed. If none happen to be true no action at all is performed.

It is of interest to note a certain similarity between the above and the conditional statement of section 2.1. Just as the if ... then ... construction could be given an otherwise part so we imagine another form of case statement

```
Case
        test 1: action if test 1 is true;
        test 2: action if test 2 is true;
              ...
        test n: action is true;
otherwise
        action if none of previous tests is true;
end case.
```

Let us now examine some problems whose solutions might benefit from the existence of the case construction.

Example 2.2.1 Finding the sign

Design a program which produces +1, 0 or -1 depending on whether the integer N that is supplied as data is positive, zero or negative respectively.

```
Case
        N is positive: set SIGN to +1;
        N is zero    : set SIGN to 0;
        N is negative: set SIGN to -1;
end case.
Print out a suitable message involving N and SIGN.
```

2.3 Remarks about testing

Due to the more complex nature of the programs we are now considering, certain other remarks should be made about the testing of such programs. Briefly the introduction of conditionals means that in effect there are now several possible routes through a program. Different sets of test data should be used to test or exercise the different routes through the program.

In very complicated programs there is likely to be a very large number of different routes through a program. It then becomes very tedious, even not feasible, to test them all. Then some other technique has to be devised in an attempt to master the complexity: the idea of stepwise refinement will be introduced in chapter four. In the meantime, the testing methods we have discussed above will suffice.

One of the very important roles that conditionals can play is in the testing and checking of input data. A programmer might expect that a pair of integers supplied as data should represent a measurement of length, say. Yet if the precise specification of the program merely states that a pair of integers is supplied then the programmer should include a test to check that the integers are indeed non-negative. This should be a complete and thorough test.

2.4 Miscellaneous exercises

1 Write a program which inputs 2 numbers and outputs the value of the smaller.

2 A bus company has the following charges for a tour. If a person buys less than 5 tickets they cost $1 each, otherwise they cost $0.75 each. Write a program which calculates a customers bill given the number of tickets as data.

3 Write a program which reads the co-ordinates of a

point, the co-ordinates of the centre of a circle and the radius of the circle, and determines whether or not the point is inside the circle.

4 Write a program which reads the co-ordinates of three points and determines whether or not they lie on a straight line.

5 A certain gas company computes its bills in the following manner. The number of cubic feet consumed in a 3 month period is found by taking a meter reading at the beginning (R1) and the end (R2) of that time. The number of cubic feet is multiplied by the calorific value (C) of a cubic foot to give the number of therms consumed. The charge for a quarter is made up of a fixed charge (S) plus a charge for the therms used. The first N therms are charged at P1 pence per therm and the remainder at P2 per therm.
   Write a program which reads R1,R2,C,S,N,P1 and P2 and produces an annotated bill.

6 Write a program which, given the height and co-ordinates of a stationary object, the height and co-ordinates of the starting point of an aeroplane and its heading (in degrees east of north), determines whether or not the plane will collide with the object.

7 In a certain country overseas, the post office charges parcel-senders according to the weight of their parcel. For a parcel weighing 2 kilograms or less the charge is 3.25 dollars. For each kilogram or part of a kilogram above 2 there is an additional charge of 1.05 dollars. Thus for example the sender of a parcel weighing 5.63 kilograms is charged 7.45 dollars.
   Write a program which inputs the weight of a parcel and outputs the amount the sender is charged.

8 The pension rules in a certain country state that a man receives $50 a week if he is over 65 and an extra $20 if he is over 70. A woman receives $45 a week if she is over 60 with an extra $25 if she is over 65.
   Write a program which reads in the sex and age of a

person and prints out the amount of their pension. If the person is under pensionable age a suitable message should be output.

9 Write a program which inputs the height, direction, speed and starting point of each of 2 planes and determines whether or not they collide. Assume they start simultaneously.

10 The Post Office issues postal orders for which the purchaser pays a fee. For example the fee for an order valued $10 might be $0.50. The amount received when the receiver cashes the order depends on the time elapsed from the last day of the month of purchase:
   (a) if this elapsed time is less than or equal to 3 months then the full amount of the order is paid;
   (b) if more than 3 months have elapsed then an amount equal to the purchase fee is withheld for each 3 month period (or part of a 3 month period) beyond the 3 months.
For example if a $7.50 postal order (fee payable $0.35) were bought in July 1976 and cashed in May 1977 then the Post Office would pay $6.45.
   Write a program which inputs

   (i) the month and year of purchase
   (ii) the month and year when the order is cashed
   (iii) the face value of the postal order
   (iv) the fee paid

and outputs the amount paid by the Post Office to the receiver.

11 Write a program which reads in the 3 coefficients of a quadratic equation and determines whether it has
   (a) no real roots
   (b) a single real root - if so, prints it
   (c) 2 real roots - if so prints them.

12 Write a program which inputs 3 numbers and outputs the value of the smallest.

13 A baby sitter charges $2 an hour between 18.00 and 21.30 and $4 an hour between 21.30 and midnight. She will not sit before 18.00 or after midnight. Write a program which reads in the times at which she started and finished sitting and calculates how much she earned. Your program should check for invalid starting and finishing times.

14 A student sits three examinations.
    (i) He is awarded a pass if he scores at least 50 in each of the examinations.
   (ii) He is awarded a pass by compensation in all three examinations if he passes in two, the average of the three marks is at least 50 and the lowest of the three marks is at least 40.
  (iii) He fails if neither (i) nor (ii) applies.

Write a program which inputs the three marks and outputs either PASS or PASS BY COMPENSATION or FAIL.

15 Read in three quantities A,B,C being the numbers shown on the three wheels of a one-armed bandit. Each quantity is an integer in the range 1 to 9. The payout is as follows

  (a) three wheels the same   80
  (b) three numbers are consecutive
       (not necessarily in order)   16
  (c) exactly two wheels the same   3

Output the payoff for the three numbers read.

16 Write a program which reads in four quantities a_1, a_2, b_1, b_2, these being the coefficients in the two equations

$$y = a_1 x + a_2$$

$$y = b_1 x + b_2$$

and determines whether
  (a) there is no solution to the equations
  (b) there is a single solution
  (c) there is an infinity of solutions.

17 Gauss derived a formula to determine the day (D) and
month (M) on which Easter Day falls given the year
(T).

If k = [T/100]
    a = T modulo 19
    b = T modulo 4
    c = T modulo 7
    q = [k/4]
    p = [(13 + 8k) / 25]
    m = (15 - p + k - q) modulo 30
    d = (19a + m) modulo 30
    n = (4 + k - q) modulo 7
    e = (2b + 4c + 6d + n) modulo 7

where [x] is the largest integer not greater than x
then D and M are determined as follows.

If d+e $\leq$ 19 then D = 22+d+e and M=3,
if d=29 and e=6 then D=19 and M=4,
if d=28 and e=6 and a>10 then D=18 and M=4,
otherwise D=d+e-9 and M=4.

Write a program which reads T and outputs the date of
Easter in a readable form, e.g. March 29th.

18 Write a program which reads the co-ordinates of a
point and the co-ordinates of the vertices of a
triangle and determines whether or not the point is
inside the triangle.

19 Write a program which reads the co-ordinates of the
centres of two circles and their radii and determines
whether or not they intersect. If the circles do
intersect the program should print out the common
area.

20 Simple arithmetic expressions can be written as a
constant followed by an operator followed by a second
constant. Given that the operator can be +, -, x or
/, write a program to evaluate simple expressions of
the kind described.

21 Write a program that reads in three positive integers

representing day, month and year and indicates whether or not these form a legitimate date.

22 Write a program which reads in the lengths of 3 lines and determines
   (a) whether or not they can form a triangle
   (b) if the sides can form a triangle what sort of triangle
      (1) right angled
      (2) equilateral
      (3) isosceles
      (4) scaline
      (5) obtuse angled

23 Write a program which reads in the co-ordinates of four points and determines whether or not they form a rectangle. If they do the program should print the area of the rectangle.

24 Write a program which reads in the co-ordinates of four points and determines whether or not they form a square. If they do the program should output the co-ordinates of the centre.

25 Write a program which reads the 4 coefficients (i.e. a,b,p and q) of each of 2 ellipses in the following equation

$$\frac{(x-p)^2}{a^2} + \frac{(y-q)^2}{b^2} = 1$$

Do the ellipses intersect? If so, what is the common area?

26 Write a program which given the direction, speed and starting point of each of 2 planes and an arbitrary distance (R) determines whether the distance between the planes is ever less than R. Assume they start simultaneously.

27 Write a program which given the direction, speed, height and starting point of each of 2 planes, determines the minimum distance between them. Assume the planes start simultaneously.

28 Write a program which given the co-ordinates of the vertices of two triangles as data, determines whether or not they are similar triangles.

29 In a computer graphics system, one problem is to determine which part of an arbitrary line segment is visible through an arbitrary rectangular window.
   Write a program which reads in
   (i) the position (X,Y co-ordinates) of the lower left hand corner of the window
   (ii) the width and height of the window
   (iii) the position of the end-points of the line segment

   and outputs the co-ordinates of the end-points of the visible part of the line segment (or a suitable message if no part is visible).

30 Write a program which, given the co-ordinates of the three vertices of a triangle together with the co-ordinates of a fourth point, decides whether or not the fourth point lies within the perimeter, on the perimeter or outside the triangle.

31 A triangle can be represented by three equations, each equation representing a different side of a triangle; none of the three lines may be parallel.
   Write a program which accepts data of the form specified together with the co-ordinates of a point; it should then decide if the lines form a triangle and if so, whether or not the point lies within the perimeter of the triangle.

3 | Loops

In this chapter we shall look at programs which make use of loops. These loops - also known for example as "repetitive statements", "loop clauses", "do statements" - allow a programmer to repeat certain actions a number of times. This idea may seem rather limiting but as the variations unfold we shall see that the number and kinds of possibilities present a formidable concept. Looping enables the number of instruction executions to exceed the number of instructions in the program and for the first time the true power of the computer will become available.

As we progress through this chapter we shall present sections each of which examines one particular kind of loop. Each section will be followed by a few examples which provide exercises on the material of the preceding section alone. At the end of the chapter there is a large set of graded miscellaneous problems. In some cases these will require application of a single process previously described, in other cases various ideas may have to be combined. Some of the more difficult examples may require a certain amount of innovation on the part of the programmer.

3.1 Repeating a process several times

The simplest kinds of loops are those which merely involve repeating some task a particular number of times, for example 10 times, 100 times or N times where N is some known quantity. In situations such as this, the general structure of the program will be something of the form

```
Preliminary instructions.
Perform N times
   the following task :
      statements describing the
      task to be performed;
   end of task.
Final instructions.
```

For convenience we shall refer to the task to be performed as the **loop body**. Effectively 'the following task' and 'end of task' delimit the loop body.

Particular programming languages have their own individual style of notation for the loop body and delimiters. The following are some examples (the order of languages is simply alphabetic not on merit).

ADA   : **for** I **in** 1..N **loop**
                task to be performed
             end loop ;

ALGOL 60   : **for** I:=1 **step** 1 **until** N **do**
             begin
                task to be performed
             end

ALGOL 68   : **to** N **do** task to be performed **od**

BASIC   : FOR I=1 TO N
                task to be performed
             NEXT I

FORTRAN 77 :   DO 100 I=1,N
                     task to be performed
             100 CONTINUE

PASCAL   : **for** I:=1 **to** N **do**
             begin
                task to be performed
             end

PL/1   : DO I=1 TO N;
                task to be performed;
             END

In all these cases the essential structure of the program is the same.

A frequently used kind of loop is one that requires a set of data for each execution of the task to be performed. The various sets of data will therefore appear in the input file in the order in which they have to be processed. We illustrate this with two examples.

Example 3.1.1   Solving 10 sets of equations

Suppose it is required to solve 10 pairs of simple simultaneous equations of the form

$$a_1 x + b_1 y = c_1$$
$$a_2 x + b_2 y = c_2$$

where each of $a_1, b_1, c_1, a_2, b_2, c_2$ is supplied as data.

The data for the complete program will consist of 60 numbers. The first set of 6 will represent $a_1, b_1, c_1, a_2, b_2, c_2$ for the first set of equations, the next set of 6 will define the second pair of equations and so on. The program therefore takes the form

```
Perform 10 times
  the following task :
    read a₁,b₁,c₁,a₂,b₂,c₂;

    solve the simultaneous equations;
    print results;
  end of task.
```

The task can be coded simply (see exercise 16 in chapter two).

One of the qualities which good programs should exhibit is a certain sensible amount of flexibility. The example above does not possess this. If the occasion arose when just 4 pairs of simultaneous equations had to be solved then either a different program would have to be written or 6 sets of superfluous numbers would have to be invented. It is desirable to arrange that some arbitrary number of pairs of equations can be solved. In the next example, we show how this can be accomplished.

Example 3.1.2   Solving N sets of equations

It is imperative that the program is given information about the number of pairs of equations to be solved. Accordingly we shall arrange that the first item of data is the integer N (that is 10 or 4 or whatever) giving this information. This will be followed by 6*N numbers, one set of 6 for each of the N pairs of equations.

The general structure of the program becomes

```
Read N.
Perform N times
   the following task:
      .
      .
   end of task.
```

Performing the task involves reading data, solving the appropriate equations and then printing the result.

In the examples above, the values that the variables have in one execution of the loop bear no relationship to the values in any other execution. There is no concept of a previously computed value being carried forward for use in the next execution. This idea, the idea of carrying forward values, the idea of **iteration** will be introduced in the next example.

Example 3.1.3   Finding the largest of a set

A non-empty set of numbers is represented in the data as a positive integer N (the size of the set) followed by N other numbers (the elements of the set). Write a program which prints the largest number in the set.

A solution to this problem is of the form

```
Read N.
Read the first element and store it in MAX.
Perform N-1 times
   the following task:
      read an item and store it in ITEM;
      if ITEM > MAX then
         alter MAX to hold ITEM;
```

```
        end if;
    end of task.
Print out the value of MAX.
```

Note that as execution progresses, on completion of each execution of the loop body, MAX holds the largest member of the set that has so far been encountered. It follows that when a new item is read it is necessary to compare that item and MAX and if necessary alter MAX accordingly.

Example 3.1.4 Finding the average of a set of numbers

In this example a set of numbers again appears as some positive integer N followed by N numbers. We want a program which finds the average of the numbers in the set.

A solution takes the form

```
Read N.
Set SUM to 0.
Perform N times
  the following task:
     read an item and store in X;
     add X to the current value of SUM
     to produce a new value for SUM;
  end of task.
Print SUM divided by N.
```

The interesting part of this program is just the calculation of the sum of the elements of the set. On completion of each execution of the loop body the variable SUM will hold the value corresponding to the accumulated sum of all the elements of the set so far read. Thus whenever an item is read it must be added to SUM to give the new accumulated sum. Initially SUM is zero, the accumulated sum of no elements of the set. On completion of the first execution of the loop body SUM will hold the value of the first element, on completion of the second execution it holds the sum of the first two elements, on completion of the third execution it holds the sum of the first three elements and so on. In this way execution progresses until all the elements have been read.

Note that

> in example 3.1.3 MAX held the maximum of all the elements so far read;
>
> in example 3.1.4 SUM held the accumulated sum of all the elements so far read.

In other examples the situation is often similar, the programmer has to ask:

> if after, say, R circuits of a loop a variable P has some property with respect to the first R elements of a set, how can we arrange that after R+1 circuits the variable will have that same property with respect to the first R+1 elements of the set?

This is very often the question that has to be answered when iteration is involved. The mathematically inclined reader will recognise induction.

Exercises 3.1

1 Code the solutions of examples 3.1.1 to 3.1.4 in a programming language of your choice.

2 Write a program which inputs N followed by the prices of N items. The program should output the price at which each item is offered in a sale. The sale price is calculated as follows. The original price is reduced by 10%, the resulting quantity raised to the nearest pound and then 1 penny subtracted from it. If the resulting quantity is less than the original price then the new price is output, otherwise the old price is output together with a warning message.

3 Write a program which inputs N followed by N pairs of numbers. The first of each pair represents the price of an item on a menu, the second the quantity eaten by a customer. The restaurant imposes a 10% service

charge. The output from your program should be an itemised bill.

4 Write a program which reads N followed by N numbers and outputs the positive difference between the two largest numbers.

5 Write a program which inputs N followed by a set of N numbers and outputs the variance of the set given by

$$V = \frac{1}{N-1} \left(\sum_{i}^{N} x_i^2 - 2X \sum_{i}^{N} x_i + NX^2 \right)$$

where X is the average of the set.

3.2 Control variables

There are situations in which it is advantageous to have available a control variable (also called "index loop counter", "control constant" and so on) which keeps some sort of record of the number of times a loop body has been executed. We illustrate several cases where this is relevant.

Example 3.2.1 Calculating factorial

Suppose we are required to write a program which evaluates the factorial function N! = 1 x 2 x ..... x N where N is some non-negative integer supplied as data.
The following program does what is required.

    Read N.
    Let PRODUCT be initialised to 1.
    Using control variable I starting at 1 and
    increasing in steps of 1 to N perform

>   the following task:
>   replace PRODUCT by PRODUCT times I;
>   end of task.
> Print the value of PRODUCT.

For each individual value of I the loop body is executed before the next value is considered. At the end of each execution of the loop body PRODUCT has the value 1 x 2 x ...x I. Again the loop body represents the answer to the question:

>   if at some stage PRODUCT holds the value (I-1)! how do we then ensure that it receives the value I! ?

Example 3.2.2 Series summation

Suppose we are required to evaluate the following series

$$\sum_{i=1}^{100} \frac{1}{i^2} = 1 + \frac{1}{2^2} + \frac{1}{3^2} + \ldots + \frac{1}{100^2}$$

This can be done in the following way.

>   Let SUM be initialised to 0.
>   Using control variable I starting at 1 and increasing in steps of 1 to 100 perform
>   the following task:
>   replace SUM by SUM plus $1/I^2$;
>   end of task.
>   Print the value of SUM.

Note that the above is very similar to some of the examples given earlier in section 3.1 on evaluating series of numbers. In this case however the various items to be added are not read from some input file rather they are calculated using the control variable.

The next example combines the ideas outlined in the two above.

Example 3.2.3 Series summation

Consider the problem of evaluating

$$\sum_{i=1}^{100} \frac{1}{i!}$$

A possible program might have the following form

    Read X.
    Set SUM to 0. Set TERM to 1.
    Using control variable I starting at 1 and
    increasing in steps of 1 to 100 perform
      the following task:
        replace TERM by TERM/I;
        replace SUM by SUM+TERM;
      end of task.
    Print the value of SUM.

In this case an accumulated sum of terms is calculated in the usual way. Note that on each circuit of the loop TERM changes. One term is obtained from the previous one by dividing by I. This explains the alteration to TERM within the program.

The examples given so far involve the use of control variables which start at 1 and progress in steps of 1 to some upper limit. There are cases where it is inconvenient to be restricted to such a rigid format. Many programming languages permit arbitrary starting values and arbitrary (possibly negative) increments. Consider the following example.

Example 3.2.4 Testing for primality

Write a program which reads some positive integer N and determines whether or not it is prime. (An integer is prime provided it exceeds 1 and is divisible only by itself and 1.)

We adopt a solution which proceeds as follows: first look at whether N is even and greater than 2, if so take appropriate action; if N is odd then it is sufficient to test if N is divisible by 3,5,... .

    Read N.
    If N is even and N>2 then
        set PRIME to false;
    otherwise
        set PRIME to true;
        using control variable I starting at 3 and
        increasing in steps of 2 to N-1 perform
          the following task:
              if N is divisible by I
              set PRIME to false;
        end of task;
    end if.
    Print an appropriate message depending on the value of PRIME.

This solution can be improved on in at least two ways: firstly it is usually unnecessary to go as far as N-1; secondly if ever PRIME is set to false the loop can be terminated immediately. The latter possibility is dealt with later in section 3.4. So far as the former is concerned we note that if both P and Q are greater than the square root of N then PxQ > N. So, if N is not prime one of its factors must be less than its square root.

Example 3.2.5 Nested multiplication

Consider the task of evaluating the polynomial

$$A_N X^N + A_{N-1} X^{N-1} + \ldots + A_2 X^2 + A_1 X + A_0$$

given the quantities A_N, A_{N-1}, ... A_2, A_1, A_0 together with a value of X.

  A polynomial of this kind can be evaluated using the obvious approach:

    Read X. Read N.
    Set SUM to 0.
    Using control variable I starting at N and
    decreasing in steps of 1 to 0 perform
      the following task:

```
    read A;
    replace SUM by SUM + A x X^I;
  end of task.
Print SUM.
```

This approach is rather inefficient because X^I has to be calculated on each circuit of the loop - on the previous circuit X^{I+1} had been calculated and this value has not been remembered. In addition the order in which the data - the values corresponding to A_N, A_{N-1}, ... A_1, A_0 is required is unsuitable for reading for example binary numbers such as 1011. This is a disguised polynomial

$$1011 = 1 \times 2^3 + 0 \times 2^2 + 1 \times 2^1 + 1 \times 2^0$$

Both the disadvantages of the program above can be overcome by using a process called nested multiplication. Here the polynomial is restructured and on each circuit of the loop we successively evaluate

$$A_N$$

$$A_N X + A_{N-1}$$

$$(A_N X + A_{N-1})X + A_{N-2}$$

Note that each line is obtained from the previous by multiplying by X and adding in the value of the next coefficient. Thus we have

```
Read X. Read N.
Set SUM to 0.
Perform N+1 times
  the following task:
    read A;
    replace SUM by SUM x X + A;
  end of task.
Print SUM.
```

Note that now we do not need a control variable.

Exercises 3.2

1. Code the solutions of examples 3.2.1 to 3.2.5 in a programming language of your choice.

2. In a certain country Sales Tax is charged on cars at the following rate

Net Price	Rate
<$2000	15%
$2000-$3000	$300 (flat rate)
>$3000	10%

    Write a program which prints out net price, Sales Tax and gross price for net prices between $1000 and $4000 in steps of $250.

3. Given that 1 metre = 39.37 inches and that there are 12 inches in a foot, write a program which outputs a conversion table. For each metric distance from 5.0 metres to 10.0 metres in steps of 0.2 metres, your program should output the metric distance and its British equivalent in feet and inches. Round British distances to the nearest inch. Your table should start

Metres	Feet	Inches
5.0	16	5
5.2	17	1
.	.	.

4. Write a program which given the day of the week on which the first of a month falls, together with the number of days in the month, prints out a calendar for the month in the form shown below.

Mo	Tu	We	Th	Fr	Sa	Su
		1	2	3	4	5
6	7	8	9	10	11	12
13	14	15	16	17	18	19
20	21	22	23	24	25	26
27	28	29	30			

5 If there is a group of n people then the probability that no two of them have the same birthday is

$$q = \frac{365}{365} \times \frac{364}{365} \times \frac{363}{365} \times \ldots \times \frac{365-n+1}{365}$$

The probability that at least two people have the same birthday is therefore p = 1-q.

Write a program to evaluate p and output p and n for values of n from 2 to 70.

3.3 While loops and iteration

In all the examples given so far the programmer has known precisely how often a given loop body has had to be performed. There are situations however where this is not known in advance and cannot easily be calculated. Consequently we introduce a new kind of loop to deal with this – often called a **while loop** or some other such name. In these cases the loop typically terminates not after some definite number of circuits but rather upon some condition becoming satisfied.

Example 3.3.1 Counting spaces

A piece of text is terminated by the special character #. Write a program to count the number of spaces and non-spaces which occur.

The following program does as required.

```
Set the integer variables SPACES and NONSPACES to 0.
Read character into CH.
While CH is not # perform
   the following task:
      if CH holds a space then
         add 1 to SPACES;
      otherwise add 1 to NONSPACES;
      end if;
      read character into CH;
```

end of task.
Print the values of both SPACES and NONSPACES;

Each circuit of the loop is preceded by an instruction which reads the next character from the input stream. If this is not the # character the loop body is executed, otherwise control passes to the statement after the loop.

In section 3.1 we saw that information about the amount of data to be processed by a program could be conveyed by inserting into the data information about the amount of data to follow. The example above illustrates another commonly used technique - insertion of a terminator (in this case the character #) at the end of the data. The while loop is the appropriate method of dealing with data sets of this form since there is no prior knowledge of how much information is present.

Example 3.3.2 Finding a square root

If x_n is a close approximation to the square root of A then a better one is x_{n+1} given by

$$x_{n+1} = \frac{1}{2} \left(x_n + \frac{A}{x_n} \right)$$

Write a program which reads some positive quantity A and calculates its square root to an accuracy which ensures that the result squared and A differ by at most 10^{-6}.
The following program will do this

    Set ROOT to A/2.
    While the magnitude of ROOTxROOT differs from A by more than 10^{-6} perform the following task:
        replace ROOT by (ROOT+A/ROOT)/2;
    end of task.
    Print the value of ROOT.

Iterative problems of this form are easily solved if the programmer knows how to obtain a more accurate approximation to a solution from a given one.

Example 3.3.3 Fibonacci numbers

The Fibonacci numbers F_0, F_1, ... are defined as follows:

$$F_0 = 0 \qquad F_1 = 1$$

$$F_{n+2} = F_{n+1} + F_n \quad \text{for all } n \geq 0.$$

Thus they are $0,1,1,2,3,5,8,13,\ldots$.

Write a program which reads a positive integer M and prints the first Fibonacci number which is not less than M.

The following program accomplishes the task:

```
Read M.
Set THIS to 0 and NEXT to 1.
While NEXT is less than M perform
   the following task:
      set TEMP to THIS;
      set THIS to NEXT;
      set NEXT to TEMP+NEXT;
   end of task.
```

Note that there is no need to remember all the Fibonacci numbers. It is only necessary to remember the current and previous value.

Exercises 3.3

1. Code the solutions of examples 3.3.1 to 3.3.3 in a programming language of your choice.

2. Consider
   $$1^n+6^n+7^n+17^n+18^n+23^n = 2^n+3^n+11^n+13^n+21^n+22^n$$

   What is the first value of n for which the equation fails to hold?

3 Write a program which reads an integer N and determines whether or not it is a Fibonacci number.

4 Write a program which inputs a sequence of brackets ("[" and "]") terminated by * and determines whether or not the sequence is well-formed. A sequence is well-formed if there are equal numbers of "[" and "]" and the number of "]" read never exceeds the number of "[" read.

5 Write a program which reads a sequence of positive integers terminated by -1 and outputs a sequence in which subsequences of repeated integers are replaced by a single instance of the integer preceded by an appropriate count and *. For example if the input contained

... 4 3 3 3 2 5 5 5 9 ...

the corresponding section of the output should be

... 4 4*3 2 3*5 9 ...

The output should end with -1.

3.4 Other variations

Although we have covered the most common kinds of loop there are other possibilities - generally obtained by combining some of the previous types. For example a control variable can often be used to advantage in conjunction with some method of terminating a loop prematurely. Many programming languages permit such a combination, e.g. **for**... **while**... loops, **repeat**... **until**, even **exit** and so on.

As a first illustration we revisit the prime number program - see example 3.2.4.

Example 3.4.1 Prime numbers revisited

Consider again the problem of example 3.2.4. This

program can be made much more efficient by terminating the loop as soon as PRIME is set to false. A revised program might be:

```
Read N.
If N is even and N>2 then
    set PRIME to false;
otherwise
    set PRIME to true;
    using control variable I starting at 3 and
    increasing in steps of 2 as long as IxI≤N
    and PRIME is true perform
        the following task:
            if N is divisible by I then
                set PRIME to false;
            end if;
        end of task.
end if.
Print an appropriate message depending on the value
of PRIME.
```

In this case the loop body is executed only if a prior test shows that both IxI≤N and PRIME is true. Should either of these conditions fail to hold the loop body is not executed. The instruction to print a message is performed and the program stops.

Example 3.4.2 Finding the position of an item

A piece of text is supplied as data. Write a program which indicates the position of the first full-stop in the text. A full-stop is guaranteed to appear somewhere in the text. Consider the following program

```
Using control variable I starting at 1 and
increasing in steps of 1 perform
    the following task:
        read a character and store it in CH;
        if CH is a full-stop then
        print the value of I and terminate the loop;
        end if;
    end of task.
```

As before the control variable I starts at 1 and on successive circuits of the loop is increased each time by 1. The phrase 'terminate the loop' will involve transferring control to whatever statements follow 'end of task'. In this particular case there is nothing to be done and the program terminates.

Example 3.4.3 Summing an infinite series

Evaluate the following series

$$\sum_{i=1}^{100} \frac{1}{(i!)^2}$$

to as great an accuracy as your computer permits.

A program to achieve the above might take the form

```
Set SUM to 0. Set TERM to 1.
Using control variable I starting at 1 and
increasing in steps of 1 perform
   the following task:
      replace TERM by TERM/(IxI);
      if TERM is zero then terminate the loop; end if;
      replace SUM by SUM + TERM;
   end of task.
Print value of SUM.
```

In the above I starts as 1 and just keeps increasing by 1 on each execution of the loop. Termination of the loop occurs when TERM is zero and at that point control is transferred to the statement after the loop which causes the value of SUM to be printed. Mathematically, TERM never becomes zero but computers hold numbers only to a limited degree of precision. Consequently when TERM is very small the computer will regard it as zero. If we disregard techniques for extended-precision arithmetic then the above program gives as accurate an answer as the particular computer will normally allow.

44 GRADED PROBLEMS

Exercises 3.4

1 Code the solutions of examples 3.4.1 to 3.4.3 in a programming language of your choice.

2 Write a program which reads N and outputs the largest integer whose cube is less than N.

3 Write a program which finds a 6-digit square with the property that the numbers represented by its first three digits and last three digits are consecutive.

3.5 Nested loops

In all the programs we have given so far only a single loop has been involved. In this section we look at problems which require two or more loops, one within another. The problems though seemingly a great deal more complicated, can be solved by adopting a straightforward and systematic approach to their solution. Again we proceed by examining some examples.

Example 3.5.1 Summing double series

Evaluate the sum of the series

$$\sum_{M=1}^{100} \sum_{N=1}^{100} \frac{1}{M^4 + N^4} = \sum_{M=1}^{100} \left(\sum_{N=1}^{100} \frac{1}{M^4 + N^4} \right)$$

that is add together all elements of the form $1/(M^4+N^4)$ where both M and N span through the range 1 to 100. A sketch of the solution follows:

   Set SUM to 0.
   Using control variable M starting at 1 and
   increasing in steps of 1 to 100 perform
      the following task :

let S be the sum $\sum_{N=1}^{100} \frac{1}{M^4 + N^4}$;
    replace SUM by SUM + S;
  end of task.
Print the value of SUM.

The instruction

let S be the sum $\sum_{N=1}^{100} \frac{1}{M^4 + N^4}$;

itself involves a loop. From the earlier part of this chapter we know how to evaluate this and the appropriate instructions can be inserted. A loop statement thus appears within the loop body of an outer loop - we say that the loops are nested.

In the above case, loops of the same kind were nested one within another. This need not be the case.

Example 3.5.2 Square root of several numbers

Write a program which, using the method of example 3.3.2 prints out the square roots of all the integers between 1 and 100.

A possible solution might take the form:

  Using control variable I starting at 1 and
  increasing in steps of 1 to 100 perform
    the following task:
      set X to the square root of I;
      print both I and X and take a new line;
    end of task.

The instruction

  set X to the square root of I

is an abbreviation for a set of instructions which itself involves a loop, so again nested loops are employed.

There are cases where loops might have to be nested to a depth greater than two.

Example 3.5.3 Tabulating highest common factors

Design a progam which will produce a table containing the highest common factor of all pairs of integers A,B where $1 \leq A, B \leq N$. The positive integer N is supplied as data.

Note the highest common factor (hcf) of two positive integers A and B is defined to be the largest integer which divides both A and B. Mathematically

$$\begin{aligned} \text{hcf}(A,B) &= A \text{ if } A = B \\ &= \text{hcf}(A-B,B) \text{ if } A>B \\ &= \text{hcf}(B,A) \text{ if } B>A \end{aligned}$$

To find the hcf we will proceed to subtract repeatedly the smaller from the larger of the two numbers until such time as the numbers become equal. Thus

```
Set A1 to A and B1 to B.
While A1 is not equal to B1 perform
   the following task:
      subtract the smaller of A1 and B1
      from the larger;
   end of task.
Print A1.
```

Now let us return to the task in hand, the production of a table of values. The result we want to produce will be of the form

Table of highest common factors

	1	2	3	4	5	.	.	.	.
1	1	1	1	1	1	.	.	.	.
2	1	2	1	2	1	.	.	.	.
3	1	1	3	1	1	.	.	.	.
4	1	2	1	4	1	.	.	.	.
.	.	.	.	.	.				
N									

If we concentrate on the printing of the rows in turn the structure of the program emerges

```
Print the heading  "Table of highest common factors".
Take a new line.
Read N.
Print, suitably indented, the numbers 1,2, ..., N.
Using control variable M starting at 1 and
increasing in steps of 1 to N perform
    the following task:
        take a newline;
        print the Mth row of the table;
    end of task.
```

The only instruction which requires more elaboration is that to print the Mth row. This can be accomplished in the following way:

```
Print M.
Using control variable L starting at 1 and
increasing in steps of 1 to N perform
    the following task:
        leave some spaces;
        calculate and print hcf(M,L);
    end of task.
```

We have already produced a piece of program which calculates and prints a highest common factor. If the various pieces of program are pieced together the final version emerges, a program in which loops are nested to a depth of three.

Exercises 3.5

1 Code the solutions of examples 3.5.1 to 3.5.3 in a programming language of your choice.

2 A set of positive integers is terminated by a negative integer. Write a program which uses the technique of Example 3.3.2 to find the square roots of the numbers to as great an accuracy as your computer normally permits.

3 Evaluate the series

$$\sum_{m=1}^{\inf} \sum_{n=1}^{\inf} \frac{1}{m^4 + n^4}$$

to as great an accuracy as your computer normally permits ('inf' denotes infinity).

4 Write a program which reads in the three positive integer coefficients in the equation

$$ax^2 + by^2 = c$$

and outputs a solution (a and b non-negative integers) if any exists.

5 Write a program which reads in the four positive integer coefficients in the equation

$$ax^2 + by^2 + cz^2 = d$$

and outputs a solution (x, y and z non-negative integers) if any exists.

3.6 Miscellaneous exercises

1 A bank wishes to detect a number of counterfeit cheques which are in circulation. On each cheque 2 numbers are printed, the cheque number and the account number. On all the counterfeit cheques the cheque number lies in the range 10000 - 10010. Write a program which reads the numbers taken from a batch of cheques and prints out for each cheque the cheque number and the account number followed by 999 if the cheque is possibly counterfeit. After the last pair of numbers in the data is the integer -1.

2 Write a program which reads N followed by N numbers and for each of the N numbers outputs the number followed by the total of the numbers so far.

3 The number of distinct ways in which r objects can be selected from n distinct objects is given by

$$nCr = \frac{n!}{(n-r)! \times r!}$$

Write a program which reads n and r and outputs nCr.

4 Write a program which both encrypts and decrypts messages. The input to the program should be an integer N followed by a message terminated by *. Every letter in the message is to be replaced by the one N places further on in the alphabet. The alphabet is to be treated in a circular manner so that A is the letter after Z. Every non-letter character is to be output unaltered. N may be any integer in the range -25 to +25.

5 Data consists of N groups of 8 numbers. Print out the number of those groups of which the first 4 members form either an ascending sequence or a descending sequence.

6 An organisation wishing to encourage its employees to save energy would like to produce a table showing, for the current and previous year, running totals month by month of energy consumption. Each row of the table would also show the percentage increase in consumption for the current year over the previous one. For example

Month	This	Last	% Increase
1	300	250	20
2	450	500	-10
.	.	.	.

Write a program which reads in 12 pairs of numbers, each pair represents the consumption for a particular month in the two years. The program should output a table of the form above. (Data to produce the above table would begin 300, 250, 150, 250 ....)

7 At a certain university students take ten units and

need to average at least 60% in the best nine units to pass. Your program should read for each student his/her student number followed by ten percentages and print a list consisting of the student numbers of those who passed.

Student numbers consist of six digits (e.g. 801234) and the last student on the input list will be followed by one with 99 as the first two digits of the number.

8 In a certain ice skating event, a mark is awarded by each of N judges. The mark awarded to a competitor is obtained by ignoring the highest and lowest of the N marks and averaging the remainder. Write a program which reads N followed by the N marks and outputs the mark awarded.

9 Write a program which finds the square root of N, a positive integer supplied as data, to as great an accuracy as your computer normally permits. Use the iterative equation given in example 3.3.2.

10 If x_k is an approximation to the cube root of N then a better one is

$$x_{k+1} = (N/x_k^2 + 2x_k) / 3$$

Use this in a program which reads N and P and outputs the cube root of N correct to P decimal places.

11 Write a program which finds all the prime numbers between 1 and 100.

12 Write a program which reads a positive integer N and prints the first N Fibonacci numbers.

13 Eudoxus' numbers are defined by the following recurrence relations

$$y_r = x_{r-1} + y_{r-1}$$

$$x_r = y_r + y_{r-1}$$

where $x_0 = y_0 = 1$

Write a program which reads N and outputs y_N and x_N.

14 There is three digit base 11 number which when reversed produces a multiple of itself. Write a program which finds it.

15 Write a program which finds a four digit number AABB which is a perfect square. A and B represent different digits.

16 Write a program which finds a four digit perfect square where the number represented by the first two digits and the number represented by the last two digits are both perfect squares.

17 Twin primes are consecutive odd numbers both of which are prime numbers. Write a program which inputs two positive integers A and B and outputs all the twin primes in the range A to B.

18 Write a program which reads in a time (t) being the earliest time at which a passenger can arrive at his departure railway station, and a number (m) being the longest journey time in hours that he is prepared to tolerate. The program then reads N followed by N pairs of numbers being the departure and arrival times of N trains to the passenger's destination. Print out the departure time of his most suitable train (that arriving earliest at his destination).

19 Write a program which reads a series of pairs of numbers. Each pair represents a fraction (numerator,denominator). Your program should output the sum of the fractions in the same form; the fraction output should have the smallest possible positive denominator. To minimise the possibility of numeric overflow, your program should ensure that the numerator and denominator of any running total are always as small as possible.

20 Write a program which finds a root of an arbitrary

function using the method of bisection. The data for the program should be 2 values, A and B, such that f(A)xf(B)<0.
  A root can be found by
  (i) computing M = (A + B)/2
  (ii) replacing A by M or B by M such that it is still the case that f(A) x f(B) < 0
  (iii) repeating steps (i) and (ii) until either f(M) is sufficiently close to zero or A and B are sufficiently close together.

21 Write a program which finds two separate three digit integers which when expressed in base 17 and 19 produce integers which are multiples of themselves.

22 Estate agent advertisements frequently contain words from which all vowels (except an initial one) have been removed. Thus

   Desirable unfurnished flat in quiet residential area

might become

   Dsrbl unfrnshd flt in qt rsdntl ar

Write a program which reads in a normal description of a property terminated by # and outputs the corresponding advertisement.

23 Write, for each of the series below, a program which reads N and x and outputs the sum of the first N terms.

(a) $X = 1 + \dfrac{1}{2} + \dfrac{1}{3} + \dfrac{1}{4} \cdots$

(b) $f(x) = \dfrac{x^2}{2} + \dfrac{x^4}{3} + \dfrac{x^6}{4} + \cdots$

(c) $X = \dfrac{1}{2!} - \dfrac{1}{3!} + \dfrac{1}{4!} - \dfrac{1}{5!} \cdots$

(d) $e^x = 1 + \dfrac{x}{1!} + \dfrac{x^2}{2!} + \dfrac{x^3}{3!} \ldots$

(e) $\sin(x) = x - \dfrac{x^3}{3!} + \dfrac{x^5}{5!} - \dfrac{x^7}{7!} \ldots$

24 Write a program which takes as data a positive integer N followed by N pairs of numbers $x_1 y_1$, $x_2 y_2$, ... $x_N y_N$ representing points on a plane. The straight line best fitting the points has equation

$$y = mx + c$$

where $\quad m = \dfrac{d - (ab)/N}{c(-a^2/N)} \qquad c = \dfrac{ad - bc}{a^2 - Nc}$

and $\quad a = x_1 + x_2 + \ldots + x_N$

$b = y_1 + y_2 + \ldots + y_N$

$c = x_1^2 + x_2^2 + \ldots + x_N^2$

$d = x_1 * y_1 + x_2 * y_2 + \ldots + x_N * y_N$

The output from your program should be the values of m and c for the data read.

25 If in a collection of n objects there are m subgroups of identical items such that subgroup i has S_i members then the number of distinct permutations of the n objects is given by

$$nPr = \dfrac{n!}{S_1! * S_2! * \ldots * S_m!}$$

Write a program which reads n followed by m followed by the S_i and outputs nPr.

26 Write a program which reads 4 positive integers A, B, C and D and outputs a table of lowest common multiples. The lowest common multiple of x and y (lcm(x,y)) is the smallest integer into which both x and y divide. You should tabulate lcm(x,y) for all x

between A and B and all y between C and D inclusive.
[Note lcm(x,y) = x * y / hcf(x,y)]

27 Consider again the equation

$$1^n+6^n+7^n+17^n+18^n+23^n=2^n+3^n+11^n+13^n+21^n+22^n$$

We can add a constant (k) to each of the 12 numbers and find n - the smallest value of n for which the modified equation does not hold. Write a program which for each value of k from 2 to 12, outputs k and n.

28 Note that

$$2 + 2 = 2 \times 2$$
$$1 + 2 + 3 = 1 \times 2 \times 3$$

These observations show that there are solutions to the equation

$$y_1 + y_2 + \ldots + y_n = y_1 \times y_2 \times \ldots \times y_n$$

when n is 2 and when n is 3. Find single digit integers which give solutions in the cases n=4 and n=5.

29 The four digit integer 1089 is multiplied when its digits are reversed (9801 = 9 x 1089). There is only one other four digit integer with this property. Write a program which finds it.

30 There are three ways of adding 4 odd digits to obtain 10:

1+1+3+5=10   1+1+1+7=10   1+3+3+3=10

It is assumed that changes in the order of the digits are irrelevant. Find all 11 ways of adding 8 odd digits to obtain 20.

31 A perfect number is one which is equal to the sum of its factors other than itself. Write a program which

prints out all the perfect numbers between 1 and 2000.

32 There are 8 questions on an examination paper. Write a program which inputs the marks awarded for each question (-1 indicates that the question was not attempted) and checks that the candidate attempted no more than 5 questions, at least two from each half of the paper. If this condition is satisfied the program should print the total number of marks otherwise it should print a suitable warning message.

33 The number 40001 is divisible by 221. Write a program which determines whether or not this statement remains true if the numbers are in base b where $4 < b < 10$.

34 Write a program which reads three integers M, N and P and produces a table of x.y modulo P where $1 \leq x \leq M$ and $1 \leq y \leq N$.

35 Compute the ratio (f_{k-1}/f_k) between successive terms of the Fibonacci series until the difference between successive ratios is less than 0.0001. Output the final ratio calculated.

36 Goldbach's conjecture is that every even number greater than 2 can be expressed as the sum of 2 prime numbers.
    Write a program which for every even integer (i) from 4 to 400 attempts to find a pair of prime numbers (A,B) such that i=A+B. If successful the program should print i, A and B; otherwise it should output a message indicating that the conjecture has been disproved.

37 Every cube is the sum of a sequence of odd positive integers. For each value of n from 2 to 40, output the sequence of odd integers which sums to n^3.

38 Input will consist of a number of words separated by spaces and possibly commas. There will be a full stop after the last word and there will be no hyphens or words spread over more than one line. The program is

to determine (and print) what percentage the words are of more than 6 letters long.

39 An aeroplane flying over a flat earth follows a course consisting of straight line segments connected together. Each segment has its own speed (in km/hour), duration (in minutes) and heading (a certain number of degrees East of North).
   Write a program which reads in the details of a flight (as N followed by N triples) and calculates the co-ordinates of the aircraft at the end of each segment taking its starting position as (0,0).

40 The effective resistance R of a series of N resistors $R_1, R_2, \ldots, R_N$ connected in parallel is given by

$$\frac{1}{R} = \frac{1}{R_1} + \frac{1}{R_2} + \ldots + \frac{1}{R_N}$$

Write a program which reads N followed by $R_1 \ldots R_N$ and outputs R. Compare the results obtained using
   (a) a method involving N+1 division operations
   (b) a method involving 1 division.

41 Write a program which inputs a sequence of integers and integer groups and outputs a sequence of integers. For example if the input contained

   ... 7 6 4*9 3 2*1 5 ...

the corresponding section of the output should be

   ... 7 6 9 9 9 9 3 1 1 5 ...

   The input is terminated by -1 which should be the last number output.

42 (a) Find the first value of n for which

   $n^2 - n + 41$

   is not prime (n = 0,1,2,...)

   (b) Find the first value of n for which

$$n^2 - 79n + 1601$$

is not prime ($n = 0, 1, 2, \ldots$)

43 Calculate successive terms

$$\frac{2}{1} \times \frac{2}{3} , \quad \frac{2}{1} \times \frac{2}{3} \times \frac{4}{3} , \quad \frac{2}{1} \times \frac{2}{3} \times \frac{4}{3} \times \frac{4}{5} \quad \ldots$$

of the product

$$\frac{2}{1} \times \frac{2}{3} \times \frac{4}{3} \times \frac{4}{5} \times \frac{6}{5} \times \frac{6}{7} \times \frac{8}{7} \times \frac{8}{9} \quad \ldots$$

Stop when successive terms differ by less than 10^{-6}. If you multiply the results by 2 you may notice that the answers are coming closer and closer to a familiar constant.

44 (a) Generate the first 100 Fibonacci numbers but print out only every 3rd one thus 2,8,.... Do you notice anything about these numbers?
(b) Modify the program so that it only prints out every kth Fibonacci number. Do you notice anything about

     (i) every fourth number
    (ii) every fifth number
   (iii) every fifteenth number ?

45 It is useful to be able to generate an integer sequence

$$x_1, x_2, \ldots x_i$$

where each element x_i is in the range $[0, n-1]$ and the sequence is "consistent with" being generated by independent trials of a finite probability experiment with uniform probability.
    The most popular generator is provided by the recurrence relation

$$x_{i+1} = (a * x_i + b) \text{ modulo } n$$

where a and b are preselected integer constants. If the pair (a,b) is properly selected (see Knuth, D.E., 1971; Chapter 3) then the subsequent sequence has the required properties.

Write a program which uses values of a, b and n appropriate for your computer and generates 100 pseudo-random numbers.

46 Approximate pi by using a random number generator. Write a program which reads N and generates the positions of N points in a square. By keeping a count of the number of points which fall inside the inscribed circle the program should output an estimate of pi.

47 Using the pi estimation technique from the previous exercise, tabulate the estimate against N for N from 100 to 1000 in steps of 200.

48 Write a program which reads in N followed by N numbers and finds their lowest common multiple.

49 Data is N followed by N scores of a batsman during a cricket season. The score for a completed innings is represented by the number of runs (<999), a "not out" score of n runs is represented by the integer 1000+n.
(a) Write a program which produces a summary of the batsman's performance under the headings

<u>Innings</u>   <u>Not out</u>   <u>Runs</u>   <u>Average</u>

The batsman's average is the total number of runs scored divided by the number of completed innings. If there are no completed innings the program should leave this field blank.
(b) Extend your program so that it also outputs the highest score made during the season (followed by * if this was "not out").
(c) Extend your program so that it outputs the number of scores of 50 or over and the number of scores of 100 or over. Note that a score of, for example, 125 should be counted only in the latter category.

50 Write a program which generates all the Pythagorean triangles which have a shorter side (not the hypotenuse) of 30 or less.

51 A density plot is a way of displaying a function of 2 variables. At each point (x,y) on a 2-dimensional area a character is printed according to the value of f(x,y). If f(x,y) is large then the character printed is "dark" for example "*" or "#", if the value of f(x,y) is comparatively small then a "light" character is printed, for example "." or ":". Write a program which produces a density plot of an arbitrary function of 2 variables F(x,y)
 where x ranges from X1 in steps of XD to X2
 and y ranges from Y1 in steps of YD to Y2
(X1, XD, X2, Y1, YD and Y2 supplied as data).

52 For each of the following series, write a program which reads a suitable value of x, a positive integer N and outputs the sum of the series correct to N decimal places.

(a) $\log_e(x) = x - \frac{x^2}{2} + \frac{x^3}{3} \ldots \quad (-1 < x \leq 1)$

(b) $\cos(x) = 1 - \frac{x^2}{2!} + \frac{x^4}{4!} - \frac{x^6}{6!} \ldots$

53 Input consists of 28 real numbers giving rainfall figures for a four week period. Print the position (e.g. DAY 13 or WEEK 2) and rainfall for the wettest individual day and the driest week.

54 Consider a lamp of C candle-power suspended h metres over the centre of a road. The intensity of illumination at a horizontal distance d from a point vertically below the lamp is

$$\frac{C \times h}{(h^2 + d^2)^{1.5}}$$

 A road has a group of 4 lamp-posts 20 metres high and 50 metres apart. Each lamp is of 1000 candle power. The level of illumination at any point can be found by adding up the contributions from each of the four lamps.

Write a program which calculates and displays the level of illumination at 10 metre intervals starting under the first and ending under the last.

55 Note that

$$12 \times 42 = 21 \times 24$$
$$12 \times 63 = 21 \times 36$$
$$12 \times 84 = 21 \times 48$$

There are 14 products with the property that

$$(10a + b)(10c + d) = (10b + a)(10d + c)$$

where a and b are unequal and c and d are also unequal.
Write a program which outputs them all.

56 Write a program which finds the first 100 prime numbers.

57 Generate Pascal's triangle up to the line beginning

    1 10 . . .

58 By devising a suitable search, decode the following

```
        A B C
        B A C
       -------
        * * * *
        * * A
      * * * B
       -------
      * * * * * *
```

A, B and C represent different digits.

59 Write a program which plots the graph of an arbitrary function f(x) on a printer. Data for the program will be the limits of x and the step size. On each output line should be the value of x, the value of f(x) and a character for example "*", in such a position that joining the "*" will give a graphical representation of the function.

60 Let P(n) denote the number of primes less than or equal to the positive integer n. Tabulate the values of

   (i) n/P(n)
   (ii) $\log_e n$

   for n from 100 to 2000 in steps of 100.

61 A common test for divisibility by 3 (or 9) is to add the digits of an integer. If the resulting sum is divisible by 3 (or 9) then so is the original number. (Note that the sum of the digits may itself be subject to the same treatment.) Program this test ensuring that the final division involves some number less than 20. Your program should work for arbitrarily large integers read as data.

62 To test for divisibility by 37 a common test is to separate the integer into groups of 3 which should then be added. Thus the integer 143412 results in 143+412 = 555. If the final result is divisible by 37 then so is the original. Program this test so that it operates for integers of arbitrary size read as data.

63 Consider a number of the form

   $a_1 a_2 \ldots a_n$

   where each a_i ($1 \le i \le n$) is a digit. To test for divisibility by 11, form the sum

   $s_1 = a_1 + a_3 + a_5 + \ldots$

   $s_2 = a_2 + a_4 + a_6 + \ldots$

The original number is divisible by 11 only if s_1-s_2 or s_2-s_1 (whichever is the larger) is divisible by 11. Program this test so that it operates for integers of arbitrary magnitude read as data.

64 This problem requires knowledge of the rules of squash. Use a random number generator to decide whether or not a particular point is won by the server. Simulate a game and output a message indicating whether the game is won by the player who served first.

Extend your program so that it simulates a match which is the best of 5 games.

65 The integer 145 has the curious property that

$$145 = 1! + 4! + 5!$$

It is possible to prove mathematically that there are no integers greater than 2000000 with this property. There is one number other than 1, 2 and 145 which has it. Write a program which finds this number.

66 Write a program which given the day of the week on which the first of a month falls, together with the number of days in the month, prints out a calendar for the month in the form shown below.

```
Mo       6  13  20  27
Tu       7  14  21  28
We   1   8  15  22  29
Th   2   9  16  23  30
Fr   3  10  17  24
Sa   4  11  18  25
Su   5  12  19  26
```

67 Politicians and bankers often quote "the rule of 72" which says that if the annual rate of inflation is R% then a fixed sum of money will decline in value by

half in a period of 72/R years. Test the accuracy of this rule by tabulating, for each value of k from 1 to 36

   (i) k
   (ii) the value of 72/k
   (iii) the time at which the value of a sum is actually halved when inflation is k%.

Assume that prices increase only once a year.

68 A car speedometer is connected to the transmission and by assuming a constant tyre circumference, transforms the number of revolutions per second of the drive shaft into kilometres per hour. However the circumference of a tyre will decrease as the tread wears away, will increase as the tyre becomes hot and will vary with the amount of air inside it.
   (a) Write a program which, for a car with speedometer calibrated for a 60cm diameter tyre, outputs a table of values of
      t(s,c) = true road speed when the speedometer shows s km/hr and the actual tyre diameter is 60+c% cm.
   Tabulate the function for
      s=30,35,40,...90
      c=-10,-8,....8,10

   (b) Modify your program so that the calibrated tyre circumference is read as data.

69 Given a positive integer N write a program to determine whether or not this is of the form a^b for suitable a and b, both integral.

70 The fraction 64/16 has the unusual property that if the '6' in the numerator is cancelled with the '6' in the denominator, the value of the fraction is unaltered.
   Write a program which finds all such fractions in which the numerator and denominator are both 2-digit

integers (before cancelling). Cancelling zeroes is not allowed.

71 A clock has a second hand which remains motionless except when it moves to the next position which it does in negligible time. The second hand moves on one step every second except that when it is in the six o'clock position it sticks for one second thus causing the clock to lose one second every minute. Every time the second hand moves from the 59th position to the 0 position the minute hand moves on one step. Every time the minute hand moves from the 59th position to the 0 position the hour hand moves on one step. (Note a different size step five times as large.) The three hands are mounted on concentric axles and coincide in the 12 o'clock position when the clock is started at midnight.

Simulate the clock from this initial condition until the hands are once again in this position and print the actual times and clock times at which the hands of the clock all coincide.

72 Given two integers m and n with m>n, write a program to print the first m natural numbers in n columns reading down the page. Arrange that the last row is short if necessary. For example, for m=23 and n=5 your program should print

1	6	11	16	20
2	7	12	17	21
3	8	13	18	22
4	9	14	19	23
5	10	15		

73 A line of data consists of a sequence of characters terminated by a period. In this sequence there is a bracketed subsequence. Write a program to read the data, and copy it to the output omitting the bracketed subsequence. For example,

```
INPUT     ABC(DEF)HIJ.
OUTPUT    ABCHIJ.
```

What will happen if the data line contains no bracketed subsequence? What happens if the data contains several bracketed subsequences?

Rewrite your program to deal successfully with the more general cases; if more than one bracketed subsequence is found all are to be omitted.

74 The primes 2,3,5,7,... can be arranged on a two-dimensional plane in the form of a rectangular spiral. Thus

$$
\begin{array}{ccccc}
59 & \leftarrow 53 & \leftarrow 47 & \leftarrow 43 & \leftarrow 41 \\
\downarrow & & & & \uparrow \\
& 11 & \leftarrow 7 & \leftarrow 5 & 37 \\
& \downarrow & & \uparrow & \uparrow \\
& 13 & 2 & \rightarrow 3 & 31 \\
& \downarrow & & & \uparrow \\
& 17 & \rightarrow 19 & \rightarrow 23 & \rightarrow 29
\end{array}
$$

Assuming that the initial 2 is stored at position (0,0)
(a) write a program which inputs integers I and J and outputs the value of the number at location (I,J) on the plane.
(b) write a program which inputs a prime number N and outputs the co-ordinates of the point at which N may be found.

75 By devising a suitable search, decode the following

```
        * * *
        * 2 *
       ─────────
        * * *
      * * * *
    * 8 *
       ─────────
    * * 9 * 2 *
```

76 It has been conjectured (by Hardy and Littlewood in 1923) that the number of twin primes less than n is approximately

$$\frac{1.32\,n}{\left(\frac{1}{1} + \frac{1}{2} + \ldots\ldots \frac{1}{n}\right)^2}$$

Write a program which tabulates the value of this formula and the actual number of twin primes for n = 100, 500, 1000, 1500, 2000.

77 Input is a piece of text consisting of a large number of sentences each terminated by either "." or "!" or "?". After the final sentence terminator is the character *. The program is to print the mean and standard deviation of the lengths of the sentences (measured in words).

78 The integral of a function f over a range a to b can be evaluated in various ways. One way of estimating it is by a Monte-Carlo method. In the figure below

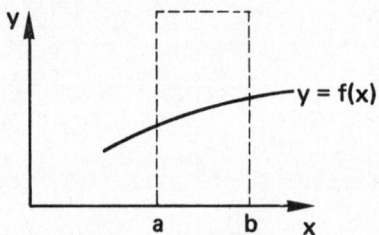

approximately half the rectangle is above the curve. If points are selected at random a count can be made of those above - call it group A - and those below - call this group B. Assuming a sufficient number of such trials, the integral may be estimated as

    B/(A+B) * area of rectangle

Test the validity of this method by using several different functions and using a variety of numbers of trails.

79 A piece of equipment has been fitted with a recorder to ascertain usage. The recorder adds to a sequential file when certain actions occur, a record of the form
       (time , action type)

The actions recorded are
- Equipment switched on   (action type S)
- Program load started   (L)
- Load ended   (E)
- Equipment switched off   (F)

Write a program which analyses the file (assume the file is terminated by a record with negative time field) and prints a report as follows:-

```
Number of times switched on and used      = l
Number of times switched on and not used  = m
Number of loads ended                     = n
Number of loads not ended                 = p
```

Note
  (i) the equipment has been switched on and used if there is an S record followed by at least one L record.
  (ii) the equipment has been switched on and not used if there is an S record followed by an F record without one or more intervening L records.
  (iii) an F record will never appear without a preceding S record.
  (iv) a load ended is an L record followed by an E record.
  (v) a load not ended is an L record which is not followed by an E record.

80 A large flat water tank has cross section as follows:

(hole)

The tank has a horizontal cross-section of 5 square metres. At the bottom there is a hole of area

1 square metre. A separate overflow pipe, also of cross section 1 square metre, starts 0.2 metre above the bottom of the tank.

The flow of water through a hole or pipe 1 metre in cross section depends on h, the height of water above it and is given (in cubic metres per second) by the formula

$$f = \frac{h^{0.5}}{10}$$

The tank starts empty, and water is run in at 0.08 cubic metres per second; how long will it take for the depth to reach 0.4 metres ?

Hint: assume that the height of water changes only at the end of each second.

81 Write a program which inputs a positive integer N and outputs its prime factorisation. For example if the number input were 980 the output should be

Prime	Power
2	2
5	1
7	2

82 If an interval A,B is divided into n equal parts and if we let

$$h = (B - A) / n$$
$$x_0 = A$$
$$x_i = x_0 + i * h$$

then the following are approximations to the integral

$$\int_A^B f(x) \, dx$$

(i) using the Trapezium Rule

$$\int_A^B f(x)\,dx \approx \sum_{i=1}^n h * [\,f(x_{i-1}) + f(x_i)\,]\,/2$$

(ii) using the Midpoint Rule

$$\int_A^B f(x)\,dx \approx \sum_{i=1}^n h * f((x_i + x_{i-1})\,/\,2)$$

Now
 (a) compose a polynomial f(x) of at least order 2
 (b) choose 2 values A and B
 (c) write a program which tabulates the value of the integral of your polynomial in the chosen range as approximated by each of the two rules. Use values of n from 2 to 40 in steps of 2.

83 Write a program which reads a Roman numeral representing a number less than 5000 and outputs the Arabic equivalent. Roman numerals are formed in the following manner.
 The alternatives for any 'units' part are composed of the letters I, V and X as follows:

I = 1, II = 2, III = 3, IV = 4, V = 5, VI = 6, VII = 7, VIII = 8, IX = 9.

 In a similar way

X=10, L=50, C=100, D=500, M=1000.

Thus, for example, LXX=70 and CD=400 and

 MCMDXVIII = 1968 MI = 1001 DCCCVI = 806

84 There is a mathematical theorem which states that the equation

$$x^2 + y^2 = r$$

has a solution in integers only if all the prime factors of r (which occur an odd number of times) are of the form 4n+1 for some integer n. Thus for example

$980 = 2 \times 2 \times 5 \times 7 \times 7$

The only odd prime factor occurring an odd number of times is 5 and since this is 4x1+1 there is a solution to the equation (980 = 14x14 + 28x28).

$504 = 2 \times 2 \times 2 \times 7 \times 9$

The only odd prime factors occurring an odd number of times are 7 and 9; 9 is of the form 4n+1 but 7 is not, therefore there is no solution to the equation for r=504.

Write a program which reads an integer r and determines whether or not the above equation has a solution.

85 (a) Given that f_n denotes the nth Fibonacci number, output in different columns

(i) $f_1 + f_2 + \ldots + f_n$

(ii) f_{n+2}

for values of n from 1 to 100.

(b) Output in different columns

(i) $f_1^2 + f_2^2 + \ldots + f_n^2$

(ii) $f_n \times f_{n+1}$

for values of n from 1 to 100.

(c) By using output similar to that employed above, compare the values of

(i) $f_1+f_3+\ldots+f_{2n-1}$ and f_{2n}

(ii) $f_2+f_4+\ldots+f_{2n}$ and f_{2n+1}

(iii) $f_n^2+f_{n+1}^2$ and f_{2n+1}

for values of n from 1 to 100.

86
$$16 = 4^2$$
$$1156 = 34^2$$
$$111556 = 334^2$$
$$11115556 = 3334^2$$

No matter how often 15 (n-1) is inserted in the middle of the number on the left (n), a digit (3) can be added to the right and the equation remains correct. So 16 is a curious square in this respect. There is only one other two-digit square with this property. Find it, and check its uniqueness.

87 This problem requires knowledge of the rules of tennis.
(a) Use a random number generator to decide whether or not a particular point is won by the server. Simulate a set and output a message indicating whether the set is won by the player who served first.
(b) Extend your program to simulate a Wimbledon men's final (best of 5 sets). Remember that a tie-breaker may operate in all but the fifth set.
(c) Modify your program so that associated with each of the two players is a (possibly different) probability that he wins the point when serving.
(d) Extend your program so that it simulates the game down to each stroke. For example a stroke could be either "good" or "bad". A bad stroke would lose the point or be a fault if serving.

88 (a) Write a program which reads in 3 integers A, B and C. A and C are positive. The number B is to be interpreted as a number in base A (your program should read B character by character and make the appropriate checks). The program outputs the equivalent number in base C.
(b) Extend the program so that B may be a real number.

89 Consider the function defined inductively by

$$f(1) = 1$$
$$f(2n) = f(n)$$
$$f(2n+1) = f(n) + f(n+1)$$

Write a program which inputs a positive integer N and outputs f(N).

4 | Subprograms

In previous chapters we have used standard functions and we have come to look upon them as a logical and useful extension of the idea of an operand - as something that could appear naturally in expressions. We have used standard functions but we have certainly not been concerned about their internal workings. The problem of designing and implementing them has been the responsibility of another person and it has been his duty to do this task properly. It has been important that his work has been of a high quality since standard functions are used often and by many people.

Note the separate tasks implied by the above discussion. There is the designer of a function and a user of that function. The designer prepares his function without undue concern about how it will be used; he is concerned only with implementing the function properly and then indicating to users the manner in which it should be used. The user, on the other hand, is not concerned at all about the means whereby the function achieves its stated aim; he merely follows the rules and expects the results to be correct.

The need for input and output facilities in programming languages tends to result in the provision of routines whereby programmers can communicate with the outside world, by reading data and printing results. These routines tend to differ from functions in certain special ways. As before they will be supplied by some designer who stipulates the way in which they must be used.

In this chapter we shall investigate the means whereby a programmer can introduce his own subprograms, alternatively called by such names as functions, procedures and subroutines. In these circumstances the designer and the user become effectively the same person. However, it is convenient to continue to regard them as different people - or rather to regard them as performing different roles at different times. In this

73

way we can concentrate on designing subprograms properly and then using them properly.

4.1 Functions

Programming languages provide standard functions for performing certain commonly required calculations or tasks. Typically there will be functions such as SIN and COS, perhaps inverse trigonometric functions, functions for finding square roots, functions for finding logarithms, functions for finding exponentials, and so on.

No matter how many such functions are provided there is no guarantee that the set provided will satisfy all the needs of every programmer. Nor is it reasonable to expect this. Most programming languages provide a means whereby a programmer can, in effect, introduce his own extra functions as required. In this way the apparent deficiency is overcome.

Let us begin by asking what characteristics user-defined functions should possess. It is natural to look for guidance on this to the standard functions themselves. What important characteristics do these possess? What lessons can be learned?

1. Each function produces a value of some type (and perhaps within some range).

2. Each function performs the calculation of one value and this is the only task that it performs.

3. Functions are self-contained in that they do not alter the values of the other variables which exist within a program; moreover the parameters of the function do not alter.

4. Functions generally do not read information or write information.

5. Functions are introduced in such a way that once working the programmer using them can forget completely about the internal workings of the

function.

6. Using the function is straightforward; this must not be a complicated or error-prone process.

It is important that all these rules are observed, even by user-defined functions. Good programming is all about simplicity. These rules ensure that functions are simple to use.

Let us now concentrate on one standard function, SIN, and examine it closely. We have typically written function calls such as SIN(0.0), SIN(PI/4.0), and so on. The (actual) parameter, the 0.0 or the PI/4.0, is an expression which produces a REAL value. Thus SIN takes REAL numbers and it produces as its result some REAL value in the range -1.0 to 1.0. We say that SIN takes a REAL parameter and delivers a REAL result. Thus there is a type associated with the parameter and a type associated with the result. Attempts to misuse types will usually lead to errors: thus SIN(TRUE), i.e. SIN applied to a BOOLEAN or logical quantity, is nonsense and will usually be flagged as a grammatical or syntax error by the compiler.

For user-defined functions one might hope for a similar story. A user might hope that attempts to use his function wrongly might lead to syntax errors. This can be arranged only if the user defines his functions in such a way that he specifies the type of the parameter and the type of the result when he introduces or defines his function. The parameters used at this definition stage are usually referred to as formal parameters. In effect then, these formal parameters and the actual parameters used in function calls should match in type.

Let us illustrate these ideas with an example.

Example 4.1.1 The SINH function

Define a function SINH which takes a REAL parameter and gives a REAL result; moreover

$$SINH(X) = (EXP(X)-EXP(-X))/2$$

Most programming languages have a mechanism of the

following kind:

>   function SINH (take a REAL parameter X)
>   give a REAL result:
>   begin   now do calculation necessary to produce
>
>   (EXP(X)-EXP(-X))/2;
>
>   return this as the result of the function
>   end.

Note the specification of the type in the parameter and also in the result; in this particular case the same type is used in both cases but they could be different. Any attempt to ask for SINH(TRUE), for instance, will result in a syntax error. For the actual parameter, TRUE, will not agree in type with the formal parameter - the former is BOOLEAN, the latter REAL.

With the aid of this definition a user can now make use of SINH in the same way as he would use a standard function. He could tabulate its values and do all the usual kinds of evaluations.

Example 4.1.2 The factorial function

Define a function FACTORIAL which takes a non-negative integer as a parameter and produces an integer result.

>   function FACTORIAL (takes a non-negative integer N)
>   gives a positive integer result:
>   begin   insert here instructions to
>   calculate 1x2x3x...xN and place the result
>   in PRODUCT, say;
>   return PRODUCT as the result of
>   the function;
>   end.

Again, once this definition has been introduced a user can treat FACTORIAL as if it were a standard function.

There is one difficulty with the above definition of FACTORIAL. What happens if, when FACTORIAL is being called or used within a program, the value of the parameter is negative? Should the possibility be ignored or should a check be included to ensure that N is not negative? Opinion on this would vary.

(a) One argument says: yes, of course; catch any errors, include checks, insert firewalls wherever possible, be defensive.

(b) The other argument says: no; the checks can be performed before the calls if necessary; there is no need to introduce checks if they are only going to introduce complexity. Why not also check that N is not too large? What should be done if N is negative, anyway? Print messages? Where? On what file, in what format?

In programming languages such as Pascal or Ada there are facilities for specifying ranges and the problem all but disappears. By stating the range of values of the parameter the difficulty can be overcome. Violation of the range constraint causes range errors and these will be detected by the compiler or at the time the program is being executed. Otherwise (b) is the correct course of action. Design a function to perform one task only. Specify clearly what that task is and use this specification. If there is a need to check information, e.g. data, then write a routine or whatever to do that, specify this clearly and do it properly.

At this stage let us note that functions provide a very important means whereby a programmer again performs the abstraction process. Typically he will realise that there is some task that will have to be performed perhaps several times in his program. He will remove all unnecessary detail, concentrate on the one operation and arrive at a decision about the precise nature of his function. Having designed and implemented it properly he can and must forget about the details of the implementation; he just uses the specification of the function in the proper manner. In a sense therefore, the programmer has created for himself a higher level of programming language. This is the essence of programming.

In later sections and later chapters we shall come into contact with other ways in which the programmer can introduce higher and higher levels of programming language.

Exercises 4.1

1. Design a function SINH in a programming language of your choice. Check that the function indeed performs the expected calculation by printing a range of its values.

2. Implement a function which converts a measurement in metres and centimetres into an equivalent measurement in centimetres.

3. Write a program which contains an implementation of the factorial function, and prints the factorial of any positive integer supplied as data.

4. Design and test a function which finds the position of a letter in the alphabet.

5. Design a function to produce inverse factorials, i.e. 1/N!, where N is a positive integer parameter. Print out the inverse factorials of 1,2,...,M where M is a positive integer supplied as data.

6. Implement functions to test whether
    (a) a character is a space
    (b) a character is a digit
    (c) a character is a vowel
   Test these in a suitable way.

7. Design and test a function to deliver the maximum of its three integer parameters.

4.2 Subroutines or procedures

Looking for guidance to the standard environment when thinking of subroutines or procedures can be frustrating. Most standard environments provide few illustrations. Those that do exist tend to relate to reading and printing, the opening and closing of files, and so on; in short, they tend to be concerned with input and output.

Input and output routines can be relatively complex. Usually there will be routines for performing simple forms of input and output for novices; more complex forms allow a programmer to exercise a great deal of control over the precise form of output. Generally there will be a certain symmetry about input and output routines in well designed programming languages. If information is printed using some form of OUTPUT or WRITE statement then an INPUT or READ statement of a similar kind should suffice to read in that information should the occasion demand.

Though the examples are few there are certain characteristics that one should look for in procedures:

> each procedure should perform one task

> each should be self-contained and should not affect any global program variables

> each should be designed in such a way that the programmer need not be concerned about how the procedure is implemented

> the method of using (or calling) the procedure should be straightforward and not error-prone.

When we introduce user-defined procedures it is important that rules such as these continue to be observed. Clear and unambiguous specification of the effect of the procedures are again essential.

Note that the above list contains no mention of changes to the actual parameter. Indeed it would be senseless to do so. Given also that procedures should not alter global variables, it would then not be possible for procedures to communicate with the outside world other than by performing printing of some output, i.e. our interest would be confined to output routines. Such a limitation would be too restrictive.

Example 4.2.1 Output of new lines

Design a procedure which will cause N new lines to be taken on output.

>   procedure NEWLINE(takes a non-negative integer N)
>   begin
>   Perform N times the following task:
>   take 1 new line on output;
>   end of task.
>   end of NEWLINE.

In the cases we have encountered so far we could observe the following:

> in the standard output routines, and in NEWLINE as defined above, none of the parameters was altered as a result of the execution of the routine; the effect was not on the parameters but was on the state of the files or output devices receiving the output

> in the standard input routines the parameters would be altered; they would receive new values taken from the appropriate input stream or file or whatever.

If we now turn to the writing of routines which are not concerned with input and output then it would be unreasonable to expect all parameters to remain constant or unaltered as a result of the execution of the routine. Otherwise how could the routine possibly have an effect of any kind? How could it communicate with the outside world? So we must expect at least some of the parameters to change. In well-designed programming languages there ought to be some means whereby the programmer can indicate those parameters that are likely to change and those that ought to remain constant. Then type checking of the appropriate kind can be performed by the compiler.

Example 4.2.2 Interchanging values

Design a procedure to interchange the values in two integer variables.

>   procedure SWAP(the integer variables A and B):
>   begin
>   Introduce a new integer variable C.
>   Place the value of A in C.
>   Place the value of B in A.
>   Place the value of C in B.
>   end the procedure SWAP.

The reader should note that we have used a very general method for solving this problem. It is possible to achieve the same effect by a curious combination of additions and subtractions of the values of A and B; this removes any need for the introduction of a temporary variable C. However this particular method uses special properties of the integers and may lead to unexpected overflow! The method we have outlined can be employed to interchange the values of integers, reals, characters and so on, values of almost any kind. As such it is more useful and better.

Exercises 4.2

1 Implement the SWAP procedure in a language of your choice and test it.

2 Design a procedure to convert a measurement in centimetres into an equivalent measurement in metres and centimetres. Include this in a program which reads several measurements in centimetres and does the necessary conversions.

3 Design and test a procedure to rotate circularly to

the right the values in its three real parameters.

4 Implement a procedure that prints a signed integer N at the right of a field of M characters. Incorporate appropriate checks.

5 Design a routine which reads single characters and can be used for reading integers.

6 Modify the routine of the previous example to allow the insertion of spaces or commas at every third character position starting from the right.

7 Design a routine which reads single characters and which can be used for reading real numbers of the form:

  optional sign
  some digits (possibly zero) before the decimal
      point
  a decimal point
  at least one digit after the decimal point.

8 Modify the routine of the previous exercise to allow the possibility of an exponent part.

4.3 Simple recursion

We have already looked at the simple uses of subprograms (functions, procedures, operators, etc.) We have encountered subprograms which have used other subprograms - for example in example 4.1.1 the function SINH would make use of EXP. We have not yet encountered subprograms which are defined in terms of themselves, a straightforward extension of the earlier idea.

A subprogram is said to be recursive if it is defined in terms of itself. Such subprograms can be particularly useful. Their use can often lead to short simple and elegant solutions to seemingly difficult problems.

Many people will argue that recursion should be used only sparingly since its use will often involve overheads in terms of time and storage, i.e. it will produce unacceptable inefficiency. We shall adopt the view that our main aim is to write programs which are correct. Other aims are secondary. If recursion helps with this main aim so much the better.

It is somewhat unfortunate that some programming languages - for example Fortran - do not support recursion. This may provide the reader with some problems. (However, it should be mentioned that there do exist techniques for translating recursive procedures into iterative procedures.)

In many ways recursive functions in computing correspond to inductive definitions of functions in mathematics. The most commonly cited example of a recursive function is the factorial function.

Example 4.3.1 Factorial function

In mathematics the following definition is usually given

$$N! = \begin{cases} 1 & \text{if } N=0 \\ N \times (N-1)! & \text{if } N>0 \end{cases}$$

Thus N! is defined inductively, in terms of (N-1)! The corresponding situation in computing is to introduce a function F, say, and to define F(N) in terms of F(N-1). Typically F(N) will be defined as

    if N=0 then 1 else N x F(N-1) end if

i.e. F(N) is defined in terms of F(N-1) and so is recursive.

In cases such as the above the construction of recursive subprograms is relatively straightforward. As long as the programmer can deduce from his mathematical experience an inductive definition he can produce a corresponding recursive function. Note that a condition is a basic and essential part of a recursive definition; absence of a condition would lead to a never-ending loop.

Exercises 4.3

1. Show how the factorial function might be implemented in a language of your choice.

2. Design a function which given a non-negative integer N produced the Nth Fibonacci number F_N. Recall that

$$F_{N+1} = F_N + F_{N-1} \quad \text{if } N > 0$$

   and that $F_0 = F_1 = 1$.

3. The highest common factor HCF of two non-negative integers M and N can be defined as follows

$$\text{HCF}(M,N) = \begin{array}{l} \text{if } M<N \text{ then HCF}(N,M) \\ \text{if } N=0 \text{ then } M \\ \text{otherwise HCF}(N, M \bmod N) \end{array}$$

   where M mod N is the remainder on dividing M by N. Show how this can be implemented in a recursive manner.

4. Use the function defined in the previous example to produce an implementation of an LCM, least common multiple, function. Use the fact that

$$\text{HCF}(M,N) \times \text{LCM}(M,N) = M \times N$$

   Test the LCM function for various sets of data.

4.4 Divide-and-conquer

The more interesting uses of recursion are in solving problems where the recursion is not obvious but is hidden. It is then the task of the programmer to discover the recursive nature of the problem and to construct his program accordingly.

Example 4.4.1 Printing an integer

Consider the task of printing a positive integer in just as much space as its decimal representation requires.

Suppose that 12345 has to be printed. This can be done by printing 1234 followed by 5. Let N be an arbitrary positive integer. Then to print it we can proceed as follows:

>   if N is non-zero then
>   print the value of N divided by 10;
>   print the single character corresponding to
>   the remainder obtained by dividing N by 10;
>   end if.

In the above example, and in many similar cases, a process called divide-and-conquer is actually being employed. The term has military origins; it was coined by Julius Caesar to describe a certain kind of military strategy whereby the enemy forces were first of all fragmented and then the smaller fragments were individually destroyed. The analogy in computing is striking.

In employing this technique to computing problems we take a task of a particular size and we split it into smaller problems which have to be solved. In printing out integers, for example, we essentially split the integer so reducing the size of the quantity we had to manage; the individual fragments were then printed. Note that this example illustrated a recursive procedure whereas previous examples dealt with recursive functions.

In splitting a problem into subproblems it is often the case that the programmer can exercise some choice in deciding where or how the split should occur. More efficient algorithms tend to result when the sizes of the subproblems are approximately equal – we say that **balancing** should occur.

Exercises 4.4

1. Implement the procedure for outputting a positive integer in just as much room as its decimal representation needs. Incorporate this in a more general routine for printing an arbitrary integer in the minimum space necessary.

2. Test and implement a routine similar to the one described above but employing a base B where $1 < B \leq 10$.

3. A partition of the integer N is a collection of positive integers whose sum is N. The partitions of N can be written as

     4
     3 1
     2 2
     2 1 1
     1 1 1 1

   Write a program which prints out the partitions of an arbitrary positive integer N.

4.5 Stepwise refinement

We have seen that divide-and-conquer is a process whereby a problem of a particular size can be split into subproblems of a smaller size which can then be managed more easily.

When faced with a large programming task (indeed a large task of any kind) it is natural to think in terms of splitting this into smaller tasks which are more manageable. Those new tasks themselves may have to go through several processes of splitting into smaller and smaller subtasks until such time as coding in some programming language can take place. The various tasks and their interrelationship then form a hierarchy of tasks which represent a solution to the problem. This is often referred to as a top-down approach to problem solving.

The process described above is usually referred to as stepwise refinement. It is divide-and-conquer with a difference. The main difference is that the resulting subtasks are not necessarily of the same nature as the original task.

In this discussion we have spoken about subtasks being 'more manageable'. By this we mean that they are simpler in some sense, easier to program. Further, if the process is carried out properly, it will be the case that the job of testing subtasks individually will be far simpler than the job of testing the final program in its entirety. This observation is crucial. Thus divide-and-conquer applies to the testing process as well as to the programming process. Of course, in truth the two are inseparable.

Testing of subroutines can be performed by creating a main program - often called a driver program - which exercises the routines. Ideally the driver program should accomplish several tasks:

> it should create values for which the routine will be tested; these should include the limiting values of ranges, exceptional values, and so on
>
> it should call the routine
>
> if possible, it should test that the results are indeed correct; otherwise the results should be printed for the scrutiny of the programmer himself.

The crude description we have given here pays little attention to how the division into subtasks should be performed. It is not possible to give a completely general set of rules which describe how this should be accomplished. Indeed several possible decompositions may be equally valid. These observations imply a certain creative element in programming.

Decomposition is made easier if the programmer can impose a structure of some kind on the initial problem. Sometimes the structure is very clear; occasionally the structure is lurking in the background, e.g. in the form of mathematical concepts and has to be unearthed; in difficult cases the structure has to be imposed. Whenever subtasks are divided it should be possible to specify the action of each subtask in a simple and convenient manner. When put together these subtasks should then provide a solution to the original problem.

It is often possible to frame individual subtasks as routines or sets of routines. These can then be programmed and tested individually. Gradually the pieces can be fitted together and tested to provide eventually a complete solution. Thus generally stepwise refinement leads to a process of top-down refinement but bottom-up programming, testing and assembly.

Exercises 4.5

1 Write a procedure which determines whether or not any two of its four integer parameters have the same value.

2 A common method of evaluating powers is merely to perform repeated multiplications. A more efficient method of evaluating X^N is possible:

    Initialise PRODUCT to 1, POWER to X and M to N.
    While M is non-zero repeat
      the following task:
          if M is odd then
            replace PRODUCT by PRODUCT x POWER;
          end if;
          replace M by M/2;
          replace POWER by POWER x POWER;
      end task.

The required result is then in POWER.

Show how this might be implemented in a language of your choice.

3 Let F_N denote the Nth Fibonacci number and let HCF and LCM represent the highest common factor and lowest common multiple. Tabulate the values of

$HCF(F_M, F_N)$, $F_{HCF(M,N)}$, $LCM(F_M, F_N)$, $F_{LCM(M,N)}$

for some range of values of N and M. What do you notice about the results?

4 The decimal expansion of the fraction 1/p where p is some odd prime integer, will be recurring or (equivalently) repeating. The sequence of digits will start to repeat after at most (p-1) digits; the length of the repeating block is called the period of the infinite repeating decimal.

Design a procedure which, given an odd prime p, determines the period of the decimal expansion of 1/p.

4.6 Miscellaneous exercises

1 Design a routine to find the smallest prime factor of an integer N.
   Incorporate this routine in a program to read an integer and print out its prime decomposition.

2 Write a program to tabulate the number of letters and other characters occurring in a sentence.

3 Write a program to compare the numbers of vowels and consonants occurring in a sentence.

4 Design a program to count the number of words occurring in a sentence and to find the average number of characters in each word.

5 Write a procedure which takes 3 parameters (A, B and C) and when called, prints a block of asterisks A wide and B deep, C character positions in from the left-hand side of the page.

6 Write and test a procedure which accepts the number of a day in a year of your choice and prints out the

date and day of the week. For example if you choose 1978 and call the procedure with parameter 54 the output should be

> Thursday, February 23rd

7 Write a procedure which takes 2 parameters - the number of a day in a year and the number of the year. The procedure should output the day of the week, month, day number and year. For example, if called with 65 and 1981, the output should be

> Friday, March 6th, 1981

See Zeller's congruence in Chapter 1.

8 In Hanoi (according to legend) stand 3 rods. When the world was created, 64 pierced discs of varying diameter were placed on one of the rods. The largest was next to the ground and no disc was on top of one smaller than itself. Monks transfer the discs to another of the rods during which process

   (i) only one disc is moved at a time
   (ii) no disc is ever on top of one smaller than itself
   (iii) discs are only ever moved from one rod to another.

The algorithm for transferring N discs from rod x to rod y can be expressed recursively as follows

   (1) if N>1 then transfer (N-1) discs from rod x to the third rod
   (2) move the remaining disc from rod x to rod y
   (3) if N>1 then transfer (N-1) discs from the third rod to rod y.

Write a procedure which takes 3 parameters

   (a) the number of discs to be transferred
   (b) the number of the starting rod (1,2 or 3)
   (c) the number of the destination rod (1,2 or 3)

and outputs the disc moves required. A typical move could be expressed

Move top disc on rod 3 to rod 1

9   Ackermann's function is defined by:

$$A(m,n) = n+1 \quad \text{if } m=0$$
$$= A(m-1,1) \quad \text{if } m \neq 0 \text{ and } n=0$$
$$= A(m-1, A(m,n-1)) \quad \text{if } m \neq 0 \text{ and } n \neq 0$$

Write a routine which given m and n returns A(m,n).
Tabulate the values of A(m,n) for all m in the range 1 to 4 and all n in the range 1 to 10.

10 Design a function to find the largest prime factor of a positive integer N.
Incorporate this in an appropriate driver routine to test the function.

11 On a conventional dartboard, a single dart may score any integer i in the range 1 to 20 also 2*i, 3*i, 25 or 50.
(a) Write a procedure which takes a single parameter N and determines whether or not N can be scored with 3 or fewer darts.
(b) Modify your procedure so that it outputs the minimum number of darts needed to score N.
(c) Modify your procedure to output the score required by each of the minimum number of darts. For example if the parameter were 120, the output should be
120
        Treble 20
        Treble 20

(d) In certain games, a player must finish by throwing a "double". Write a procedure which, given N, determines whether or not N can be scored under such conditions and if so, outputs the scores required by each of the minimum number of darts. For example if the parameter were 120, a possible output would be

120
        Treble 12
        Inner bull (50)
        Double 17

12 Write a procedure which, given M and N outputs the disc configuration on each of the three towers of Hanoi after N moves when the total number of discs is M.

13 Design and implement a function (perhaps called INTEGRATE) which evaluates definite integrals of functions over a specified range. A typical call should take the form

        INTEGRATE(LOG,1,2)

and this will evaluate the definite integral of the LOG function over the range 1 to 2.
  State clearly any assumptions you make, e.g. about the sign of LOG over the range of integration.

14 Design and implement a recursive version of the INTEGRATE function described in the previous exercise; use divide-and-conquer techniques.
  Compare the efficiency and effectiveness (e.g. accuracy) if this routine with that constructed in the previous example.

15 An integration function I might be called in the form

        I(F,A,B,ERROR)

and this integrates the function F over the interval A to B, giving a maximum ERROR.
  Design and implement a recursive version of I and compare its effectiveness with the routines produced in the two preceding examples.

16 A partition of a positive integer N (e.g. 6) is a sequence of positive integers whose sum is N (e.g. 1,2,3 or 2,2,2). Two partitions are regarded as the same if one is merely a permutation of the other

(e.g. 1,2,3 and 3,1,2). Another way of expressing this is to say that the sequence must be non-decreasing (e.g. 1,3,2 and 3,1,2 must both be written as 1,2,3).

Write a procedure which given N determines how many partitions of N there are.

17 Write a function which takes as parameters two positive integers and returns TRUE if the numbers are 'amicable' and FALSE otherwise. A pair of numbers is said to be amicable if the sum of the divisors of each of the numbers (excluding the number itself) is equal to the other number.

Your test data could include the amicable pair 1184 and 1210.

18 A cuckoo clock counts the hour and counts once on the half hour. After each hour is counted, a ten second melody is played. The motive force for the pendulum is supplied by a weight suspended by a chain. A similar weight-chain system supplies motive force for the cuckoo-music box combination.

Given that

  (i) a rewind places both weights in their topmost positions (and that these positions are equal elevation)
  (ii) the maximum distance either weight can travel is 1 metre
  (iii) the pendulum driving weight moves at a constant velocity and requires five hours to travel its maximum distance
  (iv) the cuckoo-music box driving weight moves only during its duty cycle and then at a constant velocity
  (v) the cycle referred to in (iv) is a function of the number of cuckoos plus the melody. The cuckoo rate is one per second. The weight velocity during the duty cycle is 1 centimetre per second.

Write a program which inputs the time at which the clock is rewound and outputs

(1) the times of intersection of the two weights
(2) the distances from the rewind position at which they intersect.

Allow time to continue until one of the weights has travelled its maximum distance.

19 The Mobius function M(N) is defined as

$M(N) = 1$ if $N = 1$
$= 0$ if any prime factor is contained in N more than once

$= (-1)^p$ if N is the product of p different prime factors

Thus for example
$M(78) = -1$ [$78 = 2 * 3 * 13$]
$M(34) = 1$ [$34 = 2 * 17$]
$M(45) = 0$ [$45 = 3 * 3 * 5$]

Write a function MOBIUS as specified above.

5 | Arrays

Many aspects of computation are concerned with accessing or scanning through sets of items all of which are of a similar kind. One can immediately think of looking through examination marks to put them into order of merit, sorting names to put them into alphabetical order, searching records to find the number of unemployed people and so on.

Arrays are used in programming languages for holding sets of items all of the same kind. Their usefulness derives from the general ways in which individual elements can be accessed. The process of abstraction that we discussed in chapter one will naturally cause vectors and matrices to be mapped into arrays of an appropriate form. Perhaps less obvious is the observation that chess boards, names of people, road networks, polynomials of particular kinds and so on can also be represented as arrays: names can be represented as arrays of characters and polynomials as arrays of coefficients.

In this chapter we look at various aspects of using arrays. We begin with simple examples that involve scanning arrays in various ways; later we progress to the more sophisticated realms of sorting techniques. Most aspects of array manipulation involve loops in some form or another (explicit or implicit). The correspondence between data structures (the arrays) and the pieces of program that access them (the loops) is particularly noteworthy. Similar correspondences will appear in other areas of programming.

The space requirements of arrays can be large. Each element naturally occupies a certain amount of space and if there are large numbers of elements the space requirements become large. Good programming practice dictates that arrays should not be used unless there is good reason for their introduction. Good reasons clearly include the necessity of arrays in order to solve a problem, i.e. remember a set of values. Other good reasons include efficiency considerations and the naturalness derived from the abstraction process.

5.1 Scanning arrays

We examine the problems of scanning arrays with a view to inspecting or processing the elements of arrays in a variety of ways. In practice arrays tend to be used in a rather limited number of ways. We highlight this by subdividing the examples in a particular fashion.

In a variety of programming languages an integer array A could be introduced in the following manner:

    Ada   A:array(1..8)of integer;

    Basic   DIM A(8)

    Fortran   INTEGER A(8)

    Pascal   A:array[1..8] of integer

    PL/I   DCL A(1:8)

As a consequence of such declarations there are then available a set of integer variables which can be written typically as A(1),A(2),...,A(8). In writing A(I), the I is referred to as the index or subscript and naturally this should be constrained to lie within the range 1 to 8, i.e. between the lower bound of 1 and the upper bound of 8 inclusive.

We shall now examine how we might perform various actions on all the elements of array A. Each piece of program required in the solutions to exercises 5.1(i) should take the form

      Using control variable I starting at the lower
      bound of A and increasing in steps of 1
      to the upper bound of A perform
      the following task:
         perform some operation on the Ith element of A;
      end of task.

To be more particular, all the elements of A could be given initial values in the following manner

> Using control variable I starting at 1 and
> increasing in steps of 1 to 8 perform
> the following task:
>   read in the next number and place it in A(I);
> end of task.

In general, of course, the bounds of an array might be other than 1 and 8. Moreover, the loop may have to run in the reverse direction with I having the initial value 8 and then successively 7,6,...,2,1. There are many variations.

Exercises 5.1(i)

1 By using one loop to read in integers and another to print them out, design a piece of program to read in eight integers and print them out in reverse order.

2 Write a program that reads in 57 integers and outputs them in reverse order three to a line.

3 Write a program that reads in 57 integers and outputs only the odd integers in reverse order seven to a line.

4 Read in 55 integers and output them in reverse order in the form of a triangle; one integer should appear on the first line, two integers should appear on the second line and so on.

The next set of problems will be characterised by the initialisation of the elements of an array in some special way. Essentially there will be a loop of the form:

> Using control variable I starting at the lower
> bound of A and increasing in steps of 1 to
> the upper bound of A perform
> the following task:

let A(I) be same quantity;
end of task.

In some cases there will be considerable savings if the reader notices a simple relationship between the value of A(I) and the value of A(I-1). There is a clear connection between such cases and iterative examples.

Exercises 5.1(ii)

In the group of examples that follow a procedure or subroutine should be designed to perform the particular task. They should be incorporated in suitable pieces of programs to test them.

1 Set all the elements of an array to zero.

2 Put into each element A(I) of array A the quantity

$1 + 2 + 3 + \ldots + I.$

3 Put into each element A(I) of array A the quantity

$1^2 + 2^2 + 3^2 + \ldots + I^2.$

4 Place in each element A(I) of array A the quantity I! (the factorial quantity).

5 Arrange that 2^I is placed in each element A(I) of array A.

6 Arrange that the quantity $I! \times 2^I$ is placed in each element A(I) of array A.

Calculating the sum of all the elements in an array A is relatively straightforward. Thus

Let SUM be 0.
Using control variable I starting at the lower bound of A and increasing in steps of 1 to

ARRAYS

the upper bound of A perform
the following task:
  replace SUM by SUM + A(I);
end of task.

As the evaluation of the loop proceeds so the sum of the elements in array A is accumulated in SUM.

Exercises 5.1(iii)

Design functions which, given an array of integers as parameter, evaluate certain quantities described below. We use $a_1, a_2, \ldots$ to denote the values held in $A(1)$, $A(2), \ldots$. Test these functions by incorporating them in appropriate driver programs.

1 Find the average of all the elements in an array.

2 Evaluate $a_1 - a_2 + a_3 - \ldots$

3 Evaluate $1/a_1 + 1/a_2 + 1/a_3 + \ldots$

4 Evaluate $1 \times a_1 + 2 \times a_2 + 3 \times a_3 + \ldots$

5 Evaluate $1 \times a_1 + 2 \times a_2 + 2^2 \times a_3 + 2^3 \times a_4 + \ldots$

6 Evaluate $a_1 \times a_2 \times a_3 \times \ldots$

7 Evaluate $1/(a_1 \times a_2 \times a_3 \times \ldots)$

8 Evaluate $a_1 \times 2a_2 \times 3a_3 \times \ldots$

9 Evaluate $(a_1 \times a_2 \times a_3 \times \ldots)/(a_2 \times a_4 \times a_6 \times \ldots)$

10 Evaluate $1!/a_1 + 2!/a_2 + 3!/a_3 + \ldots$

It is frequently necessary in computing to find the maximum or minimum of a set of values. Thus we might wish to find the top examination mark, the lowest temperature, the highest mountain, and so on. We shall again assume the existence of some non-empty array A of numerical quantities; let it have lower bound LOWER and upper bound UPPER. The maximum value and the position this occupies within the array can be found in the following fashion:

>   Let MAXIMUM be A(LOWER).
>   Let POSITION be LOWER.
>   Using control variable I starting at LOWER + 1
>   and increasing in steps of I to UPPER perform
>   the following task:
>   if A(I) > MAXIMUM then
>   replace MAXIMUM by A(I);
>   replace POSITION by I;
>   end if;
>   end of task.

As we scan through the elements of A, MAXIMUM is compared with each individual element and altered if necessary; appropriate adjustments are also made to POSITION.

Exercises 5.1(iv)

> We now look at some examples which are similar to the above. Devise subprograms (functions, procedures, subroutines, or whatever) to accomplish each of the following tasks. Incorporate these in pieces of program and test them.

1 Find the maximum of all the values held in an array.

2 Find the minimum of all the values held in an array together with a position this minimum occupies (there may be several). State clearly the effect of your routine.

3 Find both the maximum and the minimum of a set of

elements held in an array.

4 Determine the range spanned by the set of numerical quantities in an array.

5 Determine whether all the quantities in an array are equal.

6 Determine the maximum of the values held in an array and the number of times that maximum occurs.

7 Find the top two elements in an array of elements.

The examples we have just given involve the programmer in comparing each element of an array against some quantity such as MAXIMUM. Examples in the next set involve comparisons between the elements of the array itself!

Exercises 5.1(v)

1 Design a function which indicates whether or not all the elements of its integer array parameter are strictly in increasing order; equality between adjacent elements is not strictly increasing order. Incorporate this in a program to test it.

2 Design a function which indicates whether or not all the elements of its integer array parameter are ordered (either strictly increasing or strictly decreasing). Incorporate this function in a program to test it.

3 A word is said to be a palindrome if it reads the same forwards as backwards. Thus DAD, DEED, and MADAM are all palindromes. Write a program which accepts a single word (at most 20 characters in length and terminated by a character other than a letter) and determines whether or not it is palindromic.

5.2 Frequency counts

One of the common uses of arrays is in counting the frequency with which items arise in certain situations.

Example 5.2.1 Letter count

Consider the problem of finding the number of occurrences in a piece of text of each of the letters. one at a time. If 'G', for example, occurs then we have somehow to note that one more 'G' has appeared; an appropriate variable will take care of the number of occurrences of 'G'. In a similar way there will be variables for the other 25 letters 'A', 'B', ..., 'F', 'H', ...'Z'. Thus an array of 26 elements appears appropriate.

Initially all the elements of the array are set to zero. On reading a character and encountering a 'G', for example

   the 'G'th element of the array is increased by 1;

on encountering an occurrence of the letter 'Q'

   the 'Q'th element of the array is increased by 1.

On encountering a character CH which is a letter, the variable corresponding to CH is increased by 1.

Following this discussion it can be seen that the structure of the required program might be

      Set all elements of array to 0.
      Read a character into CH.
      While CH is not a terminator perform
         the following task:
            if CH is a letter then
               increase the CH element of the array by 1;
            end if;
            read a character into CH;
         end of task.
      Print out the letters and the corresponding
      elements of the array in an appropriate way.

Exercises 5.2(i)

1. Code the solution to example 5.2.1 in a language of your own choosing.

2. Write a program which reads a set of characters terminated by a question mark. It should then print out the number of occurrences of each vowel.

3. Write a program which takes a piece of text and prints out the frequency of occurrence of consonants, vowels, spaces and, lastly, other punctuation marks such as periods, spaces and commas.

4. Given a set of ages in the range 0 to 100 print out the number of occurrences of each age. Assume some suitable terminator.

5. Given a set of ages in the range 0 to 100 use the frequency count idea to sort them into increasing order and output them.

In dealing with frequency counts it often happens that the programmer is not interested in particular values but rather in ranges of values. For instance, he may wish to find the number of ages in each of the ranges

    0-9, 10-19, 20-29,...,90-99.

In such cases some computation has to be performed on a value to discover the appropriate range. Let AGE be an integer variable which holds some age. We have to discover the appropriate range for this value. In typical programming languages it is usually possible to relate the range to the result of a calculation of the form AGE/10+1 where / denotes integer division. Hence

    Let SLOT be AGE/10+1.
    Increase the SLOT component of the array by 1.

The examples which follow require a computation of this nature.

Exercises 5.2(ii)

1. Given a set of ages in the range 0-109 calculate the number in each of the ranges 0-9, 10-19,...,90-99, 100-109. Assume the data is terminated by some negative integer.

2. Assuming data in the form used in the previous example find the number of occurrences of ages in the ranges

    0-4, 5-14, 15-24, ..., 85-94, 95-100.

    Ignore ages greater than 100.

3. Again, assuming data in the form of the example immediately above, find the frequency of ages in the ranges 0-2, 3-7, 8-12, 13-17, ...

4. Assume a set of data consisting of measurements, all of which can be regarded as real numbers lying in the range 0 metres to 100 metres. Calculate the number of measurements lying in each of the ranges.

    0-10, 10-20, ..., 90-100

    (Include the lower bound in the range but not the upper bound.)

5. Assume data in the form described in the previous example. Calculate the number of measurements in each of the ranges

    0-5, 5-15, 15-25,..., 85-95, 95-105

    (include the lower bound in the range but not the upper bound).

6. Assume data consisting of text in the form of words separated by spaces and terminated by a full-stop. Find the number of words starting with each of the letters 'A', 'B', ..., 'Z' and the number of words of size 1,2,... .

5.3 String processing

One particularly interesting use of arrays is in the area of string handling or string processing. Informally a string is a piece of text of some kind and can be regarded as an array of characters. Note that we are not implying that an array is the only possible way of representing strings; it is one of the possible ways, even a very common method.

String processing arises naturally in many important areas of computing. Word processing facilities are used for the proper layout and presentation of letters and other pieces of text; indeed many books are prepared in this way. With these facilities it is typically possible to correct misspellings, rearrange text, properly indent paragraphs and other pieces of text, arrange words in lines (properly justified) and lines in pages, etc.

There are many other areas of applicability for string processing ideas, for example, editors, command interpreters, macro processors and document retrieval systems. We proceed by asking the reader to prepare some typical string processing routines. In this particular area he may find himself unduly constrained by the particular programming language being used. Then, however, restrictions should be clearly documented.

We leave it to the reader to design the particular uses to which he wishes to put his routines. Remember that these routines will have to be models of good programming and they must be carefully written and tested.

We shall return to string processing at a later stage and look at alternative ways of representing strings.

Exercises 5.3

1 Design a function to calculate the size of (i.e. the number of characters in) a given string.
  State clearly any assumptions you might make.

2 Design appropriate routines to

(a) convert a character to a string
(b) concatenate (i.e. join together by laying end to end) characters and strings in any combination.

3 Design a routine to produce an array in which a single character supplied as parameter is duplicated throughout the array.

4 Design a function which calculates the number of occurrences of some given character in a string.

5 Design a function to determine whether or not a character is present in a string.

6 Design a function to determine the most frequently occurring character in a string.

7 Design a function to determine the most frequently occurring letter in a string.

8 Design a routine to determine whether or not a character is present in a string; if it is the routine should determine the position of the first occurrence of that character.

9 Design a routine to produce an array in which a string can be repeated throughout the array. In general the array may not hold an integral number of copies of the string.

10 Design a routine to determine whether or not a particular string is present within a (presumably) larger string. If it is, the routine should pass out information about its position.

11 Design routines for inserting one string at a particular position within another. Permit the position to be stated in several different ways

(a) by number, e.g. after the 10th character
(b) by context, e.g. after the first occurrence

of the character string 'ABC'
(c) by context, e.g. before the first occurrence of the character string 'ABC'.

12 Design a routine to produce the string that corresponds to an integer; the string should hold the representation that might be produced on printing the integer. Provide a careful statement of the effect of the routine.

13 Design a routine to produce the integer value corresponding to a string of appropriate characters. State clearly the limitations of the routine.

14 Design an appropriate routine to determine whether two strings are in alphabetical order; state clearly what you understand by alphabetical order. Note that the routine should work for strings of differing sizes.

15 Design a routine for replacing part of one string by another string. Ensure that your routine works even if the new string is a different size from the string it replaces; in particular the new string could be empty.

16 Design routines to produce the positions of all occurrences of

   (a) a given character
   (b) a given string

in a string of characters.

17 Design a routine to remove from a string all occurrences of

   (a) a particular character
   (b) a particular string
   (c) all the characters within a particular string.

5.4 Sorting and related topics

In computing it frequently happens that names have to be listed alphabetically, that numbers such as examination marks have to be arranged in order of merit, that records of different kinds have to be ordered in some way, and so on. All of these involve sorting a set of items into a particular order.

We have already seen a method of sorting (see for instance example 5 of Exercises 5.2(i)). This method was of rather limited applicability. It worked only because the range and number of values was known and was of reasonable and manageable size. In general this is not the case and it is not feasible to adopt this as a general method. The usual reason for failure of this method is that the set of possible alternative values is too vast; consider, for example, the total number of possible names of students in a class, of accurate measurements less than one metre, and so on.

Most of the usual methods of sorting the elements in an array involve interchanging pairs of elements in the array. Basically they work by putting in order pairs of elements that were previously out of order. Repetition of this process will eventually lead to a completely sorted array. Let us examine several methods in turn.

Suppose we adopt the convention that array A has lower and upper bounds 1 and N respectively. We let $A(I..J)$ denote all the elements between $A(I)$ and $A(J)$ inclusive.

A simple-minded algorithm for sorting the elements of A into descending order can be described crudely as follows:

```
     Find the largest element in A(1..N); let it
         occupy position J in A.
     Interchange the values in A(J) and  A(1).

     Find the largest element in A(2..N); let it
         occupy position J in A.
     Interchange the values in A(J) and A(2).

     ....continue in this vein.
```

In this way the largest element of A is positioned in

A(1), the second largest is positioned in A(2), and so on. The algorithm stops when the (N-1)th largest element is correctly positioned for, by that time, the Nth element must itself be in the correct position. The elements of A are then in descending order, the ordering being determined by the ordering used in finding the largest element (alphabetic, numeric or whatever).

A more precise and formally described algorithm can be written using this outline. We have already seen how to determine the maximum element in a set, we know how to perform interchanges and we know about inserting pieces of program into a loop. The resulting sort process (sometimes called the linear selection method) is applicable to a wide variety of problems - to sorting names, numbers, characters and so on. Variations involving the production of increasing sequences are also easily handled.

The method outlined above can be criticised on the grounds of inefficiency. Basically various scans of the array (or part of it) are performed. After each successive scan the next element is placed in position. The next method we look at, somewhat imaginatively called bubblesort, likewise involves successive scans. After each such scan the next element is in position as before but some secondary sorting of the other elements has also occurred. The name derives from the analogy with bubbles floating to the top in water.

Let us use the same notation for array A as above. In the bubblesort process a scan of the array A will essentially take the following form:

If A(1) and A(2) are out of order interchange them.
If A(2) and A(3) are out of order interchange them.
    ...   .
If A(N-1) and A(N) are out of order interchange them.

At the end of this process A(N) will hold its final value (it will be the largest or smallest element of the array depending on the comparison that occurred). Indeed after this first scan there is no need even to examine A(N). Thus the second scan need only examine A(1..N-1), the third need only look at A(1..N-2), and so on. At most (N-1) such scans are needed.

Again the programming of this process should be

relatively straightforward. All the various steps that we have described have been examined before at some stage.

It is worth noting an apparent optimisation that can be included in the above. If a scan is performed and no interchange takes place during the entire scan then all the elements of the array must be in their correct order. A flag of some description can be inserted (a Boolean variable or an integer variable) to indicate that an interchange has occurred; care should be taken to ensure that the flag is reset before each scan commences.

A far more impressive sorting method is called Quicksort. The design of this method is based on the observation that it seems to be more effective to perform interchanges of elements over longer distances rather than the very short distances (indeed adjacent elements) in bubblesort. This is certainly a valid observation when the initial arrangement of the elements is the reverse of the intended final arrangement.

Using the notation of the previous discussion, Quicksort (to produce increasing order in the elements) can be described in the following terms

> Pick any element in A at random and call it X.
> Set UP to 1 and DOWN to N.
> Scan up array A, increasing UP by 1, until encountering an element A(UP) which satisfies A(UP)>X.
> Scan down A, decreasing DOWN by 1, until encountering an element A(DOWN) which satisfies A(DOWN) <X.
> Now exchange the values in A(UP) and A(DOWN) so restoring the situation whereby A(I) <= X for all I <= UP and A(J) > X for all J >= DOWN.
> Continue this process of scanning up and down, from the present values of UP and DOWN and exchanging values until UP and DOWN pass (i.e. UP > DOWN)

On completion of this scan the array will be partitioned into three sets - the lower set all less than X, the upper set all greater than X and the middle set all equal to X.

To complete the sorting process both the lower and upper sets of elements have themselves to be sorted. A recursive solution leads to the lower and upper sets being themselves processed by such scans. In this way the entire array is sorted in a particularly efficient manner.

In the examples given so far, sorting has been seen as an end in itself. But there are circumstances where sorting is used as a means of achieving another goal. When items are sorted it often happens that they can be more efficiently processed in some manner. For example, the process of discovering whether or not an item is present in an array can be programmed using the binary chop algorithm which we now investigate.

Example 5.4.1   Binary chop

Let A be a sorted (into increasing order) set of N elements which are placed in an array A(1), A(2), ..., A(N). To discover whether or not the item X is present in A we proceed as follows:

    compare X and the middle element of A, A(N/2);

this comparison produces one of three possible outcomes - either

        (a) X=A(N/2)
        (b) X lies in the range below A(N/2)
        (c) X lies in the range above A(N/2)

In cases (b) and (c) we proceed as before but using a smaller array. This binary chop process, as it is called, can be programmed in the following fashion:

```
Set LOWER to lower bound of A.
Set UPPER to upper bound of A.
Set PRESENT to FALSE.
While LOWER <= UPPER and PRESENT is false
      perform the following task:
          set MIDDLE to (LOWER+UPPER)/2;
          if X=A(MIDDLE) then
              set PRESENT to TRUE;
          otherwise if X<A(MIDDLE) then
```

```
            set UPPER to MIDDLE - 1;
         otherwise set LOWER to MIDDLE + 1;
         end if;
      end of task.
```

Example 5.4.2   Merging

Let $A(1),...,A(M)$ be an ordered set of items in increasing order and let $B(1),...,B(N)$ be a similarly ordered set of items. Write a section of program which combines the elements in A and B into an ordered array C.

Of course it is possible to put the elements of A and B in C in some arbitrary order and then sort them. But this does not take advantage of the fact that the elements of A and B are already ordered.

Let us assume that the elements of A and B are in increasing order of magnitude. Then a more sensible solution proceeds as follows:

```
      Set A.INDEX, B.INDEX and C.INDEX to 1.
      While A.INDEX <= M and B.INDEX <= N
         the following task:
            if A(A.INDEX) < B(B.INDEX) then
               place A(A.INDEX) in C(C.INDEX);
               increase A.INDEX by 1;
            otherwise
               place B(B.INDEX) in C(C.INDEX);
               increase B.INDEX by 1;
            end if;
            increase C.INDEX by 1;
         end of task.
      If A.INDEX <= M then
         copy remaining elements of A to C;
      otherwise
         copy remaining elements of B to C;
      end if.
```

Example 5.4.3   Merge sort

Consider the task of sorting a set S of elements into some order. It is possible to proceed as follows:

```
   if the size of S is greater than 1 then
      split S into 2 subsets which we
         denote by S1 and S2;
      sort S1; sort S2;
      merge S1 and S2 together;
   end if.
```

Here divide-and-conquer leads us to divide S into two smaller sets S1 and S2, so reducing the size of the problem. S1 and S2 are themselves sorted (recursively). We then assume the existence of a merging procedure which combines S1 and S2 to provide the required sorted set.

5.5 Multi-dimensional arrays

We have already seen the various uses of one-dimensional arrays. When one of these has to be accessed in such a way that all its elements have to be inspected this was accomplished by means of a simple loop which scanned from one end to the other.

Two-dimensional arrays are available in most programming languages. The abstraction process, which we have constantly referred to, is likely to lead to items of the following kind all being represented by two-dimensional arrays:

   objects such as chess boards

   matrices in mathematics

   sets of examination marks (for various subjects and for various students)

   grids such as maps and

   sets of elements of some kind

and so on. Sets of names may also fall into this category though usually it is more convenient to regard these as one-dimensional arrays of strings.

To access or otherwise process all the elements in a

two-dimensional array usually requires a pair of loops, one rested within the other. Consider the following argument. A two-dimensional array A can be regarded as a one-dimensional array of elements A (I = 1,2,...,N) each A(I) being itself a one dimensional array of items. To process or scan all the items of A requires a loop of the following kind

>   Using control variable I
>   process the Ith row of array A

Here the remark

>   process the Ith row of array A

can be looked upon as a kind of procedure call the body of which will take the form

>   Using control variable J
>   process all the elements of the form A(I,J)

Replacing the procedure call by the body of the procedure in the original produces the following

>   Using the control variable I to span the rows
>   perform the following task:
>   using the control variable J to span the
>   columns perform the following task:
>   process the element A(I,J);
>   end of task;
>   end of task.

Thus we have a double loop being used in a natural way to process all the elements in a two-dimensional array.

The argument we have just put forward has been derived by viewing a two-dimensional array as a set of rows. An alternative view would be to regard the two-dimensional array as a set of columns. Again a double loop would have materialised.

There is another very important but less obvious use of a two-dimensional array. It concerns the idea of an algebraic structure called a graph. A graph can be represented pictorially as a set of nodes joined by arcs. See Figure 5.1.

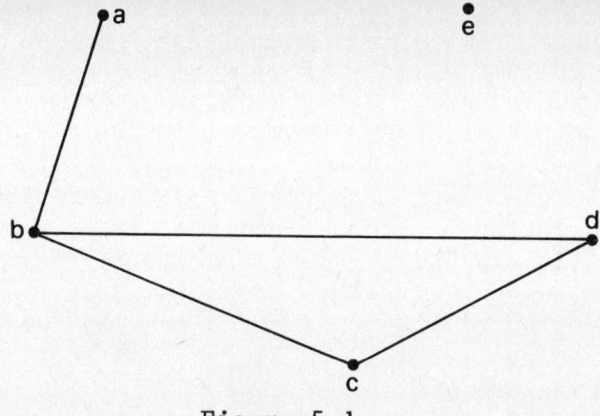

Figure 5.1

In certain cases direction can be associated with the arcs (an arrow can be used to indicate this) and then the graph is said to be directed; otherwise it is termed undirected.

Nodes and arcs might represent a variety of situations, for example,

towns and the roads between them

computers and the communication lines between them

subroutines and the fact that one is defined in terms of another

real numbers and the relationship 'is the square root of'.

Briefly, relationships of all kinds can be represented by a graph.

The examples given above illustrate the power and importance of the idea of a graph. The abstraction process can therefore lead to apparently different situations being represented in the same way and thus to apparently different problems being amenable to the same algorithm or method of solution.

We have already remarked that direction can be associated with arcs. Further it is possible to attribute weights or costs to each arc; this might represent the distance between two towns or the density of traffic between them, for example. In this way weighted graphs result.

The pictorial representation of a graph may not be the basis of a convenient representation in a program. Two-dimensional arrays provide a more promising alternative. We look at two such possibilities.

Suppose the nodes of a graph are represented by the distinct letters a,b,c,... and the edges or arcs by the numbers 1,2,3... The incidence matrix representation of a graph holds in the (c,3) position, for instance, the representation of the node which can be reached from node c using arc 3; where no such node exists some suitable character will be present.

An alternative representation is called the adjacency matrix. The (x,y) entry is

1   if there is an arc connecting node x and node y

0   if there is no arc connecting nodes x and y

Note that undirected graphs produce symmetric adjacency matrices. Of course the 1,0 above can be replaced by TRUE, FALSE or indeed any reasonable pair of alternatives. In the particular case of weighted graphs 1 may be replaced by the appropriate weight.

We can talk about paths through graphs in the obvious way. Paths connect nodes and are constructed from a sequence of traversals of arcs. In the graph given in Figure 5.1 there is a path joining nodes a and c. We say that this path is of length 2 since it is made up of the arcs ab and bc. (In the special case of weighted graphs we can talk about a weight being associated with each path; this might indicate the distance between two towns or some such quantity.)

Adjacency matrices possess some very important properties. Let A be the adjacency matrix of some graph and let it contain entries which are 0 or 1. Then the matrix product A x A can be formed. Non-zero (x,y) entries indicate the number of paths of length 2 between the nodes x and y. In general non-zero entries in A^N = A x A x ... x A indicate paths of length N.

If it is of interest to find out whether paths exist between nodes then of course $I + A + A^2 + A^3$ will indicate the existence of paths of length 3 or less. If paths of any length are required there is no need to go beyond A^N in a graph containing N nodes and $I + A + A^2 + A^3 + \ldots + A^N$ is the quantity of interest.

The ideas we have expounded here can be generalised in various ways. Perhaps the most obvious extension is to arrays of dimension higher than two. Though the need for such facilities is rare there are circumstances in which three and more dimensions are useful. The processing of such structures usually results in loops that are nested to a depth of three or more. Reasoning similar to that used in the two-dimensional case will illustrate the point.

When discussing items like sets of names it frequently, indeed usually, happens that the names will be of differing lengths. Thus rectangular two-dimensional arrays are not ideal but instead one-dimensional arrays whose elements are themselves one-dimensional arrays are more appropriate. Again double loops can be used in the processing of these objects.

5.6 Miscellaneous exercises

1. Write a program which reads N followed by details of N students - name and examination mark. The output should be a list of the names of those students whose mark is above the average.

2. Given some set of real numbers S show how one might find the member of that set closest to some quantity X.

3. Write a program which reads a positive integer N followed by a piece of text which is terminated by +. Your program should output the text exactly as read except that every N-letter word is replaced by N asterisks.

4 Data consists of N pairs (name,profession). Write a program to count professions and output (i) the name of most popular profession, (ii) the names of the people with that profession.

5 Write a program which inputs N followed by N examination marks and outputs the highest pass mark which allows at least 75% of the students to pass.

6 This program is to read a 20 by 20 array of real numbers representing heights above sea level at grid points and to print a map of the area covered as a 20 by 20 pattern of characters. The map is to show sea by space characters and land by "." characters except for the highest point which is to be a "*" character. The map is to be surrounded by "X" characters and followed by a line stating the height of the highest point.

7 In a certain university, students are classified according to the range into which their final mark falls. The ranges are 0-29, 30-45, 46-59, 60-69, 70-85, 86-100.
   Write a program which reads N followed by the marks of N students and outputs the number that fall into each range.

8 The mains voltage supplied by a sub-station is measured at hourly intervals over a 72 hour time period.
   Write a program to find
   (i) the mean voltage measured
   (ii) the hours (numbered 1 to 72) at which the recorded voltage varies from the mean by more than 10%
   (iii) any adjacent hours when the change from one reading to the next was greater than 15% of the mean value.

9 This question relates to the formation of histograms for statistical purposes.
   (a) Write a program which constructs a histogram of the ages of a population. Data is N followed by the ages of N people (no age greater than 99).

Output should be the number of people in each of the age ranges 0-19, 20-39, ... 80-99.

(b) Modify your program so that instead of a number (k) being output, k (or an appropriate multiple of k) asterisks are printed.

10 You are helping to introduce all-figure telephone numbers to a country where, up to the present, telephone numbers have consisted of a 3-letter exchange code followed by a 4-digit number.

Write a program which reads a series of old-style telephone numbers and converts them into their 7-figure form according to the table below. The data is terminated by the number XXX 9999.

Conversion table

```
A,B,C -> 2      D,E,F -> 3      G,H,I -> 4
J,K,L -> 5      M,N   -> 6      P,R,S -> 7
T,U,V -> 8      W,X,Y -> 9      O,Q   -> 0
```

Thus for example SWI 1234 becomes 794 1234

11 Modify the solution to question 2 of these exercises so that it is possible to discover either

(a) the quantity nearest to X but above X

(b) the quantity nearest to X but below X

State clearly what assumptions you make in exceptional cases.

12 Design a routine which allows a programmer to ask for all points (in a set S of real numbers) lying within distance D of some arbitrary point X.

13 Design a routine which takes a set of real numbers and produces all pairs of points within a distance D of one another.

14 Design a facility whereby, given a set S of real numbers, it is possible to ask for the set of points in S lying between the real numbers X and Y inclusive.

15 An interesting generalisation of binomial coefficients are multinomial coefficients. We define

$$\binom{k_1 + k_2 + \ldots + k_m}{k_1, k_2, \ldots, k_m}$$

as

$$\frac{(k_1 + k_2 + \ldots k_m)!}{k_1!\, k_2! \ldots k_m!}$$

Implement and test a function which evaluates multinomial coefficients.

16 In a well-known card trick

   (i) player A displays 21 different playing cards in 3 columns of 7 cards each.
   (ii) player B secretly chooses one of the cards and tells player A the number of the column it is in.
   (iii) player A gathers up the cards, displays them in columns again and once more player B identifies the column containing the selected card.
   (iv) & (v) same as step (iii)

By gathering in the cards column by column with the selected one second of the three and by subsequently displaying the cards row by row, player A ensures that after step (v), the chosen card will be the 4th in column 2 and can thus be identified to a suitably astonished player B.

Write a program which takes the role of player A.

17 A certain instructor awards letter grades to student papers having numeric scores in the following manner. The papers with the highest and lowest marks are found, thus determining the range. Papers with marks in the top 25% of the range are awarded an A, papers with marks in the lowest 30% of the range get a C and the rest get a B.

Write a program which inputs

   (i) a positive integer N
   (ii) the mark for each of N papers

and outputs each of the marks together with the letter that a paper with that score would be awarded by this instructor.

18 Write a program which reads a piece of text terminated by * and outputs any palindromes that it contains. A palindrome is a word that reads the same forwards and backwards. For example, if the input were

   I AM SURE THE DEED IS ON THE LEVEL MADAM*

output would be

   I DEED LEVEL MADAM

19 Read in a sentence composed of words separated by at least one space, and print them out again with only one space between each word and every second word reversed. The sentence on input and output is to be concluded with a full stop. Thus sample output might be:
This si an elpmaxe of tahw is tnaem.

20 One simple but effective coding system depends on an arrangement of 25 letters of the alphabet in a square depending on a keyword. The remaining letter is transmitted as itself. For example if the keyword were BREAK and the letter to be sent unaltered were J then the square would be

            B R E A K
            C D F G H
            I L M N O
            P Q S T U
            V W X Y Z

   A pair of successive letters is coded by replacing

each one by the one in the same row but in the column of the other. For example the message

> CO-MP-UT-ER-SC-IE-NC-E

> becomes

> HI-IS-TU-RE-PF-MB-IG-E

the final letter is left unaltered.

Write a program that first reads a five letter keyword, then the letter to be sent unaltered, then reads and codes a message terminated by *. All punctuation and spaces are to be ignored. Show how you would modify your program to decode a message given the keyword.

21 Write a program which reads the current year followed by N followed by a list of N employee numbers and their current ages. Produce a list showing the years in which the employees retire (become 65 years old). If more than one employee retires in a given year then include them all under the same heading, for example

Year	Number
1986	896743
1988	674501
	450926

If you have character arrays available then use employee names rather than numbers.

22 Write a program to form and print a histogram. Data for the program is an integer N followed by N numbers. This is preceded by another integer M followed by M pairs of numbers, the ith pair being the lower and upper bounds of the ith disjoint range of values. Your program should output a table showing for each range, the lower and upper bounds of that range and the number of the N values falling within it. A warning message should be printed for any data value not in any of the M ranges.

ARRAYS 123

23 Data for the program consists of integers M, N and P followed by an MxN matrix and an NxP matrix. Multiply the matrices and output the MxP result.

24 Write a program which reads a pair of positive integers P and N followed by N numbers x_1, x_2, ... , x_N. After having read x_i ($i \geq P$) the program should output the average of x_{i-P+1}, ... , x_i, thus producing the P-point moving average of the data items.

25 Imagine that you are producing a Sex * Age * Marital Status table for a census. Read in data for a large number of persons giving their name, age and whether or not they are married. The program should output tables showing the number of people in each category. For example part of the "male" table might look like

   Sex = Male

Age =	0- 5	6-10	11-15	16-20	21-25	...
Single	10	5	7	10	5	
Married	0	0	0	4	5	

26 Write a program which reads a text terminated by *. The text may include any character apart from *. Your program is to calculate the frequency of each individual letter and of each pair of adjacent letters as a percentage of the total number of letters and of the total number of pairs respectively. Print out the individual letter frequencies and the three most common pairs.

27 One way of sorting a table of numbers (a version of bubblesort described in section 5.4) is to swap round the members of any pair of numbers which are out of order. Repeated scans are made through the table until there are no out-of-order pairs.
   Write a program which generates 40 random numbers and outputs the numbers in decreasing order.

28 Write a program which reads N followed by N numbers, M followed by M numbers and determines whether or not every element of the first set is in the second and

vice versa. The program should output a suitable message if any set member is not in the other set.

29 Suppose it is necessary to search an array of N elements to determine whether or not an item X is present. Compare the following methods for efficiency by running programs and testing them over a sensible variety of alternative situations:

   (a) perform the usual linear search - compare the item with the first element, then the second element, and so on; note that the element may or may not be present and the programmer must guard against running off the end of the array

   (b) introduce a (N+1)st element and initialise it to X; then perform a linear search merely looking for the index of the first occurrence of X in the array and using the information that at least one such occurrence exists.

30 In a possible tax system, income earners might pay (for instance) nothing on their first $4000 income, 15% on the next $5000, 30% on the next $6000 and 50% on the remainder. Write a program which reads the income levels and percentages for such a four part system and then prints a table of tax payable on incomes from 0 to $25000 in steps of $250.

31 In Italy, banknotes are issued for 50000, 20000, 10000, 5000, 2000, 1000 and 500 lire, coins are available for 100, 50, 20, 10 and 5 lire.

   Write a program which reads in any sum of money and prints out a breakdown into the smallest possible number of notes and coins needed to make it up. Your program should print an error message if the sum is over 2000000 or not a multiple of 5.

32 Trimming can be described as a process of removing from the end of a string of characters some selection of characters. Examples include

   (a) removing all occurrences of some letter, e.g.

all trailing spaces

(b) removing all occurrences of members of a set of letters, represented by an array.

Design and test routines to perform trimming. State clearly any assumptions you make.

33 A string which is balanced with respect to the characters (and) has the following properties:

(a) it contains the same number of occurrences of both (and)

(b) in a left-to-right scan of the string the number of occurrences of) never exceeds the number of occurrences of (.

Thus arithmetic expressions are always balanced with respect to (and).

Design a generalised routine for determining whether a string is balanced with respect to two (different but) arbitrary characters which are supplied as parameters.

34 Design a routine for determining the maximum of a set of integers together with the positions at which these maxima occur.

Test your routine in some appropriate manner.

35 Design a routine which will indicate whether a piece of text (which contains only letters and spaces) contains an occurrence of some particular word. Do this by adding space characters at the start and end of the text and at the start and end of the word.

36 Design a routine that will take a string consisting of digits, a decimal point and perhaps an initial sign and convert this into a corresponding real number. State clearly any limitations and provide accompanying documentation.

37 Design (and test) two separate routines for changing

(a) all the lower case characters in a string to upper case

(b) all the upper case characters in a string to lower case.

38 Generalise the ideas in the previous example in the following way. Design a routine which takes as parameters three strings S1, S2 and S3 and does the following: each character in S1 that is contained at some position in S2 is replaced by the character at the corresponding position in S3.

Test your routine by checking that it performs both of the functions described in example 37.

39 In the binary system there are only two positive integers in which no digit is repeated, these are 1 and 10. In the ternary (base 3) system there are 10 positive integers with this property, namely 1,2,10,12,20,21, 102,120,201 and 210.

Write a procedure NOREP which takes a positive integer parameter k and returns the number of positive base k integers with the property described above. Thus for example NOREP(3) should return 10.

40 A sequence of integers is generated using the following algorithm:

(a) an initial number N_0 is picked.
(b) for j>0 N_{j+1} is the sum of the squares of the digits of N_j (base 10)

It is known that the sequence $N_1, N_2 \ldots$ will eventually cycle for any choice of N_0, i.e. there are integers i and j with i<j where $N_i = N_j$.

Definition: suppose that i and j are the smallest integers with 0<i<j and $N_i = N_j$. Then the insipid cycle length of N_0 is defined to be j-i and the insipid chain length of N_0 is j, the number of distinct elements in the sequence. Further, the integer N_0 is called insipid if the integer 1 occurs in the sequence.

Write a program which inputs

(i) a positive integer N
(ii) N positive integers $M_1 \ldots M_N$

and for each of the M_i outputs

(a) the insipid cycle length of M_i
(b) the insipid chain length of M_i^1
(c) a message indicating whether or not M_i is insipid.

41 In a game of ten-pin bowling each player in turn bowls a frame. The game ends after the last player has bowled his tenth frame.

In each frame a player may have up to 2 shots at the ten pins and his score is determined as follows:

(a) if his first shot is a 'strike' (knocks down all ten pins), he does not take a second shot and his score for the frame is 10 points plus the number of pins knocked down on his next two shots. Normally these will be in subsequent frames, in the case of the 10th frame they are taken immediately

if his first shot is not a strike, the player takes a second shot to try and knock down the remaining pins

(b) if this second shot leaves at least one pin standing then the score for the frame is the number knocked down by his first and second shots

if the second shot succeeds in clearing the pins then the score for this frame is 10 plus the pins knocked down on his next shot. Normally this shot will be in the next frame, in the case of the tenth frame however, the extra shot is taken immediately.

Write a program which, given

(i) a positive integer N (the number of players)
(ii) a stream of integers representing the number of pins knocked down by successive balls bowled down the alley outputs a score card showing for each player
    (1) the score obtained in each frame
    (2) the total score
    (3) the total score as a percentage of the best possible score
    (4) the number of strikes bowled.

[The stream of integers (ii) could be generated from within the program using a random number generator, but you would have to ensure that the number of pins knocked down by a ball did not exceed the number standing before the ball was bowled.]

42 Write a program which reads a word and outputs it in large format. For example if the input word were HELLO the output should be

```
X    X  XXXXXX  X       X         XXXX
X    X  X       X       X        X    X
XXXXXX  XXXXX   X       X        X    X
X    X  X       X       X        X    X
X    X  X       X       X        X    X
X    X  XXXXXX  XXXXXX  XXXXXX    XXXX
```

    Modify your program so that each letter is made up of smaller ones of the same type, so for example a large T is made up of normal size Ts.

    Extend your program so that it accepts a series of words (terminated by *) and outputs it in large format, how you split the series will depend on the width of your output device.

    Extend your program so that it can cope with digits and punctuation characters.

    If your program can output to a paper tape punch, extend your program so that it optionally produces large format text by punching appropriate patterns of holes on the tape.

43 Write a program which reads two strings of characters and finds the largest common subsequence.

44 An NxN latin square contains the integers 1 to N with no repetition of an integer in any row or column. The following is a possible 6x6 latin square.

```
6  3  1  4  2  5
1  4  5  6  3  2
5  6  2  1  4  3
2  1  3  5  6  4
3  5  4  2  1  6
4  2  6  3  5  1
```

An algorithm for producing an NxN latin square is
  (i) fill the first row with an arbitrary permutation of the integers 1 to N.
  (ii) treat the first row as a list of indexes and fill in the appropriate integer. In the example above the first row indicates that the integer which appears in 6th position in the first row, appears in 3rd position in the second row, in 1st position in the third row and so on; thus it determines the position of the 5's.
  (iii) use the first row cyclically shifted one place to fill in another integer. In the example, the sequence 314256 is used to fill in the 1's.
  (iv) repeat step (iii) using a different cyclic ordering of the first row each time until the square is full.

Write a program which reads N and outputs an NxN latin square.

45 Data for this program is an integer N and an integer S, which is either (1 or 0), followed by an N-element vector and an N x N matrix. Write a program which, if S is 1 treats the vector as a column vector and outputs the product of the matrix and the vector, otherwise treats it as a row vector and outputs the product of the vector and the matrix.

46 Write a program which reads an odd positive integer N and outputs an NxN magic square. An NxN magic square contains the integers 1, 2, ..., NxN so arranged that

the total of each row and column and main diagonal is the same.

An algorithm for constructing the square is as follows
- (i) set R = (N+1)/2 and C = N
- (ii) enter 1 at row R column C of the matrix
- (iii) enter the integers 2, 3, ... NxN sequentially, increasing both R and C by 1 (modulo N) each time for N-1 steps and decreasing R by 1 (modulo N) and leaving C unchanged in every Nth step.

47 Write a program which sorts the contents of a two-dimensional array so that they are in ascending order when the array is scanned row by row left to right. Your program should not use any storage for additional arrays.

48 Given as data N followed by a set of 2xN integers, write a program which determines whether or not they can be split into two subsets of N integers each totalling half the sum of the numbers in the original set.

49 There is a single track railway running from A to B. At various points along the track there are passing places. No train may enter a single line section if there is another train already in it. If two trains arrive simultaneously at opposite ends of a section an arbitrary choice is made to decide which proceeds. Write a program which reads in
- (i) the distance between A and B
- (ii) an integer N
- (iii) the distances of N crossover points from A
- (iv) the speeds of the two trains

and outputs the arrival time of each train at its destination assuming they leave simultaneously and that zero time is needed for starting and stopping.

50 Write a program which reads N followed by a set of N distinct numbers and outputs all the proper subsets of the set.

51 Two measurements of rank correlation are Spearman's

Rho and Kendall's Tau. Suppose we have N pairs of measurements $x_1, y_1, \ldots x_N, y_N$, for example (traffic volume, road casualties).

Spearman's Rho is defined

$$\text{Rho} = 1 - \frac{6 \sum_{i=1}^{N} d_i^2}{N(N^2-1)}$$

where d_i = (rank of x_i amongst the x)-(rank of y_i amongst the y).

Kendall's Tau is defined

$$\text{Tau} = \frac{\sum_{i=1}^{N-1} \sum_{j=i+1}^{N} S(i,j)}{N(N-1)}$$

where

$S(i,j) =$

  2 if $(x_i > x_j$ and $y_i > y_j)$ or $(x_i < x_j$ and $y_i < y_j)$

 −2 otherwise.

Write a program which reads N followed by N pairs of measurements and outputs the value of Spearman's Rho and Kendall's Tau.

52 Data for this problem is
    (i) an integer N
   (ii) N pairs of integers representing the stock in a warehouse (catalogue number, number in stock).
  (iii) an integer M
  (iv) M integers each being the catalogue number of an item in a customer query.

Write a program which reads the stock list, sorts it into order by catalogue number and then processes the query list. For each query the program should report either the quantity of the item in stock or that the item is out of stock.

There are various ways of searching the stock list. Compare the performance of linear searching with the binary chop algorithm for stock lists of a variety of lengths.

53 Write a program which inputs N followed by a set of N arbitrary numbers, followed by M followed by a set of M arbitrary numbers. The output from the program should be a list (in ascending order) of those numbers which appear either in the first set, in the second set or in both sets.

54 The k-generalised Fibonacci numbers are defined by

$$f_0 = f_1 = \ldots = f_{k-1} = 0 \qquad f_k = 1$$

$$f_{n+k+1} = f_{n+k} + f_{n+k-1} + \ldots + f_n \quad \text{for all } n \geq 0$$

Write a program which reads integers k and N and generates the first N k-generalised Fibonacci numbers.

55 Suppose that m objects are arranged in a circle and are numbered from 1 to m. The numbering may be clockwise or anti-clockwise but whichever is chosen, all subsequent counting around the circle is carried out in the same direction.

Starting with object number 1 and counting each object in turn around the circle every kth object is eliminated. After m-1 eliminations have been carried out in the manner described above there is only one object left. Denote the number of this object by $P(m,k)$.

Write a program which reads m and k and outputs $P(m,k)$.

56 Primes from 1 to N can be found using the following sieve method due to Aristosthenes

    (i) construct a list of the numbers from 2 to N
    (ii) examine each number in turn starting from 2;
        if unmarked, output it and mark all multiples

of it, otherwise move on to the next number. The numbers output will be the prime numbers between 1 and N.

Write a program which reads a positive integer N (N>1) and outputs the prime numbers between 1 and N using this method.

57 A playing card can be represented by a pair consisting of a number (2-14) and a suit; Ace = 14, King = 13, Queen = 12, Jack = 11,.... Read details of five such cards, form the appropriate records and print a description of the cards as a poker hand (e.g. FULL HOUSE, FLUSH or EIGHT HIGH etc.).

58 Data is a sequence of integers terminated by -999. Write a program which outputs the longest increasing subsequence in the data. You may assume that there are fewer than 50 integers in the data.

59 There are various ways in which a deck of cards may be shuffled, for example the deck may be split in two and the halves interleaved. The resulting pack may then be subject to the same process.

Write a program which takes an ordered deck and outputs the results of applying the shuffle method above k times for k=2, ..., 20.

60 In the game of bridge, bidding is related more or less to the point value of a hand (Ace=4, King=3, Queen=2, Jack=1), each player receiving 13 cards. Let us say that a player may "open" a hand with 13 or more points and that a team (2 players) can expect to get "game" if they have 25 or more points between them. By using a random number generator, simulate a number of deals and determine:

   (i) the probability that none of the four players can open,
   (ii) the probability that 1,2 or 3 players can open,
   (iii) the probability that a team will have enough points for a game.

61 An efficient method of searching an array can be

designed if the probabilities with which the various items in the list occur are known in advance.

Design suitable routines which take advantage of this knowledge by ordering items by probability so that a linear search is efficient.

62 The binary chop algorithm can be improved or generalised to produce the Interpolation Search or the Estimated Entry algorithm. Instead of examining the middle of an array (or a section of it) use the value being sought together with the values of the first and last entries to guess a more accurate position.

Indicate how this can be implemented.

63 The Interpolation Sequential Search algorithm combines the linear search and the ideas of the previous example. An initial probe into the sorted array can be made by using an estimate of the kind implied in the previous example. Then a sequential search (forwards or backwards depending on the circumstances) can be performed.

Show how this can be implemented.

64 In the self-organising sequential search method a list of elements is searched sequentially as in the linear search. However if an item is encountered the list is altered in the hope that further searches for this element will be more efficient. Two variations on this are

(a) the element that is found is moved to the front of the list

(b) the element that is found and the previous element (assuming such exists) are interchanged.

Show how these ideas can be implemented by designing two suitable routines.

65 Design a routine which will take a real number and convert it into a string of characters, i.e. a string

of digits containing a decimal point and perhaps
signs. Specify (by means of appropriate accompanying
documentation) the limits of your routine, especially
the circumstances surrounding rounding, accuracy,
magnitude and so on. (Take as a model the literature
that describes the routines from the programming
language you are using.) Incorporate the routine in
a program and test it.

66 For the purposes of this example a 'character set'
can be defined to be a set of characters (repetitions
are not permitted). Thus the upper case letters, the
lower case letters and the digits are all examples of
legitimate character sets. On these sets various
operations can typically be performed

(a) the union of two sets - this produces the set
of characters which includes all the
characters in the two sets (and no
repetitions)

(b) the intersection of two sets - this produces
the set of characters common to both sets

(c) the difference between two sets - the set of
characters in one set and not in the other

(d) the complement of a set (related to (c)
above) with respect to some universal set
which should be described.

Apart from facilities for performing these operations
it is necessary to be able to

(e) form a character set

(f) test if a character is in a character set

(g) given a string of characters and a character
set, determine either the position within the
string of the first character within the
character set or indicate if no member of the
string is in the character set.

Design routines to accomplish the tasks outlined above.

67 A permutation of N objects is an ordering of the N objects. Thus 14235, 54321, 12345 are all permutations of objects 1,2,3,4 and 5. More generally let the objects be called X_1, X_2, ... ,X_N. Then one permutation of these objects can be obtained from a previous permutation in the following way:

   find the largest I for which $X_{I-1} < X_I$

   find the largest J for which $X_{I-1} < X_J$

   interchange X_{I-1} and X_J

   reverse the order of X_I, X_{I+1}, ... ,X_N

Repeated application of this procedure leads to a lexicographic (related to alphabetic) ordering of the permutations of X_1, X_2, ... ,X_N.
  Write a program which reads in N characters in alphabetical order and prints out the N! permutations of these characters. State clearly any restrictions on the nature of your program.

68 Each side of each of six triangles is labelled with a positive integer. Write a program which inputs 6 groups of 3 numbers - each group the clockwise ordering of the labels on one of the triangles, and outputs the number of distinct ways in which the triangles may be formed into a hexagon. Constraints on hexagon forming are

   (i) the integers on co-linear sides must be relatively prime
   (ii) the triangles may be rotated but not reflected.

A hexagon which is the rotation of another is regarded as equivalent. The following data should produce an output of 4:

2,3,30 6,6,5 30,35,30 15,7,210 21,14,30 29,30,22

69 Write a program which reads positive integers M, N and P (N>M) and outputs the contents of main memory locations M to N inclusive (if necessary use an array to simulate main memory). Each line of your output should contain information about a group of P consecutive words as follows

   (i) the address of the first word in the group
   (ii) each of the P words interpreted as a signed decimal integer
   (iii) each of the P words interpreted as an unsigned octal integer
   (iv) each of the P words interpreted as k b-bit characters (where k and b are chosen appropriately for your computer).

For a certain hypothetical machine, a dump of locations 320 onwards might begin in the following fashion

Address   Decimal   Octal   Character

320   1230 -1811 1731   2316 4355 3303   /! PZ H3

If a number of consecutive rows of the 'dump' are identical then only the first and last rows of such a sequence should be output separated by a message indicating the number of rows that have been omitted.

70 Given a set of n points representing the co-ordinates of an n-sided polygon, find a point which lies outside the polygon.

71 To correct typing mistakes the following scheme is adopted:

!C removes the previous character that has been typed on that line; several occurrences of !C will delete an appropriate number of characters on the current line but will not go beyond the start of the line

!L deletes any characters that have been typed so far on the current line

!W deletes all characters backwards to the next space character or the start of line whichever appears first

!Z terminates the input.

It is customary to say that ! is an escape character; it essentially implies a new mode of operation for the input routine. If the ! character itself is needed this should be typed as !!.

Write a program which accepts input with typing errors and occurrences of !C, !!, etc. but outputs an edited version of the input. State clearly any assumptions you make and document clearly the effect of your program.

72 The number 142857 (generated by the decimal representation of 1/7) has a curious property; the digits are rotated cyclically when the number is multiplied by 2,3,4,5 and 6.

Write a program which finds the next prime number of the form $6k+1$ with the property that the 6k digits obtained from the decimal representation of $1/(6k+1)$ are rotated cyclically on multiplication by $2,3,4,\ldots,6k$.

73 Write a program which takes another as data and removes commentary from it.
   (a) First assume that commentary is everything between the word COMMENT and the following semi-colon. The word COMMENT and the semi-colon should also be removed.
   (b) Modify your program to deal with input programs where commentary is everything between CO and the next CO or between # and the following # or between COMMENT and the following COMMENT.

74 Write a program which reads a positive integer N and outputs a calendar for year N. Your program should print as many months as possible across the page. At the end of the calendar should be the day and date of Easter and Christmas (see exercise 17 of Chapter two).

ARRAYS 139

75 Write a program which takes a pattern (P) and a dictionary of words (D) and outputs a list of those words in D that match P. P may be composed of letters plus 2 special characters:
> . matches any single character
> * matches any sequence of characters including the empty string.

For example
> the pattern CAT matches the word CAT
> the pattern C.T matches the words CAT, COT, etc.
> the pattern C.T*S matches the words CATS, CATCHES, etc.

76 A certain programming contest involves each of a number of teams attempting to solve, in a 6 hour period, as many as possible of 4 programming problems.

In developing solutions, teams submit for running

> (i) test runs
> (ii) judged runs.

The results of a judged run are examined by the contest judges. If the results are satisfactory the team is deemed to have solved that problem. If the results are not satisfactory, the output is returned to the team.

At the end of the 6 hour period the teams are ranked by the number of problems solved. Amongst teams solving the same number of problems, ranking is determined by assigning each team a score which is:

> sum of the times (in minutes from the contest start) at which each solved problem was judged correct
> + 10 * number of test runs
> + 20 * number of judged runs.

The lower scoring of two teams is ranked higher.

Write a program which inputs

(i) a positive integer N (the number of teams)
(ii) a list of event records in which each record consists of
   (a) time of event (in minutes after the contest start)
   (b) event type
      TR = test run
      JS = solution judged correct
      JN = solution judged unsatisfactory
   (c) team number
   (d) problem number.

The list is terminated by a record with a negative time field. Your program should output a ranked list of the team numbers with the winner of the competition first.

77 In the game of cribbage, in its 2-player version, each player has a "hand" of 4 cards, the players alternately have an additional set of 4 cards (the "crib") and 1 card (the "starter") from the remainder of the pack is exposed.

At a certain stage in the game, each player evaluates his hand and, if appropriate his crib, in the following way:

(a) Each combination of cards totalling 15 scores 2 points.
(b) Each pair of the same rank scores 2 points.
(c) A "run" of 3 or more consecutive ranks scores 1 point per card.
(d) A Jack of the same suit as the starter scores 1 point.
(e) Four cards of the same suit as the starter scores 5 points.
(f) All 4 cards in a hand (but not in a crib) having the same suit scores 4 points.

Note: A hand may not score under both (e) and (f). Combinations for (a),(b) or (c) may include the starter. Ace counts as 1. Face cards, when totalling a hand, count 10.

Example: Hand   8 Hearts, 9 Diamonds, 7 Spades, 7 Clubs
         Starter 7 Spades

Score of the hand is 21 points made up as follows

    3 sets totalling 15 (7+8, 7+8, 7+8)......6 points
    3 pairs of 7s............................6 points
    3 runs of 3 cards each (789, 789, 789)...9 points

Write a procedure which takes as parameters

   (i) representations of 4 cards (a hand or crib)
  (ii) a representation of the starter
 (iii) a flag indicating whether (i) represents a hand or a crib

and returns as result the score of the hand or crib.

78 Write a program which reads a positive integer N and simulates a game of bingo between N people. Bingo may be played in the following way.

Each player has a bingo card which is a 5 by 5 matrix of positive integers with the centre entry absent. The first column contains entries in the range 1 to 16 inclusive, the second column's entries are in the range 17 to 32 and so on. The centre position is considered "covered" at the outset of the game.

A sequence of numbers is "called". Each number is in the range 1-80 inclusive. A player with a card on which a called number appears, "covers" the corresponding element on his card. The called numbers give a card a bingo as soon as all the elements in any of the 13 winning coverings are covered. The winning coverings are:

        each of the five rows
        each of the five columns
        each of the two principal diagonals
        the four corners

Your program should generate random cards for the

players (subject to the constraints described above) and then generate a stream of "called" numbers until one or more players has a bingo.

The output from the program should be

   (i) the number of numbers that had to be called before a card got a bingo
   (ii) for each card getting a bingo at this point, the numbers (and only those) which had been covered to give that card a bingo.

79 A set of positive integers E has the property that

   (i) 1 is in E
   (ii) whenever x and y are in E (the case x=y being allowed), 2x + 5y is also in E

Given that these are the only rules for generating elements of E, write a program to generate all the elements of E less than some quantity N which is supplied as data.

80 Write a program which generates a random bridge deal (13 cards to each of 4 players) and displays it in the form commonly used in newspaper columns. Using the abbreviations S,H,C and D for Spades, Hearts, Clubs and Diamonds respectively, a typical display would be

```
                      S K 7 5
                      H A Q 8
                      D Q 9 6 2
                      C A 7 3

   S A 9 6 3         *********         S 10 8 4 2
   H K 10 9 6 3      *   N   *         H -
   D 10 5            *W     E*         D A K 8 4
   C 8 2             *   S   *         C K J 10 9 4
                     *********

                      S Q J
                      H J 7 5 4 2
                      D J 7 3
                      C Q 6 5
```

Note that the cards in a hand are sorted within a suit. Your program should produce a sensible display no matter how skew the distribution of suits.

81 Let $a_1, a_2,\ldots,a_n$ be a sequence of integers. The first order forward differences are the elements of the sequence

$$D^1_1, D^1_2, \ldots, D^1_{n-1}$$

where $D^1_m = a_{m+1} - a_m$. In general the kth order forward difference is defined as

$$D^k_m = D^{k-1}_{m+1} - D^{k-1}_m$$

where $D^0_n = a_n$ is an element of the original sequence. For example given the sequence 4,-3,20,-2. The first order forward differences are -7,23,-22. The second order forward differences are 30, -45. The third order forward difference is -75. The fourth and higher order differences are undefined.

Write a program which reads a sequence of integers terminated by 999 and outputs all the defined forward differences up to and including the tenth order differences. Assume that every integer in the sequence is greater than -100 and less than 100.

The program should print the elements of the even sequences and the odd sequences on alternate lines, as illustrated below for the example sequence above.

```
   4
            -7
  -3                 30
            23                -75
  20                -45
           -22
  -2
```

82 Design a routine (a generalisation or extension of that designed in example 36 of this set) that will take a string representing an arbitrary real number perhaps with exponent part and convert this into a

corresponding real value.

83 Design a routine (a generalisation of example 65) for taking arbitrary real numbers and converting these into strings of characters; the string may include digits, signs, a decimal point and an exponent. Include accompanying explanatory documentation. (Take as a model the literature that describes the routines from the programming language you are using.) Incorporate the routine in programs and test them.

84 The randomness of the numbers produced by a random number generator can be tested in a variety of ways. If the generator produces integers in the range 1 to N then the following are among the possible tests.
    (a) individual numbers - count how often each number occurs
    (b) sequences - for some k, count how often each of the N^k sequences of length k occurs
    (c) digits - decompose each number generated into its digits and count how often each of the 10 digits occurs
    (d) poker test - treat a sequence of 5 generated numbers as a poker hand and count frequency of different types (straight, pair, full house etc.)

In each of these cases the goodness of the generator could be assessed by comparing the observed frequency distribution with the expected one using the chi-squared test.

Write a program which tests the generator of exercise 45 in chapter 3 in the ways described above.

85 Clock patience is played with a standard deck of 52 cards. The cards are dealt in 13 piles of 4, 12 piles as on a clock face and one in the centre.

The top card is removed from an arbitrary pile and placed at the foot of the pile where it belongs (Ace=1, Jack=11, Queen=12, King in the centre). The top card from this pile is the next to be placed. The game terminates when all four kings are in the centre. The game is successful if, at that time, all the other cards are correctly placed.

Write a program which reads N, simulates N games of

clock patience and outputs the number of successful games.

86 Data is a sequence of integers terminated by -999. Write a program which outputs the longest decreasing subsequence in the data. State clearly any assumptions you make.

87 Given a frequency distribution as N followed by N pairs (value, frequency) write a program which generates 100 random values reflecting their frequency in the given distribution. Use your program to generate "text" given
    (a) the approximate frequencies of the space and 26 letters in English texts
    (b) the approximate frequencies of the 729 (27 x 27) pairs of letters.

88 A statistical knight's tour is a sequence of moves made by a knight on a chessboard. There are usually 8 moves available to the knight and he chooses randomly from among them. The tour ends when the knight either tries to move off the board or arrives at a square which has been previously visited.
(a) Write a program which reads 2 integers A and B both in the range 1 to 8 and determines the average length of knight's tours starting at square (A,B) in 100 independent trials.
(b) Extend your program so that it outputs a bar chart showing the relative frequency of tours of each length found in the trials.
(c) Write a program which, for each of the 64 squares on the board, determines the average length of tour starting from the square in 50 trials. Display the results as a density plot (see exercise 51 in Chapter 3).

89 Write a program to solve a set of three simultaneous equations such as

$$1.5x + 2.4y + 3.2z = 5.0$$
$$2.5x + 3.4y + 4.2z = 6.5$$
$$5.1x + 1.4y + 4.7z = 15.0$$

reading the coefficient values as input.

90 Currency dealers in country X quote two rates for dealing in the currency of Y - a buying rate B and a selling rate S. These mean that when they buy $Y from you they will pay you B*$X but that when they sell you $Y they will charge you S*$X. Normally S>B.

Given the buying and selling rates operative in each of 10 countries for the currency of the other 9, determine whether you can make a quick buck (in country X or Y) by cycling your available money (assumed a positive amount) through various currencies.

91 Design and test a routine which finds the determinant of an NxN matrix.

92 Find the median of a set of integers, i.e. a value such that as many values are less than or equal to it as are greater than or equal to it. Assume that there are an odd number of integers in the set.

Extend your program in such a way that the median and the mean can be compared.

93 Write a program which reads positive integers T and N followed by a set of N numbers. If $1 \leq T \leq N$ then the program should output the Tth largest element of the set otherwise it should output a warning message.

94 Write a program which reads N followed by N pairs of numbers (A1,B1) ... (AN,BN) and determines whether or not the A elements are a permutation of the B elements.

95 Write a program which reads N followed by a set of N numbers, M followed by a set of M numbers and determines whether the second set is

   (a) a subset of the first
   (b) a proper subset of the first
   (c) neither (a) nor (b).

96 Consider the sequence of numbers

1 2 3 4 5 6 7 8 9 10 11 12 ...

Removing every second number produces the sequence

1 3 5 7 9 11 13 15 17 ...

Now removing every third number gives

1 3 7 9 13 15 19 ...

This process continues indefinitely. The integers that remain indefinitely are said to be "lucky". Write a procedure which, given an integer, determines whether or not it is a lucky number.

97 Snakes and ladders is played on a linear board divided into squares numbered 1,2,...,N. Each player has a marker which initially is on square 1. Each player in turn rolls a die the score of which determines the number of squares he advances his marker. The winner is the first person whose marker reaches square N.
However

(a) certain squares contain "ladders". If at the end of a move a player's marker is in a square (F) containing the foot of a ladder, the marker is moved to the square (T) containing the top of that ladder (T>F).
(b) certain other squares contain "snakes". If at the end of a move a player's marker is in a square (H) containing the head of a snake, the marker is moved to the square (E) containing the tail of the snake (E<H).

Write a program which reads N followed by a suitable representation of an N-square board and a positive integer P and, using a random number generator, simulates a P-person game.
Variations:
(i) no player may place his marker on square 1 until he has rolled a 6
(ii) a player must finish exactly on square N. If for example his marker is on square N-2, only

a score of 2 will finish.

98 Given as data, N followed by a permutation of the first N integers, output the lexicographic rank of the permutation. Rank is equivalent to position in the 'alphabetic' ordering of the permutations; the rank of the sequence 1, 2, ... , N is 1, the rank of the sequence N, N-1, ... , 1 is N!.

99 Note that

$$1 + 2 + 3 - 4 + 5 + 6 + 78 + 9 = 100$$

This is the only way of inserting seven plus and minus signs between the digits 0 to 9 in order to make the equation correct. Prove this.

100 Insert only three plus or minus signs between the ordered digits 0 to 9 in such a way that the arithmetic result is again 100.

101 How many pluses should be placed between the digits 0 to 9 arranged in descending order to result in 99? Where should they be positioned?

102 Write a program which processes the scores in a golf tournament as follows. Data for the program will be 18 integers representing the "par" score for each hole followed by N followed by N sets of data each representing the performance of a golfer. A set will consist of the golfer's name followed by 18 integers representing the number of shots taken at each hole.
(a) Write a program which produces a list of the golfers ordered by the total number of shots taken (lowest number first).
(b) Modify your program so that the first golfer with a particular score is preceded by that score. For example

    68 Brown,K.
    69 Trevino,L.
          Watson,T.
    71 Aoki,I.
          Ballasteros,S.

Include some form of division between those (if any) scoring below par and the rest.

(c) Extend the program so that it produces for each hole a summary of the performances of the golfers at that hole. For example if there were 50 golfers in the tournament, part of the table might be

Hole	Par	>1-under	1-under	Par	1-over	2-over	>2-over
.							
.							
15	4	0	11	30	6	2	1
.							

103 The Lilliputian railway system consists of 50 stations and a large number of lines. Provided that two stations are on the same island it is possible to travel between then but it may be necessary to use several lines and intermediate stations.

Write a program which given N and the start and finish point of each of the N lines, determines how many islands there are (excluding those with no stations).

104 Generating permutations of objects (see example 67 of this set) can be costly in terms of time; there are N! permutations of N distinct objects and the value of this rises rapidly as N increases. Substantial benefits can be derived from a routine which, given a particular value of k, generates the kth permutation within some ordering of permutations. In the lexicographic ordering of permutations the first $(N-1)!$ permutations of X_1, X_2, ... , X_N will have X_1 in the first position, the next $(N-1)!$ will have X_2 in the first position, and so on. So integer division of k will provide information about the object in the first position. On removing this object from the set analagous arguments can be used to derive the other objects.

Show how a routine for producing the kth permutation in a lexicographic ordering of permutations of N objects can be implemented.

105 Write a program which inputs equations of the form

ONE + TWO + FOUR = SEVEN
SEND + MORE = MONEY

If there is a solution to the equation - a set of letter-digit correspondences such that the equation is true, then the program should output the solution otherwise report that no solution exists. (A solution to the second equation above is the set {M=1, letter O=0, S=9, E=5, N=6, R=8, D=7, Y=2} giving 9567+1086=10652.)

106 Write a program which takes 2 poker hands and determines which of the 2 wins (if a tie, output "tied game"). Use the normal rules applied to 5-card hands.
    (i) assume no "wild" cards
    (ii) extend your program so that a 2 may represent any card of its suit
    (iii) extend your program so that a 2 may represent any card.

107 Programs can be used to read text and output it in a much neater manner. For example the text can be properly justified, i.e. the right-hand margin can be made uniform by inserting spaces in a sensible manner between words elsewhere on a line.

Write a program which reads text and outputs a neat version. Briefly, text should be absorbed and assembled into suitable lines for output. Adopt the following additional conventions

    (i) if a blank line appears on the input, any text that has been assembled should be printed and a blank line should be produced in the output

    (ii) if a line starts with N spaces or blanks (N is some positive integer) this should cause assembled text to be printed and the next line of output should start with N spaces.

108 A set of problems related to printing cheques follows:

(a) Given a number (R) and a field width (W), output W characters – the number (correct to 2 decimal places) preceded by a '$', preceded by asterisks (if necessary) to fill out the field. For example if R were 108.7 and W were 10 the output should be

        ***$108.70

(b) Given an integer print the equivalent English. If for example the integer were 1089, the output should be

    ONE THOUSAND AND EIGHTY NINE

(c) Given a real number, treat it as an amount of money (dollars and cents) and output the equivalent English. The number 108.7 thus becomes

    ONE HUNDRED AND EIGHT DOLLARS AND SEVENTY CENTS

(d) Given a date as a coded integer, output it in normal form. Thus the integer 251284 would be output as

    25TH DECEMBER 1984

(e) Write a program which, given as data a real number representing an amount of money and a date, coded as above, outputs a cheque with suitable formatting.

109 A series of problems related to reading and validating cheques follows.

(a) Convert a sequence of digits representing an integer to a number.
(b) Convert a sequence of characters representing a real number to a real. The conversion process should include checks for illegal characters, more than 1 decimal point etc.
(c) Convert a sequence of English words representing

an integer to the corresponding number. Again checks should be included.

(d) Convert a sequence of English words representing an amount of money (dollars and cents) to the corresponding real number. Check for example that there are no more than ninety nine cents.

(e) Read a date, for example "21ST MARCH 1984", check that it is valid and if so convert to an integer (in the case of the example 210384). If it is valid then also check that it is (i) not later than a given date D and (ii) not more than six months before. D is given in the same integer format.

(f) Write a program which reads a cheque presented as (i) date, (ii) amount in figures, (iii) amount in words, and checks that it is valid - that the words and figures correspond and that the date is not later than the current date nor more than six months before. Use a library procedure, if one is available, to give you the current date, otherwise read it in as data.

110 Write a program which inputs a time (e.g. 11.20) and draws a picture of an analog clock with the specified time displayed clearly.

111 Any string containing only upper case letters can be termed well-formed if the numeric values corresponding to the first occurrences of its component letters (A=1,B=2, etc.) are in strict ascending order and ill-formed otherwise. Thus for example CHINO is well-formed, BILLY and EMILY are ill-formed.

The well-formed strings of a particular length can be ordered e.g.
```
          1  A B C              1 A B C D E
          2  A B D              2 A B C D F
                 .                    .
                 .                    .
                 .                    .
       2600  X Y Z           65780 V W X Y Z
```

Write a program which inputs an arbitrary string

of upper case letters, determines whether or not it
is well-formed and, if so, outputs the index of the
string in the appropriate ordering.

112 Write a procedure PR which takes 2 integer
parameters MANTISSA and EXPONENT and outputs a
suitable representation of the number. For example

```
PR (6,4)    should output   60000
PR (6,-4)   should output   0.0006
PR (-6,-4)  should output   -0.0006
```

113 Three more problems related to the printing of
numbers follow.
(a) Write a procedure WHOLE which takes 2 integer
parameters N and W and outputs W characters - a
sign character and digits representing the
number N possibly preceded by space characters.
If N requires more than P characters then P
asterisks should be printed. For example, using
a 's' to denote a space

WHOLE(38,6) should print "sss+38" (with no quotes!)
WHOLE(-4,2) should print "-4"

(b) Write a procedure FIXED which takes a real
parameter R and two integer parameters W and A.
Calling FIXED results in W characters being
output - a sign character and a representation
of R (with A digits after the point) possibly
preceded by space characters. Again if the
parameter values make this impossible, asterisks
should be printed. For example

FIXED(-3.685,8,2) should print "sss-3.67"
FIXED (93.2,9,3) should print "ss+93.200"

(c) Write a procedure FLOAT which takes a real
parameter R and three integer parameters W, A
and E. Calling FLOAT results in W characters
being output - a representation of R in
"floating point" notation with the fraction f
$1.0 \leq f < 10.0$ preceded by a sign character

possibly preceded by space characters. In the representation of R there are A digits after the decimal point in the fraction part and E characters in total in the exponent part. For example

   FLOAT (5342.876, 14, 4, 3) should print
           "sss+5.3429es+3"

   FLOAT (0.000003261, 10, 5, 2) should print
           "3.26100e-6"

114 The Hamming distance between two bit patterns is the number of bit positions in which they differ, thus for example the Hamming distance between

   100101
and
   001110

is 4.

(a) Write a procedure which given 2 non-negative integers, returns the Hamming distance between their binary representations.
(b) Write a procedure which given 2 positive integers N and H returns the largest possible set of N-bit integers such that the Hamming distance between any 2 members of the set is H.

115 A football league consists of 2xN teams. During a season every team plays every other once at home and once away. The season lasts 4xN-2 weeks. Each week there are N games. Write a program which outputs a fixture list showing for each week the home and away team in each game.
   Try to generate a fixture list in which teams alternate between home and away games as far as possible.

116 Write a program which inputs a positive integer N and outputs Gray codes for the integers 1 to 2^N. The Gray code of 2 successive integers differs by only 1 binary digit.

117 For each of the questions below, write a program which reads appropriate data, typically N followed by N co-ordinate pairs, and outputs the answer to the question.

    (a) Do N points form a convex polygon?
    (b) Do N points form a regular polygon? If so what is its centre and area?
    (c) Do N points lie on a circle ?

Assuming that points possess three coordinates, design routines to answer the following questions.

    (d) Do 4 points represent the corners of pyramid?
    (e) Do 8 points represent the corners of a cube?

118 The following are geometric problems.
    (a) Write a program which takes as data the co-ordinates of a point and the co-ordinates of the vertices of a convex polygon. The program is to determine whether or not the point lies inside the polygon.
    (b) Modify your program so that it will deal correctly with arbitrary polygons.
    (c) Is a point inside the convex hull (see below) of a polygon?
    (d) Is one polygon wholly within another polygon?
    Note: informally, the convex hull is described by a piece of string that tightly encircles the polygon.

119 Geographical areas can be represented within a computer.
    (a) Write a program which given the shape of an island as the co-ordinates of a series of connected points on its coastline, determines whether or not an arbitrary point is within the territorial waters of the island. The territorial limit is supplied as data.
    (b) Given as data the co-ordinates of connected points on the coastline of an island, write a program which determines whether an arbitrary point is in the sea or on land. The island may be any shape including an atoll.

(c) Given the outline of an island, the co-ordinates of a sinking ship and information for each of a number of potential rescuing ships (position and maximum speed), write a program which determines which of the rescue ships can arrive at the sinking ship first. Ships are not allowed to move through the island!

120

```
         Store                        Store
          1                             1
       ┌──────┐                      ┌──────┐
       │  X   │                      │      │
       │      │ M                    │  Y   │
       ├──────┤                      │      │
P-M    │      │                      │      │
       │      │                      ├──────┤
       │  Y   │                      │  X   │
       │      │ P                    │      │ P
       └──────┘                      └──────┘
         (a)                           (b)
```

Given an integer array of elements STORE(1),...,STORE(P) with the restriction that this is the only array you are allowed to use, write a program which will move M elements X from their position in (a) to their position in (b) without destroying the order of the elements within X or the order of the elements within Y.

Since P may be large some thought should be given to the efficiency of your method and implementation.

Data is P,M followed by P integers.

121 Write a program which compresses text by replacing commonly occurring groups of characters by single characters which otherwise do not appear in the text. Ensure that the correspondence between groups and characters is stored in a suitable way with the compressed text. Check that the original text can be recovered from the compressed form.

122 Chebyshev polynomials are defined as follows

$$T_0 = 1 \qquad T_1 = x \quad T_2 = 2x^2 - 1$$

$$T_{n+1} = 2 * x * T_n - T_{n-1} \quad \text{for } n \geq 1.$$

Write a program which reads a positive integer i and calculates the coefficients of $T_i(x)$.

123 Write a program which reads N followed by N numbers, computes the mean and standard deviation of the numbers and then outputs a bar chart of the form

```
                            *
Standard deviation  =    ___*_____
                            * *
                            * * *      *
Mean value          =    ___* *_*____*____
                          * *      * * *  * *
                          * *        *    * *
Standard deviation  =    ___*_____*__
                            *
```

124 Certain characteristics of a hotel room may be coded in a simple way. For example
    (i) the number of single beds
   (ii) the number of double beds
  (iii) whether or not there is a bathroom
  (iv) whether or not there is a television.

Thus a room with 2 single beds and a television but no bathroom or double beds could be represented by 2001.

(a) Write a program which reads in the characteristics of the rooms in an N-roomed hotel and requests for bookings. A request is of the form

    Name , requirements

where requirements are coded in the same way as room characteristics. If a room meeting the requirements is available your program should reserve it and exclude it from further consideration. The hotel wishes to turn away as

few clients as possible so your program should minimise the resources allocated over those requested.
(b) Extend your program so that, depending on the outcome of the request, an appropriate letter is output. For example

> Dear <name>,
> Thank you for your letter requesting a room with <x> single beds and a television. We have pleasure in reserving you room <roomnumber>.

125 The Rhine test is designed to determine if a person has extra-sensory perception. Our variation involves a deck of 20 cards (Ace, King, Queen, Jack and Ten of each suit). The cards are mixed and the subject must guess at each card's value as it is drawn. The suit of the card is unimportant. He does this for each of the 20 cards, and we shall call this a game.

Write a program which uses a random number generator to simulate a reasonable number of games for each of the three strategies below. Produce appropriate statistics to show which is the best strategy.
(a) Cards are guessed at random.
(b) Cards are guessed at random with the restriction that each value is guessed 4 times (equivalent to the subject having a deck of his own which he attempts to match with the experimenter's deck).
(c) Cards are guessed taking into account all cards which have previously been drawn (i.e. the guess is based on probabilistic expectation).

126 An eccentric wine lover buys individual labels of wine in either 1, 3, 6, 12 or 24 bottle lots and consumes either 1 or 2 bottles of the same type at a time. Unfortunately his wine cellar can hold only 120 bottles, and he is further constrained by the fact that he wishes to keep wines of a particular label in contiguous areas of his cellar, so that he can always tell how many of a particular type are left; once positioned, bottles may not be rearranged in other locations. Assuming that storage locations

of his cellar are numbered consecutively, show how his wine stocks may vary as he buys and consumes wine. For example,

```
     Location  1 2 3 4 5 6 7 8 9 . .

Buys 3 'A'     A A A
Buys 6 'B'     A A A B B B B B B
Drinks 2 'B'   A A A   B B B B
Buys 1 'C'     A A A C B B B B
```

Data will be a series of pairs of the form {integer, wine type} where for example -2,B indicates that he drinks 2 bottles of 'B'. After the last data pair will be the integer 0. Deal with error conditions in an appropriate way.

127 The balancing idea outlined in example 33 of these exercises can be generalised to strings. Thus in many programming languages BEGIN...END pairs are balanced.
   Design a routine to generalise the notion of balancing in this way; describe carefully the effect of the routine and any limitations imposed.

128 Let there be a set of N boys and a set of N girls. Each boy ranks the girls from 1 to N and the girls likewise rank the boys. A pairing involves matching the boys and girls in pairs. A pairing is said to be stable provided that for each 2 boys b_1 and b_2 and their corresponding partners g_1 and g_2 both of the following conditions are satisfied

   (a) either b_1 ranks g_1 higher than g_2, or g_2 ranks b_2 higher than b_1

   (b) either b_2 ranks g_2 higher than g_1, or g_1 ranks b_1 higher than b_2.

Stable pairings always exist. Write an algorithm to determine one such pairing, given appropriate input.

129 John Conway's "Life" game (see for example Scientific American, Volume 223, number 4 (October

1970) pp. 120-123) involves a colony of organisms on an N by N rectangular array of cells. Each cell is either unoccupied or occupied by a single organism. Each cell has eight neighbouring cells, those with index 0 or N+1 are permanently unoccupied.

In one generation organisms may die or be created or survive according to the following rules.
   (a) an organism with fewer than 2 or more than 4 neighbours dies (is removed from the array) otherwise it survives
   (b) an unoccupied cell with exactly three neighbours has an organism placed in it in the next generation.

All births and deaths occur simultaneously and together constitute a single generation.

(a) Write a program which simulates the colony for ten generations. Data is N followed by NxN values representing the initial configuration. Print out the state of the colony after each generation.
   Try the following initial cell patterns

```
. . . . .      . . . . .      . . . . .
. * * * .      . . * . .      . * * * .
. . * . .      . . . * .      . * . * .
. . . . .      . * * * .      . * . * .
. . . . .      . . . . .      . . . . .
```

(b) Modify your program so that it will halt as soon as there are no organisms alive.
(c) Modify your program so that it halts if 2 successive generations are identical.
(d) Try to detect more subtle loops in the behaviour of the colony.
(e) Modify your program so that the initial configuration is generated randomly. What is the average number of generations before a random colony either dies out or starts to loop?

130 Write a program which reads a set of N simultaneous equations, or some representation of them, and attempts to solve them.

State clearly the limitations of your program.

131 A farmer surveys a number of fields each bounded by straight fences. For each fence he records a pair of numbers:
    (i) the direction of the fence (in degrees measured clockwise from North)
    (ii) the length of the fence (in metres).
The pairs are ordered so that they consecutively describe the perimeter of the field.

Write a program which inputs

  (a) an integer M (the number of fields)
  (b) for each field
    (1) an integer N (the number of fences)
    (2) the recorded pairs

and outputs for each field
    (i) whether or not the survey closes (the last fence terminates within 10cm of the origin of the first)
    (ii) the area of the field.

6 | Records and structures

An array is typically characterised by the fact that all its elements are logically related in some sense and are all of the same kind or type. In programming it frequently happens that there are logically related pieces of information which are of potentially different kinds or types. Records or structures are typically used in such circumstances.

6.1 Simple records

Consider the information that might be held about a person. The information one might hold might typically depend on the application but could include name, address, age, date-of-birth, height, employer and so on; the age and date-of-birth might both be included for checking purposes. All these pieces of information are logically related in that they apply to a person; it is natural to represent these within a program as a record (sometimes also called a structure) composed of fields or components for each individual piece of information. The abstraction process will lead to these fields being themselves represented as integers, reals, character strings or whatever, even simpler records, e.g. for birthdays.

Other similar examples come readily to mind. The details of a planet could be held in a record containing information about its name, size, the number of its moons, the names of these moons, and so on. The details of a boat might take the form of a record containing its name, tonnage, length, age, captain, crew, port of registration and even its last noted position.

In summary then records are used for grouping together pieces of logically related information of potentially different sorts. The abstraction process will lead to a wide variety of items being represented as records.

We saw that the individual elements of an array were

accessed by a process of subscripting or indexing. The fields or components of a record will typically be accessed by a process which is usually called selection. To access the name of a person one might typically write PERSON.NAME or NAME of PERSON; note that the fields will typically be represented by identifiers which should be carefully and sensibly chosen.

Indeed there are certain similarities between records and arrays. But there are some crucial differences. When a compiler comes to translate, the code produced for the selection process is usually much more efficient than the code produced for subscripting or indexing. Briefly in the former case the code will cause the immediate accessing of the appropriate information; in the latter case the code will often cause a calculation to be performed before the access occurs.

With these observations in mind consider the representation of a rational number, i.e. a fraction of the form P/Q where P and Q are integers. Should this be represented as an array of two elements or as a record consisting of two integer fields? In performing the addition, subtraction, etc. of rationals it is always clear at each stage of the process whether the numerator or denominator has to be accessed. Thus much greater efficiency and a more transparent program will result from use of a record rather than array; note that the meaning of RATIONAL.NUMERATOR is clearer than RATIONAL(1), for instance.

So there are situations in which records can be used to advantage where arrays might have been expected. The various fields of a record can be of the same or differing types but in all cases the information they contain is logically related.

It is worth remembering that in this chapter we shall confine our attention to relatively small records and relatively small numbers of these small records. This whole topic is really the thin edge of a very large wedge. In other situations related pieces of information are held in files and large amounts of information are often grouped together to form databases.

Programming languages will normally permit a programmer to define routines which operate on records and perhaps produce records as results. Arrays of records will normally be permitted, and so on. No unnatural limitation about the way they can be manipulated should exist.

Exercises 6.1

1. Assume that there is a set of data consisting of records representing people, with some suitable terminator. For each person there is a name (20 characters), sex (M or F indicating male or female) and age (an integer in the range 0 to 100). Write a program which processes these records and outputs the number of men and the number of women.

2. Using the data of the previous example, write a program which prints out the names of all the pensioners and the number of them. Use the convention that a man over 65 or a woman over 60 is entitled to a pension.

3. A set of entries for a telephone directory is supplied in a random order. Decide a suitable convention for your data and then write a program which processes this in such a way that an alphabetical list of the entries is produced in a convenient format.

4. A position on the Earth's surface can be represented by longitude and latitude. Given that each 15 degrees represents one hour's time difference, write a program that outputs the time difference between two points on the globe; assume the usual conventions about the specification of latitude and longitude.

6.2 Type declarations and operators

Despite the apparent simplicity of the concept of a record the precise form of records or structures is often difficult to remember. Many programming languages contain a facility whereby type or mode declarations can be introduced; in this way a programmer can then introduce his own abbreviations for some record type. Thus we might have a type RATIONAL for rational numbers or a type PERSON for the record of a person; as usual the freedom to choose appropriate identifiers for types should be exercised with care.

Type declarations combined with suitable function and routine declarations provide a convenient facility whereby a programmer can build higher and higher levels of programming facilities. But consider the type RATIONAL for example. It would surely be nice to be able to introduce, in a natural way, facilities for adding two rationals, subtracting two rationals and so on.

User-defined operators are not available in all languages; where they are not allowed functions or routines can serve a similar purpose though in a less natural manner. Where they are permitted the peculiarities that surround them tend to be heavily language dependent - thus rules about priority or precedence, rules about overloading or polymorphism, etc. all tend to exist.

Operators can be regarded as special kinds of functions. An operator which possesses a single operand is like a function with a single parameter. An operator which has two operands is like a function with two parameters.

In designing operators of different kinds, a programmer or designer should have a high regard to what a user will expect. Mathematical operators usually have connotations to a user; the algorithmic realisation of that operator should have the same properties where possible. In introducing an operator +, for instance, it might be relevant to ask:

(a) Is the + commutative or associative?

(b) What is the effect of 0+A or A+0? Is the answer just A?

(c) Is +A = A?

and so on.

Exercises 6.2

1. Design a type and an addition operator to support the addition of two rational numbers.

2. Design facilities for subtracting, multiplying and dividing rational numbers.

3. Design facilities for adding rational numbers and integers in any combinations.

4. Design facilities for adding and multiplying together matrices of arbitrary but appropriate sizes. Include checks on the sizes of the matrices.

5. Design operators for adding and multiplying complex numbers and raising a complex number to an integer power.

6. A measurement can be regarded as a record with components for metres and centimetres or components for yards, feet and inches. Design operators for the addition and subtraction of two measurements. How would you design an operator for multiplying measurements by a positive integer quantity?

7. Design facilities for dealing with a 24 hour clock. It should be possible to add times and perform some sort of subtraction. State clearly the specification of your operators, etc.

6.3 Variants or unions

Let us return to a discussion which we had at the start of this chapter. It concerned the nature of a record holding information about a person.

A record for a person can be made more complex by including more details of that person – the colour of his eyes, the size of his shoes, the names of all his brothers, and so on. In terms of programming there is little increase in difficulty in dealing with such extensions - merely add extra fields or components. Of course, such added information certainly increases the need for type or mode declarations. But let us consider an extension of a different kind.

In some situations one kind of record is perfectly adequate for all purposes. In other cases some variation becomes desirable. There might be situations where the structure of a record for a person might differ depending on whether that person was male or female, under 18 years of age or over 18 years of age, single or married, and so on. In these cases components will doubtless be needed for certain basic information such as name, age, address, etc. but many of the other components will differ.

Programming languages respond to the need described above by typically allowing variant records, united modes, or whatever. Further, in these situations it is also necessary to be able to decide which sort of record is being considered in a particular situation. To take the examples mentioned above it should be possible to inspect a record and decide if a record is that of a male or female, a young person or an old person, a single person or a married person, and so on. The facilities available for such tasks will normally resemble conditionals of one form or another - the concept of a variant record and a conditional go hand-in-hand.

Exercises 6.3

1 A routine has to calculate the area of geometric figures of different shapes. These may be rectangles, triangles or circles.
   Write and test a routine which accomplishes this task.

2 A (men's) sports club keeps elaborate computerised records of all its members. The records contain typical information such as age, address, etc. of each person. But there is also information about

whether a member is an active playing member, about whether he is married, and so on; if he is married the record contains information about his wife's name, the number of children and their names.

Write a program which demonstrates how such a system might be implemented. Show how the names of the wives of all the active playing members might be printed.

6.4 Simple linked storage

Let us consider further extensions to the ideas we have already developed. Again we take the example of a record of a person and we consider a development in yet another direction.

Suppose we wish to include information about a person's father. We do not want just the father's name or age but from a person's record we would like to be able to find out anything within reason about the father, i.e. we would like to be able to access the father's entire record. How can this be done? It is unreasonable to expect a record of a person to contain within it another record of the same or a similar size – magnitude or storage size considerations just make this impossible in general. The solution normally adopted in programming languages is to include within a person's record a pointer to the record of the father. Then we have a situation which can be depicted in the following way:

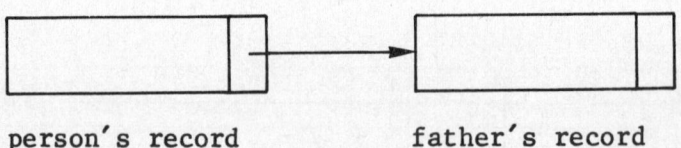

person's record   father's record

Different programming languages will adopt solutions involving references, access types and so on; essentially the concepts are similar for this purpose.

It now becomes possible to ask about AGE of FATHER or

PERSON.FATHER.AGE, for example. Indeed if the person's father's father is alive and there is another pointer we might well ask about AGE of FATHER of FATHER of PERSON or PERSON.FATHER.FATHER.AGE. If the grandfather happens to be dead we may wish a null pointer to appear in the appropriate component of the record, i.e. something which does not point to any record at all. All programming languages which admit pointers have a null pointer, usually depicted by nil or null (in diagrams we denote this by a cross).

This simple illustration of a pointer can be developed much further. It is now possible to imagine many items all linked together in the following kind of way:

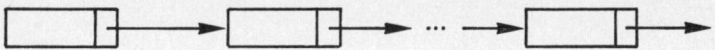

Such a structure is normally referred to as a list. This is a linear list since the arrows never point backwards to a previous element; they do not create a loop of any kind nor does a record ever have two pointers.

The reader might naturally wonder about the advantages of lists over arrays or vice versa. After all, in both cases sets of items of the same kind are involved. Moreover loops are naturally involved in the processing of both. What are the relative advantages of each and how should a programmer decide which to use in a particular situation?

With arrays it is possible to access any individual element immediately. By writing A(50) one immediately accesses the element of A whose index or subscript is 50. Arrays are therefore particularly suitable for performing frequency counts and other such operations. But we should remark that finding A(50) usually involves the computer in finding the start of A, then adding 50 or whatever and finally accessing the appropriate element. To find the 50th element of a linear list is a much more difficult and time consuming exercise.

Consider now the problem of inserting an item into a (perhaps ordered) list of items. Essentially the necessary space has to be created for the item and two pointers have to be redirected as indicated below - the

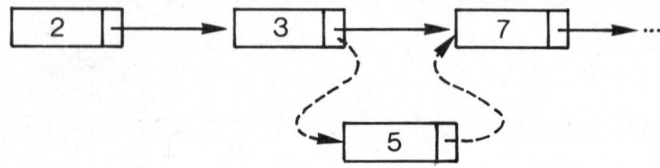

dotted lines indicate what has to be done, to give

Conceptually the insertion is particularly simple to accomplish. Deletions are also relatively easy to accomplish conceptually - merely redirect a single pointer. Compare this situation with what needs to be done when inserting or deleting an item from an array; in this case shuffling many elements up or down the array could be involved and this can be very costly.

It is worth mentioning that if sets of elements have merely to be scanned from one end to the other then lists are better than arrays, though they occupy more space. As mentioned above the process of subscripting is usually more expensive than accessing a particular field of a record and following a pointer.

The decision about what to use in a particular situation depends crucially on the kinds of operations that will have to be performed on the items involved. Using the insight gained from the abstraction process and from the discussion above appropriate and sensible decisions can be made. Note in particular that a list of characters provides an alternative representation of a string!

The examples below are intended to provide practice in performing the basic set of operations that are typically performed on lists. As such they are rather important. The reader might also like to review the different kinds of examples we gave on arrays. Many of these can be solved using lists instead of arrays. Which solution is better?

Before ending this discussion let us just note a recursive aspect to both the concept of a list (and indeed the concept of an array). A list can be regarded as either

>   null

or
>   a single element linked to another (smaller) list

This recursive nature is usually brought out by the way that programming languages traditionally permit the introduction of lists, usually a recursive type definition where the type definition is essential and not merely convenient as before. Further, recursive procedures often provide a very appropriate way of processing such items. Witness yet again the relationship between the structure of data and the structure of the routines that manipulate that data.

Exercises 6.4

1 Design a routine which inserts an item at the start of a linear list. Show also how the item might be removed from the start.

2 Design a routine to test if an element is present in a linear list.

3 Design two routines to perform the following two tasks

   (a) add an item to the end of a linear list

   (b) remove an item from the end of a linear list.

4 Prepare recursive and nonrecursive routines for reversing the elements in a linear list. Compare the relative efficiencies of them.

5 Design a routine for removing an item from an ordered list of similar items.

6 Design a routine for adding an element to an already sorted linear list in such a way that the final list is also ordered.

7 Show how two lists of elements can be combined into a single list by creating a new list containing all the elements in the other two.

8 Show how two sorted lists of elements can be combined to produce a third sorted list which contains one occurrence of each of the elements in the two original lists.

9 Given two ordered lists, show how to extract the elements common to both lists.

6.5 More complex data structures

The examples we have given so far have involved records or lists of a relatively simple kind. At most a single pointer has been involved, and there have been no loops pointing back to an earlier part of a list. There are situations where this particular simple state of affairs is not always the most appropriate. To illustrate the kinds of complexity that can arise, let us note the following possibilities.

   (a) A list can be made circular so that instead of the list ending in a null pointer there is a pointer back to the start again as illustrated below.

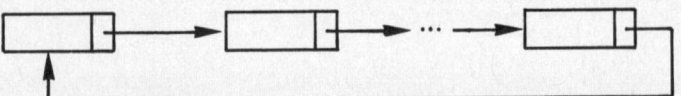

(b) There are advantages in having lists designed in such a way that in each element there are two pointers so allowing travel in two directions; thus

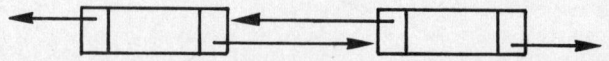

A doubly-linked list such as this might be an appropriate way of representing a polynomial or ordered list which may have to be processed in either increasing or decreasing order of its terms or items.

(c) In a family tree it might be desirable to allow pointers not only to a person's father but also to his mother, brother and sisters.

(d) In computing, general tree structures are often required; see below. Other variations using more pointers and more fields per record are also possible.

(e) Lists of items which themselves might be lists are possible. To illustrate, a polynomial in two variables X and Y can be regarded as a polynomial in one variable X where coefficients are either constants or polynomials in Y; a polynomial in a single variable can conveniently be represented as a linear list.

Exercises 6.5

1 Find the number of occurrences of each character in a list of characters.

2 Write a routine for inserting an item into a doubly-

linked list of ordered items. Incorporate this in a suitable driver program to test it.

3 Design a routine for counting the number of items in a doubly-linked list.

4 Design and test a function for counting the number of items in a list which may contain other lists as elements. You may assume that there are no loops in the list.

5 Design and test a function which indicates whether there are loops present in a list of the kind mentioned in the previous question.

Let us discuss trees in some detail.

A tree can be regarded as a record or structure with various fields. Two or more of these fields will typically be pointers to other trees. Thus if we represent a tree as a structure of the form

(left branch, information, right branch)

and if we realise that the left branch and the right branch are themselves trees with a similar structure then a picture of the following kind emerges

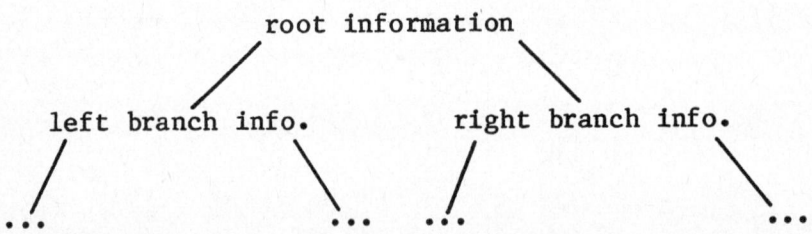

Such a structure is often used for holding family trees or expressing the ancestry of monarchs. In computing, trees are used also for representing expressions and indeed the structure of entire programs. Thus

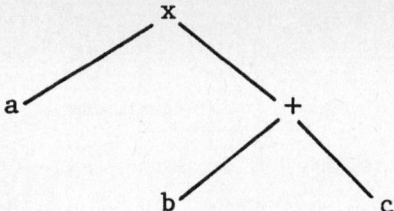

represents a x (b + c) in a bracket-free manner.

In fact a tree is nothing more than a special kind of graph. It is special in that there are no circuits or loops in the pictorial representation of the structure. Although a tree may have many branches emanating from any node the most common situation occurs when there are two branches at each node - except at the terminal nodes. Then the tree is said to be a binary tree.

6.6 Miscellaneous exercises

1 A point can be represented as a record with two real components representing x-coordinate and y-coordinate. Write a program which reads a set of points representing the vertices of a polygon (suitably ordered) and prints out the length of the perimeter of the polygon.

2 Records for a set of employees include name, address, age, etc. but also information about whether they receive a weekly or monthly salary; the amount received per week or per month is also present. Write a program which processes a set of these records and outputs

    (a) the amount of the weekly wage bill
    (b) the amount of the monthly wage bill excluding wages paid under (a) above
    (c) the total yearly wage bill
    (d) the number of employees being paid by each means.

3 An airline reservation system maintains records for possible flights consisting of

STARTING POINT
> 3 character code

DESTINATION
> 3 character code

STARTING TIME
> integer on scale 0001 - 2400

ARRIVAL TIME
> integer on scale 0001 - 2400

SEATS
> positive integer in suitable range.

Your program is to read 20 such records followed by queries of the form STARTINGPOINT-DESTINATION, one to a line. For each query find whether there is a possible flight with a seat available; if so reduce the number of seats by one and print out the flight details (or an apology).

4 A league table consists of a set of N records each representing the performance of a team. A record contains
   (i) team name
   (ii) number of games played
   (iii) number of games won
   (iv) number of games drawn
   (v) number of games lost
   (vi) number of goals scored
   (vii) number of goals conceded
   (viii) number of points awarded (2 for a win and 1 for a draw).

Write a program which inputs
   (i) a positive integer N
   (ii) N records of the form above
   (iii) a positive integer M
   (iv) the results of M games in the form
team1 goals scored team2 goals scored

e.g.   Liverpool 2 Everton 2

The program should update the records according to the results of the games and output an ordered list

of records. Records should be ordered by
   (i) number of points awarded (highest first)
   (ii) if points equal then by goal difference
        (goals scored - goals conceded)
   (iii) if both these equal then alphabetically by
         team name.

5 An organisation's payroll file consists of one line
  for each employee consisting of:

  NAME (20 characters, file arranged alphabetically)
  SEX (1 character M or F)
  SALARY (integer)
  DATE OF BIRTH (3 integers YEAR MONTH DAY)

  Your program is to read up to 10 amendments to the
  file followed by the file itself and print the
  amended file. Amendments will be in the same form as
  the file itself, will also be in alphabetical order
  and will consist of new employees (name different
  from any existing one), employees left (salary given
  as 0) and promotions, demotions and change of sex
  (name same as existing employee, other details
  changed). Your program should of course remove
  employees who have reached retirement age (65 for M,
  60 for F).

6 Design a function which finds the product of all the
  integers in a linear list.

7 Write a procedure which given a positive integer I
  and a linear list L returns as result the Ith member
  of L.

8 Write a procedure which given an item and a linear
  list returns the position of the item in the list or
  -1 if it is not present.

9 Design a function which indicates if items in a list
  appear in some order defined by a second parameter
  (which is a function).

10 Write a procedure which, given a circular list,

returns the number of items it contains.

11 Write an initial routine to determine whether a sublist is present in a larger list.
   Modify your program in such a way that there is a routine with three parameters L1, L2, and L3 all of which are lists; if L2 is present in L1 it should be replaced by L3. Ensure that this routine is tested properly.

12 Write procedures or functions to carry out the operations of insertion, deletion and search on a linked list of integers which are to be maintained in ascending order. Make your program call the procedures (or functions) according to commands read as input.

13 Write a procedure which given two lists L1 and L2 appends L2 to L1.

14 Write a program which inputs a sequence of bracket characters (for example "[" "{" "(" ">" etc.) and determines whether or not the sequence is well-formed. For example

   { [( ) ( )] < (( ) ( )) > } is well-formed

   { ((< >) ( )) [( ) } } is not well-formed.

15 Solve the elimination problem of exercise 55 from chapter 5 using lists instead of arrays.

16 Memo functions were proposed by Donald Michie (see for example "Memo functions and machine learning", Nature Vol. 218, pp. 19-22, 1968). A memo function maintains a list of argument-result pairs. When a memo function is called the list is searched to see if the argument has occurred in a previous evaluation. If it has then the corresponding result is obtained from the list otherwise the function is evaluated and the new argument-result pair added to the list.
   Write a memo function PRIME. PRIME is called with a single positive integer argument (N) and returns true

if N is a prime number and false otherwise.

17 Write a procedure which given a linear list of integers in arbitrary order rearranges the elements into ascending order.

18 Write a procedure which reverses a given linear list in situ (i.e. does not require any space for another list but merely rearranges pointers).

19 Write a function which takes as parameter a simple linear list and determines whether or not the list contains repeated items.

20 Write a procedure which given a linear list X, constructs a list of those items which appear only once in X.

21 Find all the elements that follow each occurrence of X in a list. Produce a list of the followers.

22 Represent a set as a list. Then show how the usual set operations of union, intersection, complement and membership can be implemented.

23 When the function being "memoised" is recursive, a distinction is made between top-level function calls and those originating from the body of the function itself. The argument-result list is searched in both cases but only in the former are additions to the list permitted.
   Write a memo function FACTORIAL. FACTORIAL is called with a single positive integer argument (N) and returns the value of N!.

24 The decimal expansion of any fraction of the form 1/n is either a terminating decimal or a decimal sequence which repeats.
   Design a program which reads a positive integer n and outputs the appropriate decimal expansion. Your program should output three dots to indicate a repeated expansion.

25 Design a suitable set of facilities for performing

multi-length arithmetic involving integers.

26 The problem of finding prime numbers has always interested mathematicians. The Lucas test for primes is based on the following result:

if p>2 is prime then 2^p-1 is a prime number if and only if

$$L_{p-2} = 0$$

where the L_i are defined inductively as follows

$$L_0 = 4$$
$$L_{i+1} = (L_i^2 - 2) \text{ modulo } (2^p-1) \text{ for } i = 0,1,2...$$

i.e. L_{i+1} is the remainder when L_i^2 is divided by 2^p-1.

Find all primes of the form 2^p-1 (i.e. all Mersenne primes) less than 2^{1000}.
Find the first value of n for which

$$2^{2^n} + 1$$

is not a prime number.

27 Write programs to find in each case below, a number which has the specified properties:

    (a) the number begins with the digit 3. If this digit is moved to the last place then the new number is one third of the original.
    (b) the number ends with the digit 4. When this digit is moved to the first place the new number is four times the original.
    (c) the number ends with the digit 4. When this digit is moved to the first place the new number is twice the original.

28 Design a suitable set of facilities for performing multiple length arithmetic involving real numbers.

29 Jacques Dultea calculated the square root of 2 to over a million decimal places in 1970-71 using the following technique

He let $P_0 = 6726$ $Q_0 = 4756$

and then performed 17 iterations of

$$P_{k+1} = P_k^2 - 2$$

$$Q_{k+1} = P_k Q_k$$

Then P_k/Q_k is a close approximation to the square root of 2.

Use the same technique to calculate the root of 2 to 100 decimal places.

30 Use the fact that

$$\arctan(x) = x - \frac{x^3}{3} + \frac{x^5}{5} - \frac{x^7}{7} \ldots\ldots\ldots$$

and the relationship

$$pi = 24\arctan(1/8) + 8\arctan(1/57) + 4\arctan(1/239)$$

to obtain an approximation to pi correct to 100 places.

31 Write a procedure which given an arbitrary linear list L and item I determines the number of times that I appears in L.

32 Write a procedure which produces a list which is the reverse (at all levels) of a given list. For example if the given list were

[[a1 a2 a3] b c [d1 d2] e]

the reversed list would be

[e [d2 d1] c b [a3 a2 a1]]

33 Write a procedure which given an arbitrary linear

list L and positive integer I returns the Ith item in L.

34 Input consists of the following:
    (a) a list of students together with the classes each takes
    (b) a list of times at which these classes always take place.

The program should then accept a list of students and attempt to output the times at which they can all meet (i.e. none has a class).

35 Given a file containing a book like this with key-words marked in some way and page numbers also easily identifiable, write a program which will produce an index (an alphabetically ordered list of problem titles each followed by a list of the numbers of the pages on which a problem with that title appears).

36 A buzz-phrase is a grammatical group of technical sounding words which contains very little information. Some examples of buzz-phrases are

    Locally constrained minimisation
    Desirable behavioural characteristics
    Maximising performance criteria in response to system implementation objectives.

Write a program which generates buzz-phrases. Start with short noun phrases before attempting longer sequences.

37 Write a program which inputs an arithmetic expression in reverse polish form (post-fixed notation) and outputs an equivalent expression in infixed form. Assume the input is terminated by a semi-colon. For example if the input were

    A B + C D * E F - * / ;

the output could be

    (A + B) / (C * D * (E - F))

38 (a) Show how it is possible to implement Ackermann's function as a memo function. See exercise 16 of this set.
   (b) Modify the program obtained from (a) to find the number of calls involved in the usual recursive form and the maximum depth to which normal recursion would go.

39 Write a procedure which 'flattens' an arbitrary list, that is produces a single level list of the elements of the original list in order. For example the 'flattened' list corresponding to

   [a b [c [d e] f g] h [[i j] k] l] is
   [a b c d e f g h i j k l]

40 Design a routine which allows an arbitrary function of a suitable kind to be applied to all the elements in an arbitrary list to produce a new list containing all the results in the corresponding order.
   Incorporate your routine in a suitable driver routine.

41 Design a means of counting the number of loops in an arbitrary list of integers. State clearly any limitations of your program.

42 A KWIC (key-word-in-context) index is formed by permuting the key words (i.e. words other than "the", "of", "to", "by", "a" etc.) in a book title, and then forming a sorted list of those permuted titles, for example the two titles

   Systematic programming : an introduction
   Introduction to Programming and Computer Science

   would give the following KWIC index

   ction to Programming and   Computer Science/ Introdu
             programming : an   Introduction/ systematic
    ng and Computer Science/   Introduction to Programmi
     introduction/ Systematic   programming : an
    Science/ Introduction to   Programming and Computer

Programming and Computer Science/ Introduction to an introduction/ Systematic programming :

Note that the permuted key words line up on a single column and are usually slightly separated from adjacent words. Where the title is too long to fit on one line, it is wrapped around and in these cases a "/" marks the end of the title.

Write a program to read in a series of titles and compile such a KWIC index. Make your program slightly more general by allowing for an author's name as well.

43 Write routines which will perform the following tasks.
   (a) Find the remainder when one polynomial is divided into another.
   (b) Find the HCF and LCM of two polynomials.
   (c) Differentiate a polynomial.

44 In preparing an index for a book an author decides on the following strategy. As he reads his book he types a page number followed by the list of words on that page to be included in the index. An appropriate terminator ends the input.

Write a program to process this data and produce a carefully sorted index.

45 As in the previous question we consider the problem of preparing an index for a book. Modify the scheme described above to allow an author to specify ranges of pages covering one particular topic. Provide clear documentation relating to your program and its method of operation.

46 A binary tree can be used to sort numbers if the first number input is put into the root, subsequent smaller numbers are put into the left subtree, subsequent larger numbers are put into the right subtree and the same rules are applied recursively to each subtree.

Write recursive procedures or functions to enter a number into such a tree, to print all the numbers in order and to find the height of the tree.

47 Given a list of numbers (terminated by -1) representing the a priori probabilities of messages, generate Huffman codes for the messages.

48 Write a program which creates a structure representing a French/English and an English/French dictionary. There should be no duplication of words and efficient translation should be possible both ways.
   (a) Write a procedure which given an English word returns the corresponding French word if it is the dictionary otherwise outputs a suitable message.
   (b) Generalise your procedure (a) so that a second parameter enables it to be used for translation in either direction.

49 A concordance of a piece of text is a list of all the word occurrences in the text in alphabetical order each with a certain amount of the text surrounding its occurrence to indicate the context in which the word was used. In addition the page/line/word number of the occurrence could be output.
   Write a program which inputs a piece of text terminated by # and outputs a concordance.

50 A university keeps computerised records of all its students. These differ in certain crucial ways depending on the nature of a student's course of study; however certain basic information such as name, date of birth, etc. must be held for everyone.
   If a student is an undergraduate then his course, his year of study, his passes to date, etc. will all be held.
   For diploma students there will be information about former qualifications and about course of study.
   For M.Sc. and Ph.D. students there will be information about his department, about his thesis topic and his supervisor.
   Show how such a system might be implemented.

51 Write a program to produce an examination timetable showing for each course the time, room and date of the examination.

The principal data will consist of an integer N followed by N student records. The Ith student record will consist of an integer N_i followed by the numbers of the N_i courses taken by the Ith student.

Your program should try to minimise the time between the first and last examination . Apart from the fact that no student can sit more than 1 examination at a time, possible constraints are

(i) room sizes – additional data for the program could be a list of the sizes of rooms available. No examination should be split over more than one room.

(ii) assuming that examinations are either morning (9.30) or afternoon (2.00) examinations, no student should sit more than 2 examinations in any 48-hour period.

52 A suitable description of a room with the following dimensions

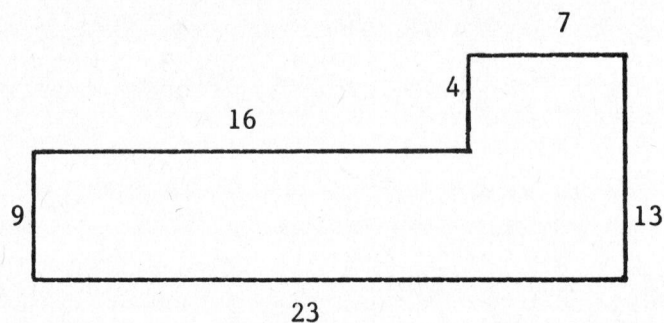

might be

((N,9) (E,16) (N,4) (E,7) (S,13) (W,23))

a series of direction-distance pairs which, if followed from the lower left-hand corner of the room, traces the perimeter.

Write a program which inputs a description of this form and outputs the area of the room. Assume that the measurements are given in metres.

You may also assume that the corners are all square and that consequently the only legal directions in the input are N,S,E and W. Ensure however that your program checks that the list of direction-distance pairs brings you back to the corner from which you started.

53 The tree

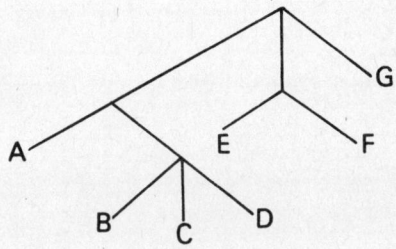

may be represented by the parenthesised expression

((A (B C D)) (E F) G)

Write a program which inputs an expression representing a tree and outputs a representation of the tree similar to that above.

54 Given as data
   (i) a positive integer N
   (ii) N pairs of the form (identifier, value)
   (iii) an expression in reverse polish form containing constants, identifiers and operators.

Write a program which outputs the value of the expression.

55 Write a program which inputs an infixed arithmetic expression and outputs an equivalent post-fixed one (that is in reverse polish form).

56 (a) Write a program which inputs an arbitrary logical expression, containing at most 4 variables, and prints out a truth table for the function.
   (b) Write a program to input an arbitrary expression and output it in

(i) disjunctive normal form
(ii) conjunctive normal form
(see for example Mowle, F.J. "A systematic approach to digital logic design", Addison-Wesley 1976).

57 Generate in increasing numerical order the members of the sequence $2^a 3^b 5^c$ where a,b and c are non-negative integers. Do this efficiently by generating the initial values and then multiplying these by 2,3 and 5 respectively. Continue in this way, by multiplying previous values by 2,3 and 5 to obtain later values.

7 | Modules and packages

Subprograms provide one means of structuring programs. An even higher level of structuring can be accomplished using the concept of the package or module. The introduction of this new idea will allow programmers to make use of, and even construct, special libraries of routines to serve special purposes.

We first consider the design of modules which gather together sets of related functions, operators and/or procedures. When we reached the corresponding stage in the design of functions, operators and so on, we looked to the standard environment for guidance. We again do likewise but in this case we view the situation with a degree of dissatisfaction. Standard environments in most programming languages contain a motley collection of items. These might include a selection or all of: input and output routines and related facilities; trigonometric functions of various kinds; logarithms, exponentials, square root and other mathematical functions; facilities for character handling and string processing; random number generators; some useful types and a set of operators, functions and so on for their manipulation.

There is usually no place in the standard environment for such functions as factorial or highest common factor. Why? Given the means of introducing functions into programs, i.e. function declaration, a programmer is at liberty to introduce his own factorial or highest common factor function if he so chooses. (In fact the same can be said of the SIN function, for example, but in view of the frequency of its use and in view of the fact that a very specialised knowledge of numerical analysis is necessary to produce a useful facility, this is beyond the experience of most programmers.) So the set of facilities is basic in some sense. Other functions and so on can be readily constructed from those provided and from the rules of the programming language.

When we design modules we shall not group items

189

together in a haphazard kind of way. All items declared within a module will share a common bond, though that bond may take one of several possible forms. It will be our intention that the module will be easy to use in the sense that

> the interface with the user is natural - there are no peculiar restrictions or unnatural restrictions or difficulties involved in using the module; the use of the module should blend naturally with the use of the programming language itself

> there will be no unnatural inefficiencies involved in the use of any of the facilities within the module

> the set of facilities will be basic in some sense and yet complete in that all the expected operations will be present.

These then are the kinds of considerations that govern what follows.

7.1 Groups of items

The most primitive forms of grouping of items are the sets of declarations of constants of a useful or familiar nature. Several sets of examples come readily to mind - groups of mathematical constants, quantities for converting one form of measurement to another, days of the week, weeks of the year and so on.

A set of possibilities is given in the following examples. The programmer should attempt to make his facilities as complete as is reasonable. If facilities are provided for converting inches into the metric equivalent the inverse facilities should also exist.

Exercises 7.1

1 Provide a package containing a set of commonly used

MODULES AND PACKAGES 191

mathematical constants.

2 The instructions in an assembly code have to be converted by an assembler into machine code. Design a facility whereby this translation is easily performed.

3 Design a facility whereby the information about the various attributes of a computer are made available. Include word length, memory capacity, speed, etc.

4 Provide a package in which a set of mathematical constants is given to a high degree of accuracy, e.g. to about 20 decimal places.

7.2 Simple packages

Let us begin by considering the design of facilities for trigonometric calculations. The bond that binds these facilities is the nature of the computations involved.

Certainly the SIN function should be included together with the other five similar functions COS, TAN, COSEC, SEC and COT. Of course, TAN can be defined using SIN and COS but to omit any of these six imposes an unnatural restriction that should not be allowed to exist.

Should the inverse trigonometric function ARCSIN, ARCCOS, etc. be included in the same package or in a different package? A strategy which leads to the latter will tend to cause a proliferation of modules all containing a relatively small number of routines. Although there are arguments in favour of this (e.g. the space requirements for package use are kept low) it is probably desirable to keep all the trigonometric functions together; the final package therefore contains the six trigonometric and the further six inverse trigonometric functions.

When libraries such as these are being assembled and programmed it is important that good quality software results. To this end it is important that routines, operators, etc. are all tested. As usual each routine should be thoroughly tested in turn; boundary conditions and peculiar situations should all be used to exercise and test the facilities.

Exercises 7.2

1 Indicate how these trigonometric routines might be implemented as a suitable package.

2 Design a package which provides an implementation of the usual hyperbolic functions.

3 To convert metres and centimetres into yards, feet and inches and vice versa, a variety of routines are required. Design and implement a package which supports a suitable set of facilities.

4 Design and implement a package for use by a number theorist who is interested in prime numbers, highest common factors, and so on.

7.3 Encapsulating data types

A very important kind of module encapsulates a data type of some sort, i.e. introduces a new type together with a set of operations and facilities applicable to objects of that type. One could envisage modules which provide an implementation of the idea of a complex number, a rational number, vectors of various kinds, matrices, and so on.

Let us take rational numbers, i.e. numbers of the form P/Q where P and Q are integers, Q being non-zero. What sort of operations or facilities would one want to provide? The following would almost inevitably be required:

   (a) a means of creating a rational number from a pair of integers

   (b) a means of finding the numerator and denominator of a rational

(c) certain arithmetic operators such as addition and subtraction, multiplication and division and so on

(d) certain comparison operators such as equality, less than and so on.

Of the above note that (a) can be described as a construction facility of some kind, (b) as a selection facility.

The reader might argue that there are certain noticeable absentees from this list. What about some means of converting an integer N into a corresponding rational number namely N/1? What about converting rationals to reals? A facility such as the latter could be provided or it could be argued that the construction facility provides a means of achieving this. To settle this argument the host programming language itself can be examined. What does it provide in the way of facilities for converting an integer into an equivalent real? Mimic the corresponding facilities in the host programming language.

Should input and output facilities be provided? Let us concentrate on the latter. If the module designer does decide to do so he should provide a certain degree of flexibility so that the users of the package can output rational numbers in a variety of ways. In this case it would probably not be wise for the module designer to supply special facilities for this. By making use of standard input/output routines for integers together with the facilities for selection, a user of the module can design his own suitable routines.

Now let us turn to the facilities for arithmetic. Let us just concentrate on addition between two quantities. The designer has at least two options:

1. he can supply various addition operators to cover: integer + rational, rational + rational, rational + integer and perhaps real + rational, rational + real.

2. he can supply only rational + rational; if a user wishes to add an integer and a rational he converts the integer to a rational and proceeds

in the obvious way.

Again the answer to this dilemma can be obtained by appealing to the host programming language. What does it provide in the way of facilities for adding integers and reals? Mimic these facilities and natural extensions of programming languages will emerge.

In this way then one can decide on the answer to most questions. By appealing to the underlying mathematics and by examining the kinds of operations and facilities usually assumed, a programmer can arrive at a sensible set of answers. As far as is possible he should arrange that the various operators, routines, etc. all possess their expected mathematical properties.

There is one further matter to consider in relation to the design of a rational arithmetic package. A rational such as 1/2 can appear also as 2/4, 3/6 etc. Should the package allow such a multiplicity of possibilities or should it permit only 1/2? Such a decision should be of little concern to the user of a package but it is certainly of concern to the designer. If a standard representation such as 1/2 is demanded then certain advantages follow:

(i) certain operations and facilities are simplified

(ii) the probability of unexpected overflow is minimised.

The corresponding disadvantages are that the designer of the package must ensure that items are reduced to standard form, i.e. that cancellation occurs wherever possible.

On balance a standard representation would normally be assumed. All operators would assume that their operands had been standardised and they would ensure that the results they produced were standardised. In this way order is maintained. By 'standard' in this context we mean that all rationals are held in the form P/Q where the highest common factor of P and Q is unity and Q is positive. If such a representation can be hidden from the user of a package so much the better. For then he cannot possibly interfere with the proper working of the package, either accidentally or deliberately. Languages

MODULES AND PACKAGES   195

such as Ada provide a means of keeping aspects of implementation hidden and secret.

In this instance note that the various facilities for manipulating rationals all share common knowledge about the way rationals are represented. This is the bond that binds together all aspects of the module.

In the case of packages supporting data types of a more complex kind another consideration has to be taken into account. Consider a package for matrix manipulation. In this case the size of the matrices is is an important consideration. Ideally the package should be designed in such a way that the various operators, routines, etc. are quite independent of matrix size. Further, a user of the package should be able to use matrices of an arbitrary size - within the limit of the size of the machine, of course.

Before ending this section we make the following very important observation. If a programmer is, for example, faced with the task of designing a module for the manipulation of polynomials whose coefficients are rational numbers, there is a great temptation to take shortcuts by confusing rational arithmetic and polynominal manipulation perhaps in an intricate way within a single package. This is a route to potential disaster. The way to proceed is to design properly a rational number module and then promptly forget about how it works. The programmer is now free to concentrate on the design of his polynominal package assured of the fact that all the necessary facilities for rational arithmetic are present. Indeed it may happen that some of the rational arithmetic facilities are not used in the polynominal manipulation but that does not matter; on a future occasion they will be used in some other way. The separation of concerns involved here is of paramount importance. Products produced in this way are most valuable.

Exercises 7.3

1 Design a simple package to support rational number arithmetic.

2 Design a package which will permit a user to perform

arithmetic involving complex numbers. The design should be such that an implementation using Cartesian products or an implementation using polar coordinates would be equally viable.

3 Design a package which will offer a user the means of easily manipulating matrices the elements of which are real numbers.

4 Design a package which will permit a user to perform arithmetic involving arbitrarily large integers.

7.4 Own variables and the use of globals

The data types we have been examining so far have all had counterparts in mathematics or in some other area of work. Choosing the set of operations has presented some difficulties but by appealing to the mathematical counterparts and by trying to blend the package and the programming language we could arrive at sensible decisions. However, there are cases where the situation is not so straightforward.

A stack can be described as a data structure which holds items: only two basic operations are permitted – either items can be added to the top of the stack or they can be removed from the top. Visualise a pile of plates: plates can be added by placing them on top and removed by taking plates from the top.

How should such a data type be brought into existence? What facilities or operations should be provided? The means whereby a stack is implemented would normally be kept hidden if possible – but would typically be an array and a pointer or a linked list. There would certainly be facilities for

   (a) creating an empty stack

   (b) placing an item on a stack

   (c) removing an item from a stack.

Note that again we have construction and selection facilities.

The ease with which stacks can be used will be increased enormously by the addition of other facilities to

(i) test if a stack is empty

(ii) read what is on the top of the stack.

Note that it is possible to accomplish both of these using the facilities already described: for (i) it is necessary to place some dummy item E on the stack initially, then read an item to test if it is E and finally replace the item read; for (ii) read an item, note it and then replace it.

Neither (i) or (ii) above permits any unauthorised access - they merely make stacks easier to use and as such are desirable.

A stack can then be implemented in the following kind of way:

(a) introduce declarations of an appropriate kind (an array and pointer or a linked list);

(b) initialise variables so that the stack is initially empty;

(c) declare procedures of various kinds for

>placing an item on the stack
>removing an item from the stack
>testing for emptiness
>reading the item on top of the stack.

If the language permits the hiding of information then only the four procedures mentioned under (c) will be made visible.

The ideas described here can be generalised in a convenient manner. We can describe (a) and (b) above as

>setting up an environment.

(c) above can be described as

> providing the only means of accessing the environment.

Ideally the environment itself is hidden, but the means of accessing or altering the environment are made public.

As described above the environment remembers information from one access to the next. Variables which possess such a property are generally referred to as own variables, a term which has its origin in Algol 60 but which has been revived in Ada.

The procedures and functions which affect an environment in the manner outlined above must access variables declared outside the procedure or function but local to the package. They must do so since they affect or access the environment. We say that side-effects occur. Normally side-effects are to be discouraged and in the earlier chapter on subprograms this aspect of their design was stressed. But side-effects of the kind which affect own variables are acceptable and can be described as benign.

There are various ways in which the own variable concept is important. In all cases an environment is installed and the means of accessing the environment is then created and made public.

Exercises 7.4

1 Demonstrate a way in which the stack mechanism used in the previous discussion might be implemented.

2 A programmer wishes to discover the number of times Ackermann's function is called whenever A(M,N) is evaluated; see example 9 of Chapter 4. Demonstrate the way in which this can be accomplished.

3 Design a method of recording the maximum depth of recursion involved in evaluating A(M,N) where A is Ackermann's function. See previous example.

7.5 Abstract data types

The stack concept we introduced in section 7.4 was important but the implementation we arrived at was of limited value. It was acceptable provided only one stack was needed. What would happen if several stacks were needed within a single program? To overcome this deficiency it is desirable to be able to introduce a new type called STACK and to arrange that certain operations such as those previously described can be performed on each stack. One further facility is needed namely the means of initialising a stack to the empty stack. All the facilities of course must now be altered in such a way that the stack they operate upon appears as a parameter. The task of introducing abstract data types such as STACK and having the necessary amount of information hidden is eased by suitable programming language facilities. In this respect Ada scores handsomely over most other common programming languages. What of the general problem of designing abstract data types such as STACK? What guidelines can be provided? Almost inevitably there will be facilities for construction and selection, for performing the basic operations and for performing certainly frequently occurring combinations of basic operations or certain other tasks (such as tests for emptiness). The precise nature of the basic operations can be found only by a careful study of the abstract data type and of the ways in which it is typically used. In short, it is necessary to perform abstraction. As with subprograms there is an important separation of concerns involved in introducing abstract data types (and indeed modules or packages in general). The designer of a new type should design without worrying unduly about use. Conversely the user of the new type should not worry about how the design was performed. The designer should design properly and provide information about how the type should be used. The user should follow the instructions. Indeed ideally it should be possible to change the method of implementing an abstract data type without having to alter (or even recompile) the programs that use it. We have now taken a very important step forward in our programming. With the introduction of abstract data types we have the facility to invent our own types and suitable functions, procedures and operators for acting on these types. We now genuinely have the means of introducing higher and higher levels of programming language. Given the existence of sufficiently many modules and packages we have the means of, in effect, making it appear that we have a programming language suited to our every need.

Exercises 7.5

1 Design a package which supports the mathematical concept of a set. Note that in a set each element appears just once – multiple instances of the same element are not permitted.

2 A bag is like a set but it possesses the ability to have elements occurring with arbitrary frequency. Design a package which would present an appropriate implementation of the concept of a bag.

3 As the name suggests, a queue is an abstract data structure with which there are associated certain operations:

   items that join the queue are placed at the end only

   items are removed from the queue only if they are at the head of the queue.

   Show how the concept of a queue might be implemented.

7.6 Note on generics

Some programming languages, notably Ada, have the concept of a generic module or package. In such cases it is possible to parameterise packages. Let us explain.

Polynomials can be of different sorts. Their coefficients might be integers, reals or complex numbers. In designing facilities for polynomials should a programmer be forced to prepare one package for polynomials with integer coefficients, another for polynomials with real coefficients and yet a third for polynomials with complex coefficients? The logic involved in all three packages would probably be identical. In such cases it is sensible to have as a parameter, the type of the coefficients (and inevitably associated operators and so on). In this way a greater degree of generality and usefulness is achieved. The argument can be applied with even more force in other respects. Should one design matrices where entries are integers, reals or whatever, stacks whose items are characters, integers, etc. and so on? The answer is, of course, no.

7.7 Miscellaneous exercises

1 Design facilities for conducting arithmetic modulo N where N is some positive integer.

2 A bit pattern within a computer can usually be interpreted in at least three ways: as an instruction, as an integer or as a string of characters. Produce a set of routines for interpreting a bit string in a suitable variety of ways.

3 It is possible to talk about numbers of the form $m+ni$ where i represents the square root of -1 and both m and n are integers. Such numbers are usually referred to as Gaussian integers.
    Design a suitable set of facilities for working with Gaussian integers.

4 A set of brackets such as (,),[and] is said to be well-formed provided that

    (i) the number of opening brackets of one kind never exceeds the number of closing brackets of that kind when scanning from the left to the right

(ii) the numbers of opening and closing brackets of a particular kind are equal.

To test whether brackets are well-formed stacks can be used. When an opening bracket occurs place it on the stack. When a closing bracket occurs a matching opening bracket should be on top of the stack and can be removed; if it is not present either because the stack is empty or because a bracket of the wrong kind is there then the brackets are not well-formed.
Write a program to implement this idea.

5 Memo functions (see question 16 in the miscellaneous exercises in Chapter 6) provide a convenient means whereby repeated evaluations of functions can be avoided. Consider the factorial function and assume that in a particular situation 1!, 2!,...,10! are likely to be requested repeatedly. In these circumstances it would be sensible to have an integer array A, say, which might hold these ten values. An implementation might then proceed as follows: to evaluate N! first inspect A(N); if the value is here extract it, otherwise perform the evaluation and when it is complete put it in A(N).

    (a) Design an iterative version of the factorial function which makes use of this memo function concept

    (b) Design a recursive version of the factorial function and implement it as a memo function

    (c) Compare the relative efficiency of these two implementations.

6 Design a package for vector manipulation.

7 Design a set of trigonometric routines for finding SIN, COS, etc. of arguments involving complex numbers.

8 Design a calendar package. Not only should this have the facility of producing a calendar for a suitable

year but it should be able to indicate important dates such as Easter, and so on.

9 Design a package to allow a user to perform character and string manipulation in a convenient manner.

10 Dates, times, etc. are often required in a variety of different formats. Produce a set of facilities which will permit ready conversion from one format to another.

11 Random integers X_0, X_1, X_2, ... between 0 and m-1, say, can be generated in the following way. X_{n+1} is derived from X_n to be the remainder on dividing $aX_n + c$ by m. To be effective choose

   *m to be a power of two and at least 2^{30}
   *a such that its remainder on division by 8 is 5, and choose a to lie between m/100 and 99xm/100
   *c should be odd and c/m approximately 0.211325

Demonstrate how this may be implemented by choosing m in such a way that m+1, say, is the largest integer that your machine can hold.

12 Demonstrate how the idea of the previous example can be used to produce random real numbers between 0 and 1.
   Check on the randomness of the results by looking at the numbers of values that fall into particular ranges.

13 The algorithm used in the two previous examples should work in such a way that numbers start to repeat only after the generation of m numbers. We say that the period should be m.
   By examining the concept for small values of m check if the period can ever be abnormally small. What advice would you give to a user of this algorithm?

14 Other methods of generating random integers calculate X_{n+1} to be the remainder on dividing

$$aX_n^2 + bX_n + c \text{ by } m$$

$$X_n + X_{n-1} \text{ by } m$$

$$aX_n + bX_{n-1} + \ldots + X_{n-k} \text{ by } m$$

Show how each of these methods can be implemented.

15 Examine each of the methods for generating random numbers described in the previous example. In particular, check the possibility of the periods being exceptionally small and the distribution of the integers throughout the entire range.

16 Design a package to support polynomial manipulation involving polynomials in a single variable with integer coefficients. As well as arithmetic and comparison capabilities, facilities should be provided for differentiation, evaluating a polynomial given that the variable has a particular value, and so on.

17 Design a set of routines that can be used for the layout of text. These should include not only facilities for taking spaces, new lines and new pages but also facilities for leaving margins, maintaining page counts, putting headings at the top of pages, and so on.

18 Design a set of facilities for use with large sparse matrices, i.e. matrices most of whose elements are zero. Do this by holding only those elements that are non-zero. Include facilities for diagonal matrices, upper triangular matrices, band matrices, and so on.

19 Design a package which will permit arithmetic involving integers of arbitrarily large magnitude.

20 Design a package which will provide facilities involving real numbers of arbitrary magnitude and precision.

21 Design a memo function implementation of Ackermann's

function.

22 A Gaussian prime is a number of the form m+ni which is divisible only by itself and no other Gaussian integer, with the possible exception of the units +1, -1, +i and -i. Gaussian primes are usually standardised by multiplying by an appropriate unit so that they are of the form m+ni where m = -1 (modulo 4).

Write a program which reads an arbitrary Gaussian integer and outputs its prime factors as suitable Gaussian integers.

23 A cross reference program will accept as input another arbitrary program. The output will be a list of the identifiers in the input program together with a note of the lines on which these identifiers were used. Write a cross reference program for a language such as Fortran which has no block structure.

24 Design a package for a number theorist interested in working with continued fractions.

25 Design a suitable set of facilities for someone interested in combinations and permutations.

26 Find pi=3.14159265... to 100 decimal places.

27 Find e (= 2.718...) to 100 decimal places.

28 Design a package for polynomials involving a single variable but with rational coefficients. Include a facility for integration.

29 Consider the set of polynomials in the single variable X with integer coefficients. The usual operations of addition, subtraction, etc. can be performed on such polynomials. Factorisation into a product of similar polynomials can also occur. Indeed there are such things as prime polynomials, e.g. X, X^2+1, and so on. Produce a suitable set of facilities for factorising polynomials of the kind described, finding highest common factors and lowest

common multiples, and so on.

30 Write a cross reference program (see exercise 23) for programs expressed in a language which does have block structure. Distinguish carefully between different variables having the same identifier.

31 A polynomial in N variables can be regarded as a polynomial in a single variable with coefficients which are polynomials in the remaining N-1 variables. Design a suitable set of facilities for the manipulation of polynomials in two variables.

32 Generalise the facilities of the previous question to allow the manipulation of polynomials in several variables.

33 The workings of a computer can be simulated by maintaining an array which represents the internal store of the machine. As instructions are decoded and obeyed the array contents are altered in appropriate ways. Design a simulator for a machine of your choice.

34 Design a set of trigonometric routines for finding the SIN, COS, etc. of very accurate real numbers, the answers being equally accurate.

35 An assembler is a program for transforming assembly code into machine code. Write an assembler for a machine of your choice.

8 | More advanced programming

In chapter four we introduced the related ideas of recursion and divide-and-conquer. The examples we dealt with at that stage were of a relatively simple kind. In this chapter we look at more advanced concepts which tend to result in a further development of both of these ideas.

In some of the problem areas we look at, it will be convenient to talk about procedures or functions accessing global variables. Now we do not intend to imply that all of what we said earlier in chapter four about the nature of routines no longer holds. We have deliberately decided to incorporate this material in a chapter which follows the discussion about modules and packages. The facilities and associated ideas contained in chapter seven should be seen as the means of providing the proper visibility.

8.1 Stepwise refinement revisited

In section 4.5 we gave a rather simplified view of the process of stepwise refinement. At that stage the process could be justified on the grounds of making large programming tasks manageable and of overcoming the problem of testing.

The crude description given then paid no attention whatsoever to the possibility that certain routines, operations or whatever may be required by several of the subtasks. So we need to modify the description of the process to take this into account. In performing the splitting then we were allowed to imagine an environment in which there are certain routines, certain operators, certain data types (perhaps even certain abstract data types), and so on.

We have seen that we need to look for structure of some

kind. This may be present in a very natural manner - see the later discussion in sections 8.4 and 8.5 where the underlying grammar, the nature of the data, provides the structure. In other more difficult cases the programmer has to adopt a view which imposes an underlying structure on the problem.

Whatever happens, the interfaces between tasks should exhibit certain desirable properties. They should be natural, clean and easily specified. Related to this is the fact that they should be narrow, i.e. the variables being passed across should normally be few in number and independent of one another.

8.2 Divide-and-conquer revisited

Let us consider a problem involving a set of points which lie in a two-dimensional plane. Let P and Q be two points whose co-ordinates are (A,B) and (S,T) respectively. We say that a point P dominates a point Q provided that

$$A > S \quad \text{and} \quad B > T$$

If neither P dominates Q nor Q dominates P we say that P and Q are incomparable.

Given a set of points we can talk about the number of points (in the set) which dominate a particular point. Alternatively we can ask whether a point is dominated by another point in the set.

Definition. Given a set of points S, the rank of a point X is defined to be the number of points in S dominated by X.

Below we give some problems which involve looking at this dominance problem. Solutions which use divide-and-conquer techniques are particularly satisfying. Given a set S of points we can divide this into two disjoint subsets S1 and S2 effectively by drawing a dividing line parallel to the y-axis in such a way that it passes through the set of points and yet no point is on the line. Then it is clear that no point to the left of the line can dominate any point to the right of the line. Further, a point P to the right of the line dominates a point Q to the left of the line if and only if the y-coordinate of P is greater than the y-coordinate of Q. Using these observations a neat recursive solution emerges and clearly it is based on divide-and-conquer techniques.

To summarise the above, we start with a two-dimensional problem involving N points. We subdivide this into two smaller two-dimensional problems together with, what is in effect, a one-dimensional problem; the one dimensional problem is a computation involving only y-coordinates.

It should be relatively clear that these ideas can be extended to deal with points in spaces of higher dimension - three, four and in general k-dimensions. More generally a point $(A_1, A_2, \ldots, A_k)$ dominates a point $(B_1, B_2, \ldots, B_k)$ provided that

$$A_i > B_i \qquad \text{for all } i=1,2,\ldots,k.$$

The idea of rank extends in a natural way. The concept of divide-and-conquer also extends. A rough outline is as follows:

> to solve a problem involving N points in k-dimensional space split this into
>
> two problems involving N/2 points in k-dimensional space together with
>
> one problem involving N points in (k-1)-dimensional space.

The idea of one point dominating another is really just a generalisation of some kind of the usual ordering relations 'less than' or 'greater than'. This observation means that a whole host of problems can now be discussed - finding maxima, finding minima, binary search, ordering, and so on. Unfortunately many of these generalisations are complicated by the fact that incomparable elements may exist. However, divide-and-conquer is the clue to the solution of many of these problems.

Consider the idea of binary search. Basically an element X is given and the task is to decide whether or not X is in some set S. In the usual rendering of this problem we sort the elements of S into some order (usually increasing or decreasing) and this allows us to decide in an efficient manner whether or not X is in S. Ideally we sort once and ask questions about the presence of quantities afterwards. Really modules should be involved to ensure the proper visibility, and so on.

Let us now look at the two-dimensional case and ask a slightly different question. Given a set of points S how can we preprocess S in such a way that the question "what is the rank of X in S?" can be answered efficiently. We can split S into two subsets S1 and S2 in the manner described previously, i.e. by drawing a line L parallel to the y-axis. Either X is to the left of L or it is to the right of L. If it is to the left then the rank of X is just the rank with respect to S1, the left-hand subset; if it is to the right then the rank of X in S is the rank with respect to S2 added to the number of points in S1 dominated by X; the latter quantity can be found by looking only at the y-coordinates of the points.

To perform the above operations efficiently we have to represent the set S in a curious manner, as a tree. The topmost node will contain information representing

- the line L (for this we need to hold only the x-coordinate)

- a pointer to the node representing S1

- a pointer to the node representing S2

- an array of the elements of S1 sorted by y-coordinates

Note yet again the recursive nature of the structure and the reflection in this of the recursive nature of the algorithm itself.

Exercises 8.2

1 Design operators or routines for determining whether

    (a) one point in two-dimensional space dominates a second point in this space

    (b) a point in k-dimensional space dominates another point in this space.

2 Design a routine for determining whether or not two points in k-dimensional space are comparable. If they are, indicate whether the first dominates the second or vice versa. Provide appropriate documentation for your routine and test it in a suitable manner.

3 Given a set S of points in the two-dimensional plane, design an algorithm to calculate the rank of each point in S using divide-and-conquer.

4 Given a set S of points in three-dimensional space show how the rank of each point can be obtained.

5 A maximum of a set of points in two-dimensional space is defined to be a point which is dominated by no other point. Write an algorithm to determine whether a given point is a maximum of a set of points.

6 Using the definition of maximum given above, write an algorithm to determine the maxima of a set of points in two-dimensional space. (Note that there may be more than one maximum but all of these will be incomparable elements.) Use divide-and-conquer techniques.

7 Create an algorithm for effectively performing the binary search process in the two-dimensional case.

8 Given a set S of elements in the two-dimensional plane preprocess these in a manner which allows one

to determine efficiently the rank of an arbitrary element X in S.

8.3 Backtracking

An interesting set of problems that have recursive solutions involves a process known as backtracking. In such cases, steps are made towards the final solution and the details recorded. If these steps do not lead to a solution some or all of them may have to be retraced and the relevant details discarded. In these circumstances it is often necessary to search through a large number of possible situations in search of feasible solutions. Let us illustrate the process by examining a particular problem.

The eight queens problem in chess is concerned with the following question: is it possible to position eight queens on a conventional chess board in such a way that no queen is under attack from any other queen by the conventional rules of chess? Basically the answer is yes, and there are 92 possible ways of doing it. In Figure 8.1 we illustrate one of the possible methods. Variations of the basic problem involve printing the first so many solutions, counting the total number of possible solutions and so on. We shall examine a method whereby all solutions can be listed.

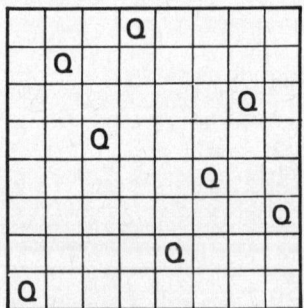

Figure 8.1

A very obvious way of approaching this problem is to

imagine that we have to consider all possible ways of positioning the queens on the chessboard; each such position has then to be examined to determine whether the queens occupy acceptable positions. Such an approach would indeed produce a solution...eventually. The total number of positions that would have to be examined is 64x63x62x...x57.

A more elegant solution can be obtained by noting that in each acceptable position of the queens each row and each column of the chessboard will contain precisely one queen. We shall use the notation (1,7,5,8,2,4,6,3) to denote the pattern indicated in Figure 8.1; thus the queen in column one is on the first row, the queen in column two is in the seventh row, the queen in the third column is in the fifth row, and so on. Thus the first coordinate in (1,7,5,8,2,4,6,3) specifies the row occupied by the queen in the first column, and so on.

Let us now investigate the problem of positioning the queens. We denote by Q1 the queen in the first column, Q2 denotes the queen in the second column, and so on. We might proceed as follows:

position Q1 in position 1, i.e. row 1

position Q2 in the first position in column 2 where it will not be under attack from Q1; Q2 goes into position 3

position Q3 in the first position in column 3 where it will not be under attack from either Q1 or Q2; Q3 goes into position 5.

Proceeding in this way Q4 goes into position 2 and Q5 goes into position 4 as illustrated in Figure 8.2.

Now try to position Q6 in column 6. It is impossible; there is no acceptable position for Q6 in this column. So we backtrack and move Q5 into its next acceptable position, namely position 8. Now try to position Q6. It is impossible. So backtrack and try to move Q5. Impossible! So backtrack further and move Q4 to its next acceptable position which turns out to be position 7. Now try to position Q5. In this way progress is made. Eventually all possibilities will have been considered and either rendered unacceptable or printed out. How do we program such a seemingly complex process?

The abstraction process will presumably result in the board being represented as a two-dimensional array. We then introduce a subprogram called POSITION for placing a queen in a column, the call POSITION(C) will position a queen in the Cth column.

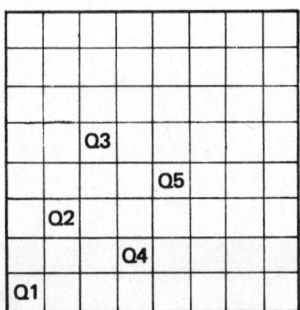

Figure 8.2

The definition of the procedure POSITION might then take the following form:

POSITION processes the COLth column of the board:
Using control variable ROW starting at 1
and increasing in steps of 1 to 8 perform
the following task:
  place a queen in position (COL,ROW) of the board;
  if the board represents an acceptable configuration
  then
    if COL is 8 then
      this is a solution; note it;
    otherwise
      process the (COL+1)th column of the board
      by calling POSITION;
    end if;
  end if;
  remove queen from position (COL,ROW);
end task.
end the processing of column COL.

The main program itself would then take the form of two instructions to:

set up the initial chess board;

call POSITION to process the first column.

The backtracking that is present in this solution is perhaps not immediately apparent. It is basically contained in the recursion.

Exercises 8.3

1. Write a program which will determine a single solution to the eight queens problem.

2. Design a program which, given a positive integer M will find M different solutions of the eight queens problem. Adopt a helpful approach if M happens to be too large.

3. The eight queens problem can be generalised in such a way that boards of size k x k with sets of k queens are considered. Write a program to determine and print out all the solutions in such cases.

4. Use a backtracking approach to generate all the permutations of the quantities 1,2,..., N.

5. Use a backtracking approach to find and produce all partitions of the integer N supplied as data.

8.4 Recursive descent

A beautiful use of recursion emerges in writing compilers for programming languages. Let us take a simple example and illustrate the technique in this way. We invent a small programming language and show how to write a piece of program which recognises legal programs written in the small language, i.e. the program fragment detects whether or not an arbitrary string is a member of the set of programs in the language.

To describe the programming language we introduce a variant of notation which is usually referred to as Backus-Naur-Form or BNF for short. We write rules such as

        `<assignment>::=<identifier>=<expression>`

to mean that an assignment is defined to be an identifier followed by an equals sign followed by an expression. Thus ::= denotes 'is defined to be'. `<assignment>`, `<identifier>` and `<expression>` are all referred to as syntactic categories; they describe a class or set of items. On the other hand the equals sign is referred to as a terminal; terminals are the objects that appear in programs. Correspondingly, non-terminals are synonyms for syntactic categories.

To complete the BNF notation we introduce other symbols with special meaning:

    | means 'or' and separates alternatives

    [ ]   are square brackets used to surround optional terms; for example, a positive number may or may not be preceded by a plus sign

    { }   are curly brackets and denote zero or more occurrences of the enclosed items.

The complete set of terminals, non-terminals and rules that describe a programming language is usually referred to as a grammar. More accurately, it describes the form or syntax rather than the meaning. There is also a special non-terminal, such as `<program>`, called the sentence symbol, which indicates the class of objects being defined. BNF is a convenient way of expressing grammars for programming languages.

With these remarks we can now give a complete BNF definition of our programming language (or at least of the form that programs take rather than their meaning):

   `<assignment>::=<identifier>=<expression>`

   `<expression>::=[-]<term>{+<term>|-<term>}`

<term>   ::=<factor>{x<factor>|/<factor>}

<factor>   ::=<constant>|<identifier>|(<expression>)

<identifier>::=A|B|C|...|Z

<constant>   ::=0|1|2|3|4|5|6|7|8|9

In recursive descent we associate a subprogram with each separate syntactic category. Thus there will be a subprogram for recognising assignments, another for recognising expressions, another for recognising terms, and so on. These we refer to as ASSIGNMENT, EXPRESSION, TERM and so on. The definitions of the various subprograms will follow from the definition of the appropriate syntactic category and will be based on them.

The routine ASSIGNMENT for recognising an assignment will call in turn routines for

    recognising an identifier, then
    recognising an equals symbol, then
    recognising an expression.

In effect the definition of ASSIGNMENT is this

    Call the routine IDENTIFIER.
    If the current character is the equals symbol then
        read the next character and let it
        be the new current character;
    otherwise
        report a syntax error;
    end if.
    Call the routine EXPRESSION.

The routines for EXPRESSION and TERM can be programmed in a similar way. The programming of FACTOR is less straightforward. However the only difficulty can be resolved by including a conditional of the form

    If the current character is a digit then
        recognise a constant;
    otherwise if the current character is a letter then
        recognise a variable;

```
        otherwise if the current character is an opening
            parenthesis read the next character and let it
            be the new current character;
        call the routine to recognise an EXPRESSION;
        check that the current character is indeed a
            closing parenthesis and read
            the next character;
        otherwise
            a syntax error has occurred;
        end if.
```

In this way the recogniser can be programmed. As recognition of different phrases or syntactic categories takes place, so other actions can be performed: code can be produced so that compilers are derived; translation from one high level language to another can occur; information about the variables, constants, etc. used can be accumulated and summary information produced at the conclusion; and so on.

Witness yet again the relationship between the structure of the data as defined by the grammar and the structure of the program that processes it. Indeed the stepwise refinement process is being guided by the nature of the underlying grammar.

We have produced a rather simplified view of what actually happens in practice. An important difference is, of course, the number of rules involved. Programming languages might need as many as 100 rules for their definition.

Another important difference is that identifiers, integers, and so on are often more complicated than we have indicated. Identifiers might consist of strings of letters and digits starting with a letter, for instance. In reality a lexical analyser (a function or routine) will remove spaces and commentary and gather together the different characters that form the identifiers, integers, and so on. In effect, the identifiers, etc. are placed in suitable tables and replaced by codes. Different identifiers might be replaced by pairs of integers such as (0,0), (0,1),(0,2),.... Different integers might be replaced by (1,0),(1,1), (1,2), and so on. The compiler writer must devise his own codes and notation for his lexical analyser. The effect of this preprocessing is to reduce significantly the number of nonterminals and to change the nature of the terminals.

It is important to be aware of the limitations of the recursive descent process. Given a rule of the form

$$A ::= B \mid C$$

where A is some nonterminal and B and C are appropriate lists of terminals and/or nonterminals, the method works only of the terminals that can start a B are completely different from the terminals that can start a C. No single terminal can start both B and C since then the parsing process will not know whether to look for a B or a C. Backtracking can be used in cases of uncertainty - i.e. look ahead for a B and if this search is unsuccessful look for a C. However this often leads to unnecessary inefficiency.

Some simple actions can be taken to counter difficult cases though in general the problem is difficult and is surrounded by a body of theory in the area of grammars. We mention just two simple cases which are worthy of brief discussion.

Firstly given a rule such as

$$A ::= a B \mid a C$$

we can replace this by two rules

$$A ::= a X$$

where

$$X ::= B \mid C$$

If it can be shown that B and C start with different sets of symbols the recursive descent method can be applied to the latter grammar.

Given a rule such as

$$A ::= b B \mid \langle empty \rangle$$

where

$$\langle empty \rangle ::=$$

then an if..then..otherwise..end if form of construction can be used to write a procedure which recognises an A. If the current symbol is a b we must seek a B; otherwise we assume that an A has occurred.

Secondly let us take rules of the form

$$A ::= A\ a\ |\ b$$

This rule is recursive in that A is defined in terms of itself. Since A appears as the left-hand symbol of one of the alternatives on the right-hand side we say that simple left recursion is present.

Grammars which contain left recursion must be transformed before recursive descent techniques can be applied; otherwise the method will fail since infinite recursion will appear. The rule given above can be replaced by

$$A ::= b\ X$$

where X is a new nonterminal defined by

$$X ::= \langle empty \rangle\ |\ a\ X$$

A more complex form of left recursion takes place in circumstances such as

$$A ::= B...|$$

$$B ::= C...|$$

$$C ::= A...$$

Even in this case (which is rather uncommon) the recursion can be removed.

We have spoken about various kinds of transformation that can be applied to grammars. All of these can be performed automatically. A grammar can be given as data and a program can be constructed to output a transformed grammar. Further, given an appropriate grammar a recogniser can be automatically produced. It is possible to devise suitable grammars for most of the common programming languages.

Exercises 8.4

1 Implement a recursive descent recogniser for the language described by the above grammar defining <assignment>.

2 Show how the program of the previous exercise can be modified to cover the following situations:

    (a) allow the presence of spaces (which have no effect) in the input

    (b) count the number of different identifiers occurring

    (c) reproduce a listing of the input.

3 Write a program which, given a suitable grammar, will detect whether or not left recursion is present.

4 Given an arbitrary grammar expressed in BNF notation demonstrate how to test for and remove simple left recursion.

5 Write a program which, given a suitable grammar with capital letters as nonterminals and small letters as terminals, will automatically produce a recogniser. State clearly the limitations of your program.

8.5 Pattern matching

In the earlier discussion on string processing in Chapter five, we saw illustrations of the kinds of operations that can typically be performed on strings. We shall now generalise these ideas and move into the realms of pattern matching. In this section we therefore examine ways of finding patterns of certain kinds within strings.

We shall always talk in terms of finding a pattern of

a particular kind within a string of characters. It will often be convenient to think of the string as being a line of text and so we shall not think of searches doing unexpected things like swallowing up an entire input file looking for an absent pattern.

We shall say that a string matches a pattern or indeed that a pattern matches a string if the string contains an occurrence of the pattern. We say that the match occurs at position I of the string if the Ith character indicates the start of the pattern.

There are certain ways in which the definitions we have given are incomplete. Several occurrences of the same pattern may exist within a string. To be definite we shall always look for the leftmost occurrence of a pattern match and the value of I will reflect this. Even at a particular position there may be several different occurrences of the same pattern. Let us take one example to illustrate. Identifiers in programming languages can typically be several characters long and the initial character is itself usually a legitimate identifier. Consequently a search for an identifier can match in more ways than one. To avoid confusion in this sense we shall imagine that a search for a particular pattern at a particular position will find the largest possible string matching the pattern.

What sort of patterns are of interest? We shall use the notation developed earlier in our discussion of BNF to describe particular combinations and sequences of characters. Since it is desirable to express patterns in as succinct a manner as possible we shall tend to use the |,{,}, etc. variations to describe patterns. Some additional notation is also helpful. For example

   ?   will denote any single character and so X?Y may match X+Y or X-Y.

  [A-Z]   will denote the set of capital letters, A B ... Z.

  [a-z] and [0-9] have a similar meaning; similarly for other character sets.

  -a   will denote any character other than the letter a; again other possibilities

MORE ADVANCED PROGRAMMING   223

> result from replacing a by a different character or set.

%   denotes the start of a line.

$ denotes the end of a line.

So briefly [] is used for character sets, - denotes complement and the start and end of strings can be specified; other variations are also possible.

Example 8.5.1

The pattern

(i)   %$ matches an empty string

(ii)   %ABC   matches a string beginning with the characters ABC

(iii)   ;$ matches a string ending with ;

(iv)   COMMENT [A-Z]* ;

matches a string containing the word COMMENT followed by some arbitrary and possibly null sequence of capital letters followed by a semicolon.

(v)   ?*   matches an arbitrary sequence of characters.

These remarks complete the brief description of what is involved in some form of pattern matching. But, in truth, they hide some of the difficulties involved in the implementation of them. Consider a pattern of the form PQ*R where P,Q and R are abbreviations for some pattern. An implementation might naturally look for the pattern P, then as many occurrences as possible of Q and finally an occurrence of R. It is conceivable that this approach leads to the recognition of too many occurrences of Q and to a subsequent failure to match R. The most helpful attitude that the pattern recogniser can adopt is to look for a smaller sequences of occurrences of Q's and then see if R matches the remaining and now larger string. Only when all possible sequence of Q's have been considered should failure be announced.

What we have described is nothing more than backtracking. It is necessary to consider this possibility whenever the star operator is involved or when the vertical bar is present in a pattern. In patterns which involve several occurrences of the star operator or the vertical bar the situation becomes relatively complex. In the backtracking process both the length of the matched string and the position of the start of the pattern can be used.

In the exercises that follow we might imagine that it is necessary to produce a program which makes searches through a (perhaps large) file looking for all occurrences of lines which match a particular pattern. On finding matches the corresponding lines have to be printed. Briefly, a request for

       FIND   COMMENT [A-Z]*;

should produce all lines containing this pattern (and perhaps the corresponding line numbers).

When we reach more complex patterns it may be advisable to hold a convenient internal representation of the pattern that is easily scanned. Thought about this ought to be stimulated by thinking about the efficient implementation of simpler patterns.

Exercises 8.5

1 Design a FIND program which will find all lines containing a specified string of characters. Print out line numbers and the contents of lines.

2 Write an efficient FIND program for finding any one of a set of strings. Note that several of the strings might start (or end) with the same sequence of characters; moreover

       FIND   BY   BYPASS

is possible. State clearly any restrictions on your system.

3 Design a FIND program which allows for the inclusion of markers to denote the start and end of a line. Describe carefully the limitations of your program.

4 Write a pattern matching program for seeking patterns which include strings, character sets such as [A-Z] and the ? facility mentioned earlier. Provide accurate documentation which describes the system and its limitations.

5 Augment the pattern matching system of the previous example by including the complement facility.

6 The escape character idea is useful in pattern matching. If it is necessary to search for a ? or an occurrence of [the notation of the previous sections is inadequate. Escape characters provide a useful means of overcoming the difficulty. Introduce a suitable notation for dealing with this situation, implement your ideas and document them carefully.

7 Implement a pattern matching facility which includes all the facilities mentioned earlier with the exception of the star facility. Note that for efficiency reasons it may be necessary to hold a special representation of the pattern.

8 Implement a FIND facility which permits (within patterns) concatenation, character sets, complements and stars. Describe carefully the limitations of your system.

8.6 Miscellaneous examples

1 Design a program which, given an arbitrary grammar expressed in BNF notation, will produce separate alphabetic listings of the terminals and

nonterminals.

2 An arithmetic expression can contain opening and closing brackets. For the expression to be syntactically legal the following conditions must hold

>   (a) the number of closing brackets is equal to the number of opening brackets

>   (b) in a left to right scan the number of closing brackets never exceeds the number of opening brackets

The string that forms the expression is then said to be balanced. (This idea stems from the programming language SNOBOL.) Introduce a pattern matching facility for recognising balanced strings of the kind described above.

3 The notion of balanced strings described in the previous question can be extended to cover square brackets, begin...end pairs and so on. Design a simple system for recognising whether this more general form of balanced string is present. Note that it may be necessary to consider strings spanning more than one line.

4 Given a positive integer N show how this might be partitioned into quantities $x_1, x_2, \ldots, x_k$ in such a way that

$$x_1 + x_2 + x_3 + \ldots + x_k = N$$

and the product $x_1 x_2 \ldots x_k$ is as large as possible. Try to ensure that your solution is efficient.

5 Given a set S of points in the k-dimensional space design an algorithm for finding the rank of each point in S.

6 Show how the binary search algorithm in k-dimensional space might be implemented.

7 The programming language LISP admits s-expressions, a simplified version of which may be defined as follows:

   (a) any letter is an s-expression.

   (b) if u and v are s-expressions so is (u,v).

   Write a piece of program which recognises s-expressions.

8 Let A be an alphabet consisting of three characters (e.g. a,b,c). Write a program which, given the positive integer N, generates a sequence of N characters with the property that no immediately adjacent substrings of characters are identical.

9 Let A and B be points in k-dimensional space with the property that A dominates B. Show how to find (by divide-and-conquer techniques) the number of points with integer coefficients lying in the box defined by A and B, i.e. find the number of points P for which A dominates P and P dominates B; coordinates of P are integers.

10 Given a set S of points in k-dimensional space show how the set of maxima of S might be found.

11 Given a set S of points in k-dimensional space show how the rank of each element of S might be found.

12 Given a set S of points in k-dimensional space show the number of points dominated by a point X might be found.

13 The data for this problem consists of a set of names of towns together with their longitude and latitude. Frequently it will be necessary to enquire which town is closest to some position. Indicate how this might be programmed.

14 In exercise 2 of Exercises 4.5, a method was given for evaluating powers in relatively few multiplications. Tabulate the least number of

multiplications needed to evaluate X^N where $1<N<100$ and, in each case, indicate the number of multiplications that produced the result. Compare these results with the method of chapter 4.

15 Design a pattern matching facility for use with arithmetic expressions. It should be possible to

    (a) remove extraneous brackets, e.g. replace (A) by A

    (b) replace 0 + A by A where appropriate

    (c) perform operations similar to those described in (b) above, e.g. replace 1 x A by A

    (d) replace expressions involving constants by a single constant, (e.g. 4x5 by 20) when appropriate.

Implement and carefully document your system.

16 Implement a pattern matching facility which includes all the facilities mentioned during the discussion of pattern matching. Thus the * operation and the vertical bar facility should be included. Describe carefully the abilities and limitations of your system.

17 Eight rooks can be placed on a conventional chess board in such a way that every position on the board comes under attack. Compare the number of ways this can be done with the number of solutions of the eight queens problem.

18 Design a program to test whether a grammar is 'clean'. Thus the following need to be checked.

    (a) Is there precisely one rule for each nonterminal?

    (b) Can each nonterminal be defined ultimately in terms of terminals?

(c) Is there at most one sentence symbol?

Note that (c) above implies that a check is made to ensure that each nonterminal (with the possible exception of a sentence symbol) is used on the right-hand side of some rule.

19 Clearly eight queens can be placed on a conventional chess board in such a way that every position on the chess board is under attack. By using a suitable search technique discover the minimum number of queens needed.

20 Generalise the idea in the previous problem in such a way that solutions for chess boards of arbitrary kxk size can be given.

21 (Knight's tour) In chess the knight can move two squares vertically and one square horizontally or two squares vertically and one square horizontally. Can a knight tour a chess board in such a way that every square is visited once and once only?

22 Can a knight tour a chess board in the manner described in the previous example but with the added constraint that in one more move he can arrive at his starting position?

23 Design a system for producing arbitrary programs for a language described by a suitable BNF grammar. Use random number generators to make choices about alternatives within the grammar; variables that are used need not be declared.

24 Consider a one-dimensional chess-board infinite in both directions:

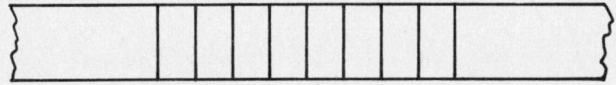

Let p stand for piece and let b stand for blank. There will be an infinite number of blank squares and a finite number of squares on which pieces will be placed. The former squares we mark with b, the latter we mark with p. A move in this game of one-dimensional checkers consists of replacing either

      ppb   by   bbp
or
      bpp   by   pbb

Effectively one piece jumps over another so removing it from play; in the first case above the leftmost piece jumps and in the second case the rightmost piece jumps. The object of the game is to leave precisely one piece on the board. Design a program which will test whether it is possible to produce a sequence of moves which will result in only one piece being left. Do this by examining the structure of the input, not simulating all the moves.

25 Prepare a program for scanning libraries of programs expressed in some suitable high-level language. Produce statistics about the frequency of occurrence of the various constructs.

26 A comma-free code is a collection of words (called a dictionary) from which sentences which contain no punctuation (spaces, commas, etc.) may be formed in an unambiguous manner. In effect therefore two or more words placed side-by-side cannot possibly be interpreted in some unexpected manner. Given an alphabet consisting of N letters there are many ways of producing words of length K. Write a program which will find the largest possible size of comma-free dictionary.

27 Lambda expressions can be defined in BNF notation in the following manner

    <var> ::= a | b | c | ... | z

    <lambda-expression> ::= λ<var><lambda-expression>
      |(<lambda-expression><lambda expression>)

Write a program to recognise legal lambda expressions. Use your program to decide whether or not (λxxy) and λxλy(xλxλyy) are legal lambda expressions.

28 Write a program to determine the sets of terminals that can start each nonterminal in a grammar.

29 Use the previous program to perform factorisation on the rules of a grammar. State clearly the limitations of your system.

30 Combine the ideas of the two previous problems to produce a system for taking a grammar in BNF notation and producing a transformed grammar which is amenable to the recursive descent approach. (Note that this can now be linked to a program to produce a recogniser automatically.)

31 Write a program which, given a grammar and a nonterminal, outputs the subset of the grammar which describes the nonterminal. State clearly any assumptions you make.

32 A salesman has to visit each of N different cities starting at his home city and returning there having visited each city precisely once on completion of his journey; the distances between all of the cities are given. Write a program which accepts suitable data and produces a route which minimises the distance the salesman has to travel.

33 Design a system for including within a program (in some suitable language such as Ada, Basic or C) statements which record the number of times each statement has been executed. On completion of the program all this information should be printed in a convenient manner.

34 Design a recogniser for the Basic programming language, i.e. a program which will decide whether a piece of text constitutes a syntactically legitimate Basic program.

35 Design a program that will produce a neat layout of and an alphabetical list of all the identifiers used in a Basic program. One might imagine, for instance,

that each FOR and accompanying NEXT, can be vertically below one another and that the intervening text is indented by some amount.

36 Design a program to produce a neat layout of programs expressed in some language more complex than Basic, e.g. Ada, Fortran, Pascal, PL/I.

37 A step-shaped object of the form

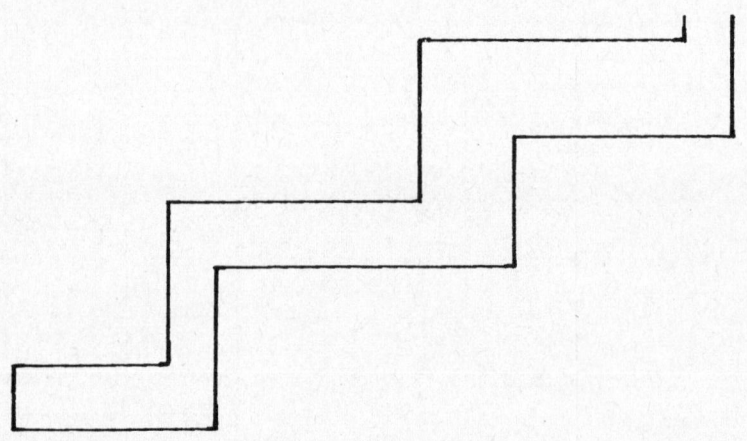

is formed by building with vertical and horizontal rectangles of varying widths and lengths.

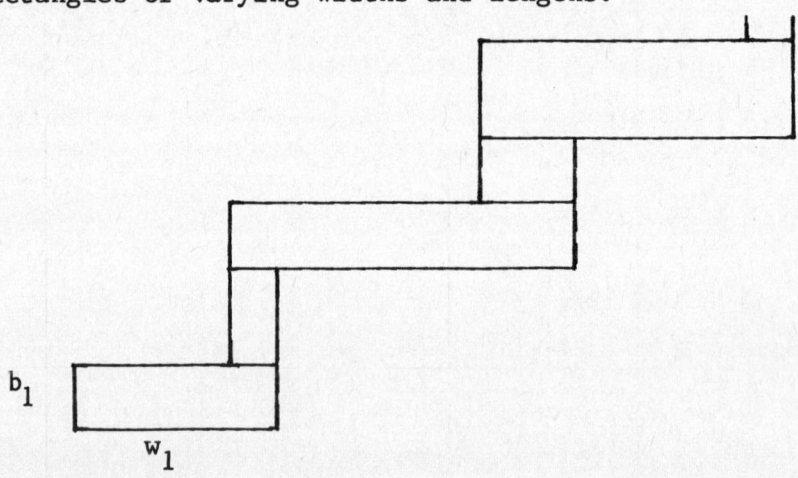

Write a program which

(a) reads a description of such an object as N followed by N pairs (w_i, b_i) the width and breadth of each rectangle starting from the base of the figure.

(b) reads the co-ordinates of two arbitrary points within the figure (assume the lower left-hand corner of the first rectangle is at location (0,0))

(c) calculates the length of the shortest path between the two points given that the path must lie wholly within the object.

38 Grammars are sometimes written in a less than satisfactory manner. For example

   (i) two rules defining a given nonterminal might be given - usually these will be combined into one rule

   (ii) the sentence symbol might not be apparent - usually this will be the first nonterminal defined

   (iii) the definition of a nonterminal is often distant from the position in which it is used

   (iv) nonterminals are introduced and defined for no apparent reason, e.g. a nonterminal might be used only once and defined in a simple way - in these circumstances there are good reasons for performing substitution and removing the nonterminal.

Design a program for cleaning up a grammar and highlighting the possible sentence symbols.

39 Design a program for generating arbitrary programs to test the compiler for a block-structured language. Allow options which could force each variable that is used to have been declared.

40 In a certain country the Post Office issues stamps in

sets of N denominations. Further no more than three stamps may be placed on any letter or parcel.

Write a program which, given N, will choose a set of denominations which will allow the greatest range of letters or parcels to be sent (starting with a one unit piece of mail and going up in steps of one.)

41 Prepare a program which will provide a convenient graphical representation of a suitable grammar expressed in BNF. Diagrams such as the Pascal syntax diagram might be produced. (See Rohl, 1980.)

42 Write a program which allocates the integers 1 to 8 to the squares in the figure below so that no two adjacent squares (vertically, diagonally or horizontally) contain consecutive integers.

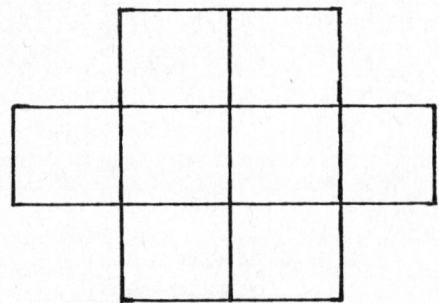

43 The "N queens problem" is to place N queens on an N*N chessboard in such a way that no two queens lie on the same vertical, horizontal or diagonal line. Assuming that N is supplied as data,

(a) write a program which will find all the solutions to the problem

(b) write an optimised version of the program which suppresses solutions that are merely symmetries of previously output solutions.

44 Consider the following configuration on a chess board.

```
              p   p   p

                  p       p

      p   p   p   p   p   p

          p       p

          p   p   p
```

Can a knight in chess capture all 16 pieces in 16 consecutive moves?

45 Can the knight move from the bottom left to the top right of a chess board visiting every square en route? Can each square be visited exactly once?

46 A maze may be represented by a two-dimensional array in which elements containing -1 represented blocked squares, elements containing 0 represent free squares, an element containing 1 represents the start and an element containing 2 the finish. Write a procedure which takes such an array and outputs the path (if any exists) from the start to the finish. Moves from one element of the path to the next must be either horizontal or vertical.

47 The following problem has been in existence for more than a thousand years. A man has to take a wolf, a goat and a cabbage across a river. The boat has room for the man plus either the goat or the wolf or the cabbage. If the man takes the cabbage with him, the wolf will eat the goat, if he takes the wolf with him, the goat will eat the cabbage. The cabbage and goat are only safe from their respective enemies if the man is present. Write a program which evaluates and outputs the sequence of moves which makes it possible for the man to transport the wolf, goat and cabbage successfully across the river.

48 Every year a Computer Science department draws up a list of M projects. Each of N students (N<M) will attempt just one project but specifies 3 that he or she would like to attempt (in order of preference).

Write a procedure which takes parameters
   (a) M
   (b) a 3xN array of student preferences
and allocates one project to each student in such a way that the sum

$$S_1 + S_2 + \ldots + S_N$$

is maximised where S_i is

   3 if the ith student is allocated first choice
   2 if allocated second choice
   1 if allocated third choice
   0 if allocated a project not on his or her list of preferences.

Your algorithm should be as fast as possible so that if for example each student states a different first preference, the solution is found very quickly.

49 Use the computer to show that in four moves the configuration

   . . W B W B W B W B

can be rearranged so that all the blacks are together and all the whites are together. A single move takes the form of moving two adjacent checkers into the gap. Similarly show how 10 checkers can be rearranged in 5 moves and 12 checkers in 6 moves.

50 There are seven positions on a line, six of which are occupied by white (W) and black (B) checkers. The initial configuration is

   W W W . B B B

A move can take one of two forms:

   a checker can be moved into an adjacent gap

   a checker can jump over one neighbour into the gap.

MORE ADVANCED PROGRAMMING   237

Show how the black and white pieces can be interchanged in 15 moves.

51 There exist a set of n cells and (n-1) occupants. No cell may have more than one occupant at a time. A table indicates which cells are linked directly together. A particular configuration of occupied cells may be altered by moving into the unoccupied cell, the occupant of any cell directly connected to it. Write a program which reads
   (a) a description of an initial configuration (I)
   (b) a description of a final configuration (F)
   (c) the connectivity table
and determines whether or not I can be transformed into F under the rules above.

52 A grammar in which no nonterminal is defined recursively describes only a finite number of possible strings.
   Write a program which accepts such a grammar, checks it for validity and outputs the complete set of strings it describes.

53 A configuration of pieces on a chess board can be represented by the contents of an 8 by 8 array. A frequent type of chess problem is that in which from a given configuration the white pieces (which have the first move) have to mate the black king in N moves against any defence. Write a program which reads a board configuration and the value of N and outputs white's first move.

54 A directed graph with N vertices V1, V2, ..., VN can be represented by an NxN matrix M.

   $M(i,j) = 1$ if there is an arc $V_i \rightarrow V_j$
   0 otherwise.

   Two directed graphs are isomorphic if the vertices of one can be labelled in such a way as to produce the other.
   Write a procedure which takes as parameters two matrices each representing a graph and determines whether or not the graphs are isomorphic.

55 Write a program which generates random arithmetic expressions
    (a) with no brackets
    (b) with brackets.

56 Given a square grid of heights above sea-level, including a mountain top, find a possible descending path from the mountain top to the lowest point of a trough on the grid. (Water does not run uphill but may run diagonally relative to the grid.)

57 Write a procedure which takes the following parameters
    (i) a two-dimensional array containing the representation of an island. Every element of the array has 1 of 2 values depending on whether or not it represents the coastline. If you only have numeric arrays use 1 and 0, if character arrays are available you could use . and *. An example is

```
. . . * . .
. . * . * .
. * . . . *
* . . . * .
* . * . * .
* * . * . .
```

    (ii) the co-ordinates of any point inside the coastline.

  Your procedure should return as result the total area of the island excluding the elements defining the coastline. The area of the island above is thus 9 units. Assume that every square of the island is connected to another square of the island along an edge.
  Write a procedure which simply takes parameter (i) and returns the same information.

58 (a) Write a procedure which takes as parameter an NxN matrix and returns as result the determinant of the matrix.
   (b) Show how to calculate determinants using a

divide-and-conquer technique and balancing i.e. express NxN as four N/2 x N/2 and proceed from there.
Is process (b) any more efficient than (a)?

59 The Diophantine equation $3x^2 + 4y^2 = 19$ has integer solutions such as $x = 1$ and $y = 2$. On the other hand $3x^2 + 4y^2 = 5$ has no integer solutions.
Write a program to determine whether an equation of the form

$$a_1 x_1^2 + \ldots + a_n x_n^2 = b$$

has any integer solutions. If it has then print them.

60 A four metre by 2 metre area can be paved with 2*1 metre slabs in any of the five ways illustrated.

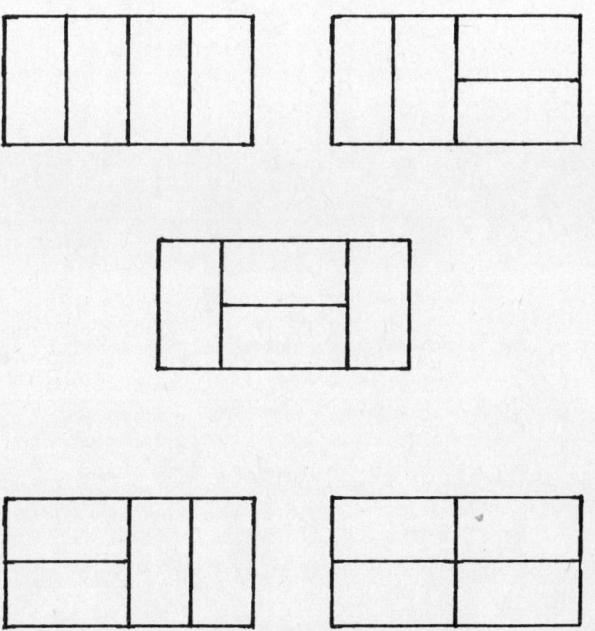

(a) Write a program which given N, determines how many ways there are of paving a 4 metre by N metre area.

(b) Write a program which given M and N, determines how many ways there are of paving a N metre by M metre area.

61 Let M and N be positive integers read in as data. The generalised postage stamp problem consists of choosing a set of N integers with the property that

 (i) each of the integers 1,2,...,S can be formed by adding together not more than M members of the set
 (ii) the number S in (i) is as large as possible.

(a) Write a program which reads M and N and outputs both S and the set of N integers.
(b) Write a program which finds the minimum value of N such that when M=3, S is at least 100. Print out the set of N stamps.

62 Both

13	1	6	10		1	2	3	4
14	2	5	9	and	13	5	6	10
	12	11	7		14	12	11	9
3	15	8	4			15	8	7

are configurations of the 15-puzzle. Show how, in 50 moves it is possible to move to

1	2	3	4		1	2	3	4
5	6	7	8	or to	5	6	7	8
9	10	11	12		9	10	11	12
13	14	15			13	15	14	

respectively.

63 Write a program which reads a grammar and outputs a finite number of strings described by the grammar. If the grammar permits two nonterminals to appear side-by-side or allows some item to appear in a particular context, the set of strings generated should include at least one instance of these.

64 Design a program that, given an initial configuration, will provide a solution of the Rubic Cube puzzle.

9 | Files

A file is essentially a data structure held on a secondary storage device rather than in main memory. When a normal program ceases execution and is removed from main memory, the contents of main memory data structures are lost. In contrast, the contents of files created are usually preserved. In this way data generated by one program is available for use by programs running at a later date. In addition, the capacity of most secondary storage devices is made virtually limitless through the use of exchangeable discs and tapes. Thus a file is a way of storing a large amount of data over a long period of time, though of course it is also a way of storing temporary results during the running of a program. Most businesses use files, for example, of stock held, of employees, of accounts payable; a university would have student files, a law enforcement agency would keep criminal records.

Access to files is typically via directories. A directory can be regarded as a file containing information about other files. For each file there may be a record of its name, size, physical location, time of last access, and so on.

There is a price to be paid for the convenience of having files. Data must be in main memory in order to be processed and access times to secondary storage devices are comparatively long. In the time that it takes to fetch data from a typical disc, 100,000 accesses can be made to a typical main memory. Great care must therefore be taken in arranging data in a file. It may often be worth performing searches and comparisons in main memory in order to avoid a secondary storage access.

The choice of file structure, as we saw with main memory data structures, depends on the types of operation that will be performed on the file contents. The following file organisations are common:

(i)   Serial
  (ii)   Sequential
 (iii)   Direct access
  (iv)   Indexed sequential

9.1 Serial files

Certain secondary storage devices (for example magnetic tapes) can be accessed only in a serial manner. To access the nth record the (n-1) preceding records must be skipped. It follows that any file held on magnetic tape is a serial file. Although a magnetic disc is a direct access device, certain programming languages (for example PASCAL) enable programmers to access files only in a serial way.

Conceptually when a serial file is opened for reading, a pointer is positioned at the beginning of the file. A read operation transfers data from the file starting at the pointer position and advances the pointer over the data read. Data is transferred into main memory. Programming languages typically provide mechanisms for detecting when the pointer is at the end of the file and for 'rewinding' the file.

A serial file opened for writing is initially empty. Data transferred from main memory to the file is added to the end of the file, so extending it.

It follows from the above that the only way of modifying a serial file is by copying it to a new file incorporating the amendments during the copying process. 'Splicing' a serial file as one might a tape or film is not in general possible.

It is important to be aware of differing conventions in different programming languages for detecting the end of a file. The programs in this book are intended to be language independent; we adopt the convention that a programmer must issue a READ or INPUT instruction and perform a test if he wishes to determine whether he has reached the end of file. In practice it may be necessary to incorporate a dummy record to ensure that the correct action takes place.

Example 9.1 Creating files

Write a program which, from a file RAWDATA of real numbers, creates two files ABOVE and REST. File ABOVE should contain those numbers in RAWDATA which are above the average of the numbers in that file; file REST should contain the remaining numbers.

A possible solution is of the form

```
open file RAWDATA for reading;
set TOTAL and NUMNUMBERS to 0;
read from RAWDATA a value for R;
while not END_OF_FILE for RAWDATA perform
     the following task:
          add 1 to NUMNUMBERS;
          add R to TOTAL;
          read from RAWDATA a value for R;
     end of task.

set AVERAGE to TOTAL/NUMNUMBERS;

open file ABOVE for writing;
open file REST for writing;
rewind file RAWDATA;

read from RAWDATA a value for R;
while not END_OF_FILE for RAWDATA perform
   the following task:
     if R>AVERAGE then
         write R to ABOVE;
     otherwise
         write R to REST;
     end if;
     read from RAWDATA a value for R;
   end of task.
close files.
```

Exercises 9.1

1. Code the program of example 9.1 in a language of your choice.

2. Write a program which copies one file to another.

3. Write a program which reads a file of integers and copies the odd integers to one file and the even integers to a second file.

4. Write a program which removes from a file of integers those which are not prime.

5. A file RESULTS contains pairs of integers. The first of each pair is a student identity-number and the second is the score obtained by the student in an examination.
   Write a program which reads RESULTS and creates 3 files:

   PASS - should contain the identity-numbers of students scoring the pass mark (50%) or better.

   FAIL - should contain the identity-numbers of students scoring below the pass mark.

   COMMENDATION - should contain the identity-numbers of students scoring one of the five highest scores obtained.

   Assume the presence of at least five students.

9.2 Jackson design method

Jackson (see Jackson, 1975) has devised a design methodology particularly suitable for data processing problems involving files. Here we will only touch on a few aspects of the design method, the reader is

encouraged to read the publication referred to.
The steps in the Jackson design method are:

(i) represent the problem environment by appropriate data structures

(ii) devise a program structure based on the data structures

(iii) break down the task to be performed into a set of primitive operations

(iv) assign the primitives to appropriate components of the program structure.

Note again the relationship between the structure of data and the structure of programs operating on it. Jackson uses the following notation:

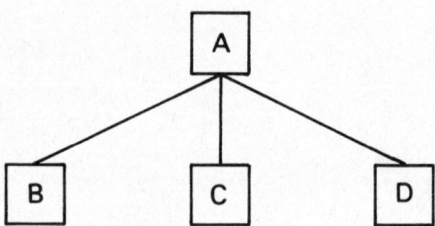

indicates that an A consists of a B followed by a C followed by a D. For example, a speech might consist of opening remarks followed by the main text followed by closing remarks.

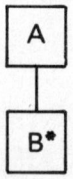

indicates that object A consists of a sequence of zero or more occurrences of object B. For example, an error report from a program compilation would consist of zero or more error messages.

Running example

Example programs in this and certain subsequent sections will describe the construction of files enabling useful queries to be answered about a set of documents. The file structures are similar to those used by the IBM STAIRS information retrieval system (see, for example, Martin, 1977).

In this first phase we consider a serial file containing the texts of a number of documents. The order of the documents is not significant. Each document is preceded in the file by a 'header' the precise form of which we ignore here but may in practice include author, title, security level and so on. The text of each document is followed by some recognisable terminator. Each document consists of a number of sentences each of which in turn contains a number of words.

Using Jackson's notation we can represent the file of documents:

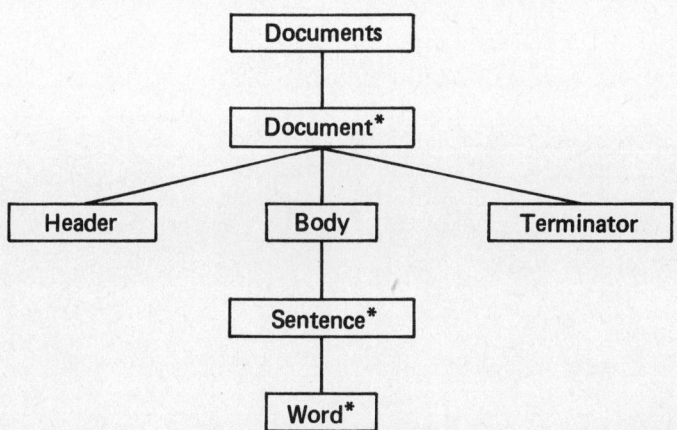

In the first phase of file construction we need to copy each of the documents to a distinct file. These files will be designated F1, F2, ... We need to keep a record of the allocation of documents to files so will create a directory file (D). The directory will contain for each document
   -its number (position in the input sequence)
   -its header
   -the name of the file to which its contents have

been copied.

Once D exists we can use integers to identify documents and use the directory to retrieve them.

The final file to be produced in the first phase will contain one record for each word occurrence in the file of documents. We will designate this file W; each record in it will contain

(a) the word
(b) the number of the document in which it occurs
(c) the number of the sentence within the document in which it occurs
(d) its position within the sentence.

The following are the primitive operations in terms of which we can define the task to be performed:

(1) open D,W and input
(2) close D,W and input

(3) set document-number to 0
(4) increase document-number by 1

(5) set sentence-number to 0
(6) increase sentence-number by 1

(7) output word record to W
(8) output word to file F_i

(9) open new file F_i
(10) close new file F_i

(11) write new directory entry

(12) set word count to 0
(13) increase word count by 1
(14) read word from input

The program structure will be similar to the file structure; assigning the primitive operations to the components gives us

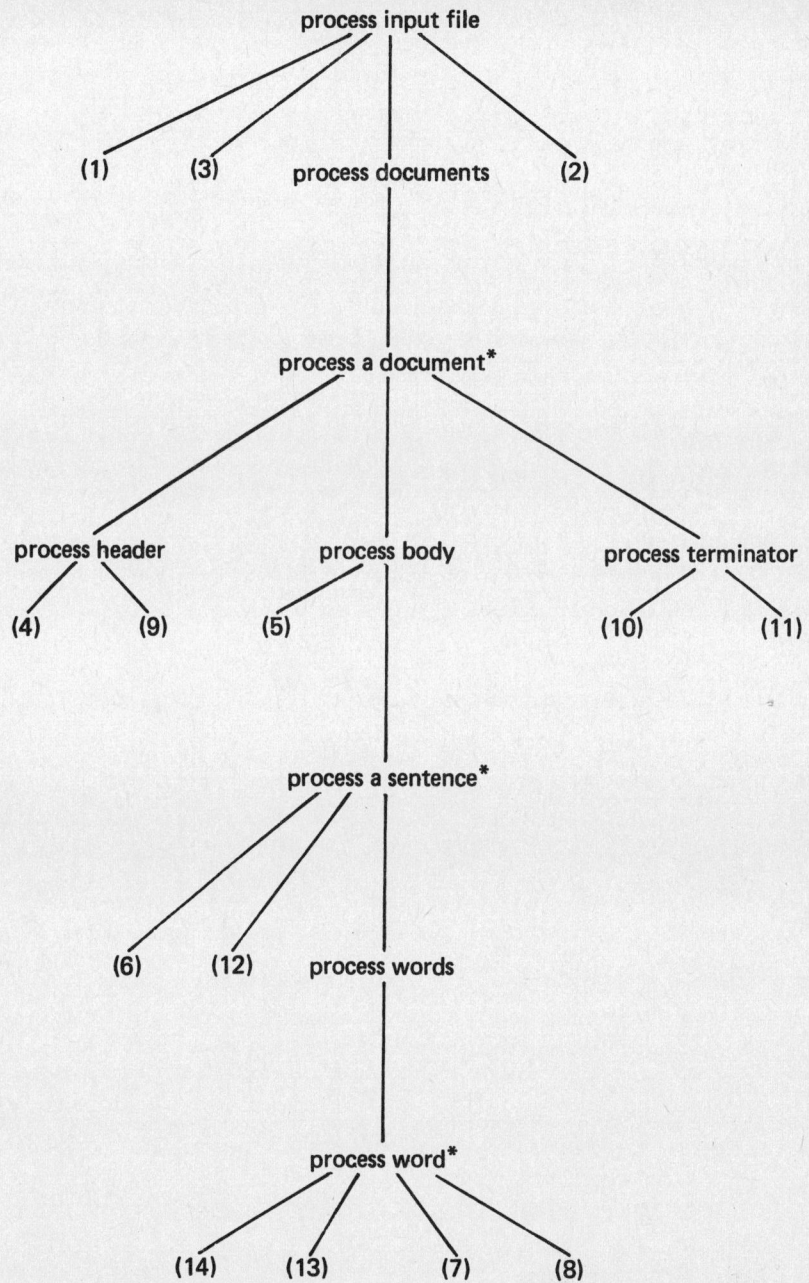

From the program structure we can derive the following

```
primitive 1;
primitive 3;
while not END_OF_FILE (documentfile) perform
the following task:
        primitive 4;
        primitive 5;
        primitive 9;
        while not end_of_document perform
        the following task:
                primitive 6;
                primitive 12;
                while not end_of_sentence perform
                the following task
                        primitive 14;
                        primitive 13;
                        primitive 7;
                        primitive 8;
                end of task.
        end of task.
        primitive 10;
        primitive 11;
end of task.
primitive 2
```

Exercises 9.2

1 Code the program above in a language of your choice.

2 A certain file consists of a set of record groups followed by ZZZZ. Each record group consists of an integer Mi followed by Mi one-line records followed by XXXX. The various Mi may have different values.
   Write a program which determines whether or not a given file is in this format. Output appropriate diagnostic messages if it is not.

3 Assuming that each one-line record in the file described above contains a student name followed by

scores in each of six examinations. Write a program which reads the file and outputs the total score for each student and the average score for each examination.

9.3 External sorting

In commercial organisations, a large amount of computer time is spent in sorting files of data. Some of the reasons for this will emerge in later sections. Typically a file is too large to be held completely in main memory; so sorting algorithms such as those described in chapter five are not by themselves adequate. When the data to be sorted will not fit in main memory, an 'external' sorting algorithm is required. Many external sorting algorithms are of the following form:

 (1) Sorted sequences of records are produced from the unsorted file. A simple way of doing this is to read as many records as possible into main memory, sort them, output the sorted sequence and then repeat with the next group of input records. (There are alternatives which on average will tend to produce longer sequences.)

 (2) The sequences from (1) are distributed as they are produced onto 2 or more files.

 (3) The sequences are merged together, in one or more 'phases', to produce a file containing the records in the desired final order.

Running example

The file W of word records described earlier will, for a reasonable document file, be very large and would normally be sorted using an external sorting algorithm. The second phase of our file production is the sorting of file W.

If, when comparing 2 records from W, either during the

internal sorting or during the merging, fields are compared in lexicographic order of words, then all records with the same word field will be brought together. Within each group of records order will be by position in sentence within sentence number within document number. Designate the sorted file W′.

Exercises 9.3

1 Implement the sorting algorithm above in a language of your choice.

2 Compare the number of read operations required to sort a given file when 2,3,4,..., etc. files are used in steps (2) and (3). Tabulate your results.

3 Devise an algorithm for step (1) above which takes advantage of any partial ordering in the input file when producing the sorted sequences. It should be possible to produce sequences which on average are about twice as long as those produced using internal sorting. Longer initial sequences lead to fewer merging phases.

9.4 Sequential files

In a sequential file records are in sequence in some sense. For example a bank might keep records of its customers in account number order, a theatre company might order a file of its patrons on the combination of name and address. These two examples are typical in that records are ordered by a field or combination of fields which uniquely identifies a record. This is termed the primary key of the record. Sequencing might be accomplished by physical positioning of the records in the file, or by pointer fields or by means of indexes (see Section 9.6).

Sequential files can be updated efficiently by being merged with a file of amendments ordered in the same way.

Example 9.4 Updating files

A file OLDMASTER contains details of current bank account balances. Each record is of the form

  account number, current balance

and records are in ascending order of account number. There is at most one record with a particular account number.

A file AMENDMENTS contains details of recent changes to accounts. Each record is of the form

  account number, change

Again records are in ascending order of account number but in this file there may be many records with the same account number.

In examples such as this, it is good practice to include checks to ensure that non-existent account numbers do not appear. See the first example in the next set of exercises. A less than satisfactory first attempt at an amendments program follows:

```
Open OLDMASTER and AMENDMENTS for reading.
Open NEWMASTER for writing ;
Read from AMENDMENTS a record called TRANSACTION.
Read from OLDMASTER a record called ACCOUNT.
While not END_OF_FILE(OLDMASTER) perform
   the following task:
     if not END_OF_FILE(AMENDMENTS) then
        if acc. no. of ACCOUNT < acc.no. of TRANSACTION
        then
           write ACCOUNT to NEWMASTER
        otherwise
           while acc. no. of ACCOUNT = acc. no. of
              TRANSACTION perform the following task:
                update ACCOUNT with information
                   in TRANSACTION;
                read from AMENDMENTS a new TRANSACTION
              end of task.
           write ACCOUNT to NEWMASTER
        end if
     end if;
```

            read from OLDMASTER a new ACCOUNT;
    end of task.
  Close files OLDMASTER,AMENDMENTS and NEWMASTER.

Exercises 9.4

1 Code the program of example 9.4 in a language of your choice extending it so that a suitable message is written to an error file for each amendment that is for a non-existent account.

2 Extend the program so that new accounts may be added and existing ones deleted.

3 Extend the program so that it reads also a third sequential file LIMITS in which records are of the form

        account number, limit

   The program is to output a suitable message if an amended account record has a balance less than the limit specified for it in LIMITS.

9.5 Direct access files

If a serial file, as far as accessing operations are concerned, is similar to a linked list of records, then a direct access file can be thought of as an array of records. The records are directly accessible in the sense that a record can be accessed without accessing any others in the file. It follows that the file must be held on a direct access device such as a disc.
  Certain accessing techniques are possible which are not feasible on serial files, for example:

    binary search - if we can calculate the position of
                    the Ith record in the file.

        hashing - for fast retrieval of arbitrary
                  records.

Running example

Consider the file W′ of sorted word records. We can use this to construct two direct access files; one of occurrence records and the second a dictionary of the words in W′.

In order that a word can be found quickly in the dictionary, one possibility is to use a hash function to place the records. A hash function is a key-to-address function; its argument is typically the primary key of a record. It transforms this, usually in some simple way, into an address in a table or file where the record should be stored. (We have to resolve collisions if the space is already occupied.) The same function is used to compute an address when we want to retrieve a record. Given good design choices retrievals can be very fast.

The input file W′ can be represented

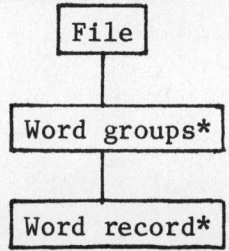

The output files we need are:

(i) In the file of word occurrences each record represents an occurrence of a word in the document file. There will be information of the following form:

    (a) document number
    (b) sentence number
    (c) position within sentence.

(ii) In the dictionary each record holds information about a different word including

    (a) pointer to (e.g. record number of) first record in the occurrence file for

256   GRADED PROBLEMS

       the word
  (b) count of occurrences
  (c) word.

Using Jackson's methodology we identify the following primitives

    (1) open W', dictionary and occurrence files
    (2) close W', dictionary and occurrence files

    (3) read record from W'
    (4) write record to occurrence file in next free space
    (5) hash record into dictionary file

    (6) set count-of-occurrences to 0
    (7) increase count-of-occurrences by 1

Assigning these to the program structure derived from the structure of the input file gives:

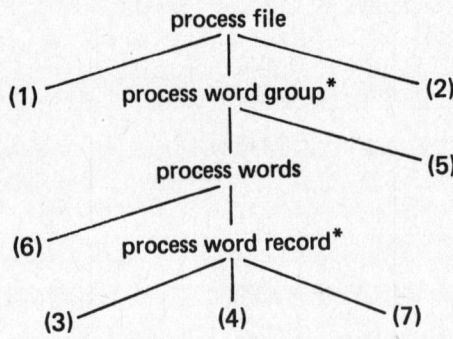

Exercises 9.5.1

1 Code the program above in a language of your choice.

2 Extend the program by recording in the dictionary entry for each word, the number of different documents in which it appears.

The two files we have generated above, together with the directory file produced earlier, are sufficient to support a useful information retrieval system. It should be clear how it is possible to identify (and, using the directory, to output if required) those documents containing an arbitrary word.

Much more usefully, the files are sufficient to enable us to identify those documents containing an arbitrary phrase. For example if the phrase were "nuclear fusion", the list of occurrence records for "nuclear" would be merged with the list for "fusion" in a special way. The merge would identify those sentences in which "fusion" occurs one position after "nuclear" and hence those documents containing the phrase. Clearly an n-word phrase would require a merge of n lists.

Exercises 9.5.2

1 Implement a retrieval system for finding those documents containing an arbitrary word.

2 Extend the system so that it can find those documents containing an arbitrary phrase. For each document containing the phrase your program should output some document identification (from the directory) and a count of the number of times that the phrase occurs. Add a feature to your program that allows a user to list the contents of an arbitrary document file.

9.6 Indexed sequential files

An indexed sequential file is a sequential file supplemented by one or more indexes. The indexes are like the table of contents or index of a book; they provide rapid access to records with a given value of a particular key. The indexes will be files of records in which there is a key value and a pointer. For a large file we may have hierarchical indexes. A common form of index is the B-tree (see, for example, Knuth, 1973) guaranteed efficient even in the worst case.

Typically a file will be indexed on the primary key. Consider the directory produced in 9.5 from file W'. An alternative to hashing the words into the dictionary is to place them in the order in which they occur in the input file (alphabetical) and create an index. The STAIRS system indexes on the first 2 characters giving an index of 702 entries (26x27 - to allow for one letter words). Thus there are pointers into the dictionary for entries "A", "AA", "AB",... .

If there are no words beginning with a particular pair, a suitable pointer is entered. Given a word to find in the dictionary, the first two letters are used to access the index directly. A region of the dictionary is identified and searched, for example using a binary search. If we remove "null" entries from the index (to some space), a direct look-up is no longer possible. Index entries would have to contain the 2-letter pair. This could be reduced to a single letter if we index the index, the higher index having perhaps 26 entries.

Other possibilities for indexes are illustrated in the following example. A stock file for a supermarket contains one record for each different type of item carried. The fields of the record include product number, product description and supplier. The records are physically ordered by product description.

We could have
- (i) an index on product number; this would be ordered by product number and allow us to process items in product number order.
- (ii) an index on the product description - which could take advantage of the ordering of the

stock file by this field and would be comparable with the STAIRS index above.

(iii) an index of suppliers. Each entry in this index might point to the first record with the particular supplier. This in turn would point to the next. In this way all records with the same value of a non-unique key could be retrieved.

Figure 9.1 shows a representation of the stock file and figure 9.2 useful indexes.

(a)	(b)	(c)	(d)
12	Apples	XYZ	2
76	Beans	XYZ	4
83	Beer	ABC	6
7	Carrots	XYZ	?
8	Cheese	MND	?
74	Cloves	ABC	?
.	.	.	.

(a) product number
(b) product name
(c) supplier name
(d) pointer to next record with the same supplier

Figure 9.1

Product number index

   (a)   (b)

   7   4
   8   5
   .   .

Key: (a) product number
       (b) pointer to stock file

Product name index

(c)

1
2
4
.

Key: (c) pointer to first record with name
         beginning with a particular letter

Supplier index

  (d)   (e)

ABC   3
MNO   5
XYZ   1
 .   .

Key: (d) supplier name
(e) pointer to first record with the
    particular supplier

Figure 9.2

Exercises 9.6

1 Implement the dictionary of the information retrieval system as an ordered direct file with a 2-level index.

2 The index effectively holds the first 2 characters of a word so there is no need to store these in the dictionary. Implement this space saving feature and verify that one-, two- and three-letter words can all be found correctly in the dictionary.

3 Modify the retrieval program so that a user may specify a word stem rather than a word in a query. For example the query "program*" should identify documents containing "program" or "programme" or "programming" and so on. Word stems should be allowed anywhere in a phrase as well.

9.7 Miscellaneous exercises

1 A publishing company holds in a file details of all books they publish. However in future they wish to maintain two distinct files (i) paperbacks (ii) hardbacks.

Write a program which reads a file containing details of both paperback and hardback books and creates two files as specified above. Assume that the first character in each input record indicates if the book is paperback (p) or hardback(h) or both (b).

2 A file EVENTS consists of records of events that have occurred during a calendar year. Each record describes one event and starts with a date field giving the number of the day in the year during which the event occurred. The file is ordered in ascending order by this day number.

A file SELECT consists of single-field records, the field being a day number. The file too is ordered in ascending sequence by this field.

Write a program which reads these 2 files and produces a report which shows, for each date in SELECT, the number of events which occurred on that date. For example

Day	Events
13	12
45	6
.	.
.	.
352	4

3 A file EXAMMARKS contains a number of 80-character records each of which should have the following format:

Column(s)	Content
1-20	Last name followed by initial
21	Blank
22-57	Nine 3-character fields each followed by a blank column. A 3-character field may be blank or may contain a right-justified unsigned integer. If present, the integer in the first field should be less than 41, any integers in subsequent fields should be less than 21.
58-80	blank

Write a program which reads EXAMMARKS and examines each record to see whether or not columns 21 to 57 are valid. Valid records should be output to file VALIDATED. Invalid records should be output to file INVALID and each followed by one or more appropriate fault messages.

4 A college maintains an alphabetically ordered file of its staff. At the beginning of each academic year an updated file is produced by a program which reads the old file and an amendments file containing the names of staff together with a code N indicating new staff

or D indicating departing staff. Write a suitable program and test it. State clearly the limitations and assumptions of your program.

5 The following is a method for encrypting a plain text file (P):
   (i) Generate a file (R) of random characters.
   (ii) Merge files R and P by reading a character at a time from each (file R may have to be re-read a number of times) and outputting a composite character to a file (C). The composite character should be formed in such a way that given either of its two components, the other is uniquely recoverable. One possibility is to perform an exclusive-or operation on the 2 character codes. File C is then an encryption of file P with respect to file R.

   File C may be decrypted by merging it with file R as described above except that this time R is used to recover the plain text from the composite character.
   (a) Write a program which generates file R. The longer this file, the more secure, in some sense, the encryption will be. Try various file sizes starting perhaps with R containing 100 characters.
   (b) Write a program which, depending on a control character read ("E" or "D"), will perform either encryption or decryption. Test your program to ensure that a suitable garbled encrypted file is produced and that the plain text can be recovered.

6 Set up a file containing vehicle records which hold registration number and owner information (name and address). Write a program which, given a vehicle's registration number, will rapidly retrieve and print the owner information.

7 Write a program to produce monthly statements for the customers of a bank. Assume that a file ordered by account number exists in which is held the balances in the accounts at the end of the previous statement period. A second file contains details of payments

to and withdrawals from accounts during the current statement period.

The program should output a statement for each customer. The statement should be headed by the account number and list the balance brought forward, the transactions and the balance carried forward. For each day on which there was a transaction the statement should list the amount in the account at the end of the day.

Ensure that your program also produces an updated balances file and records any invalid data in an error file.

8 Write a program to process a simple company payroll. An employee file ordered by employee number contains, for each employee: name, rate of pay per hour and normal work week (in hours). The program is to read this file and one similarly ordered containing the number of hours worked by each employee in the current week; assume that employees are paid overtime at twice the normal rates. Arrange that the program, using simple tables, computes the income tax witholdable and outputs a statement for each employee showing gross pay, net pay and tax withheld.

9 Extend the payroll program so that a file of deductions/bonuses is also read. Records in this file are of the form

   employee number, code, key, R

Key : F for fixed amount additions/deductions (R holds the amount)
      V for variable additions/deductions (R holds the amount as a percentage of gross pay).

Your program, apart from using the records to compute net pay should ensure that a suitable annotated statement is produced for each employee. For this purpose "code" is simply some identifying string.

10 Extend the payroll program so that it maintains a file of running totals for the current tax year. For each employee the file should contain the gross and

net pay to date as well as the totals paid or deducted under each code.

11 Statements in a certain programming language are written one to a line. Each line starts with an integer statement number in the range 0-999999. Statements in a program are in ascending statement number order.

Write a program which inputs an arbitrary program in this language and outputs an equivalent program in which the statements are numbered M, M+N, M+2N,...where M and N are supplied as data.

The language includes a GOTO statement which may appear as a statement e.g. GOTO 3245 or as part of an IF statement e.g. IF A<B THEN GOTO 3082. Clearly statements of this form may have to be modified.

12 Set up files of driver and vehicle records. Write a program which inputs a file of driver names and outputs for each, details of all vehicles owned.

13 A certain bank pays interest on current (chequing) accounts. During a monthly period, at the end of each working day, an amount equal to R/30000 of the balance in the account is accumulated in a total. This total is added to the account at the end of the month.

For this service the bank imposes a charge of S dollars a month and in addition a charge of D cents for each deposit into the account and W cents for each withdrawal from the account. If a customer keeps a minimum of M dollars in the account during a month then all charges for that month are waived otherwise they are imposed on the last day of the month.

Write a program which reads suitable files and produces appropriately annotated statements for the customers.

14 A crossword puzzle compiler would find it useful to have a file of words and puzzle clues. Design a file structure suitable for holding word-clue pairs so that stored clues for an arbitrary word may be retrieved rapidly. Write a pair of programs, one to

add word-clue pairs to the file, the other to list the clues held for each word appearing in a given file.

15 Assume that each time a book is sold in any shop the ISBN is written to a central serial file. At the end of each week the file is processed to produce a list of the ISBNs of all the different books sold during the week. This list is ordered by number of copies sold. Write and test a program which produces this bestseller list.

16 A certain bookseller sells at a discount those books currently in the New York Times bestseller list. He has a file in ascending order of ISBN of each title in stock together with the publishers price. Each week a file is sent from the NYT listing, in rank order, the ISBNs of the bestselling books. The length of this file may vary from week to week.

Assume that special discounts apply to titles in the top ten. The bestselling book of the week is discounted by 35% and the next nine by 25%. The remaining books on the list are reduced by 10%.

Write a program which produces for each discounted book, the title and discounted price.

17 Each record in a certain personnel file consists of 4 positive integers representing respectively

    (i) employee ID-NUMBER
   (ii) employee AGE
  (iii) employee WAGE (in pence per hour)
  (iv) employee JOBTYPE

Write a program which answers a series of queries about the file. The format of a proper query is given by

    { query } RECORDS WHERE field [NOT] ro intval

where query = {COUNT,LIST}
     field = { ID, AGE, WAGE, JOBTYPE }
        ro = { LT, EQ, GT }
   intval = unsigned integer value

{ } denotes "one of" and [ ] means optional. The file of queries is terminated by the word QUIT on a line by itself. For each proper query read, the program is to produce output as follows

    (a) if the query is COUNT, the number of records in the file which satisfy the query is to be output

    (b) if the query is LIST, all records (if any) satisfying the condition given in the query are to be output.

18 A useful program would be one which detected possible typographical errors in files of text. Rather than rely on a dictionary, the program could estimate the probability of a word being in error by using the appropriate probabilities of the trigraphs (3-letter groups) in the word.

  Using error-free text samples, establish a file containing the rate of occurrence in text of each of the approximately 20,000 trigraphs (remember the space character).

  Write a program that reads a text file, assigns an 'error probability' score to each different word and outputs the words ranked by this score. Experiment with different ways of arriving at the score. Speed up the program by using a small dictionary to filter out very common words.

19 At a certain university, teachers record grades for their students on machine readable preprinted forms. Each form is headed by a class identification and contains a list of the identification numbers of the students in the class. An appropriate single letter grade is entered next to each number.

  The forms are processed by the university administration which then sends to each student a grade report. The report is headed by the students identification number and contains a list of classes taken and the grade awarded for each.

  The output from the form-scanning machine is a file of the form:

    <class description 1>

```
            <student id> <grade>
            <student id> <grade>
                    .
                    .
            <class description 2>
                    .
                    .
```

Write a program which reads a file of this form and outputs the corresponding grade reports.

20 A collegiate ice hockey organisation runs a number of conferences (leagues). Write one or more programs which maintains a file of the playing records of the teams. It should be possible to input a file of results of games and have the records updated appropriately. It should also be possible to output the current rankings of the teams in each league. Teams are ranked by the percentage of possible points (2 for a win, 1 for a tie) they have obtained. Teams with equal percentages are ranked by number of wins and, if still equal, alphabetically by team name. Write, test and document update and listing programs.

21 Extend your hockey league system above to take into account the fact that matches frequently involve teams from different conferences. A distinction can therefore be made between these non-conference matches and the others. Ranking of teams is now by their performance in conference games and only if these are equal is the overall record used. Modify the file structure and programs appropriately.

22 A certain Revenue Service wishes to check the honesty of its taxpayers. It has a file on which it records details from employee income statements. Each record on this file is of the form

```
    { employee social security number,
      employer identification number,
      amount of pay received}
```

A second file contains information derived from employer returns, on this file each record is of the form

>   { employer identification number,
>   employee social security number,
>   amount of pay given }.

Write a program which, by processing the files in some way, outputs
>   (i) a list of employees who do not appear to have declared all their income
>   (ii) a list of employers who do not appear to have listed all their payments.

Note that during the tax year an employee may have several employers and that an employer will normally have more than one employee.

23 A certain instructor awards grades to students based on their class-relative performance. The class average is subtracted from each score and the results divided by the standard deviation of the scores. The standard deviation is the square root of the variance (see exercise 5 of Exercises 3.1). The grade awarded then depends on R the resulting number.

> $2.0 \leq R$ implies grade A
> $1.0 \leq R < 2.0$ implies grade B
> $-1.0 \leq R < 1.0$ produces grade C
> $-2.0 \leq R < -1.0$ results in grade D
> $R < -2.0$ produces grade F.

A file SCORES contains (id-number, score) pairs for a class, unordered in any way. Write a program which reads SCORES and outputs a grade report for the class. The report should consist of 5 columns headed A,B,C,D and F. In each column should be the id-numbers of the students awarded the particular grade arranged in decreasing score order.

24 Design files in which a radio station could keep details of its library of tape recordings. The station needs to be able to:
>   (a) list recordings by reel number and, within reel by position
>   (b) list recordings in alphabetic order of

topic/title
(c) add details of new recordings to the files
(d) remove details of recordings that have been erased
(e) produce a list of blank tape segments.

25 The programs outlined in the running example in this chapter essentially create indexes to a set of documents. Write a program which reads a file containing additional documents, copies them to individual files and updates the directory and index files.

26 Write a program which processes a file of records containing the characteristics and preferences of a group of men and women. The program should output, for each person in the file, the names of the N program most "compatible" people of the opposite sex (N, a positive integer is input as data). Experiment with different ways of computing compatibility.

27 To assist with its assessment of students, a computer science department maintains a file of records containing details of student performance in homework, examinations, projects and so on.
(a) Write a program which takes information prepared in some convenient form (for example tabular) and adds appropriate records to the file.
(b) Write a program which inputs requests for reports (specified in some suitable notation) and outputs the reports, formatted in a readable manner, to a file.

28 (a) Write a program which reads from two files each containing "runs" of integers in ascending order. Your program should output larger runs each of which is formed by merging together one run from each input file. Arrange that your program distributes the output runs alternately on two output files, i.e. the first file will contain runs 1,3,5... and the second runs 2,4,6....
For example if the input files were

```
A:  2 4 9 2 3 7 10 4 11 12 15 1 7 8 9 19 21
B:  1 3 6 8 9 10 7 9 2 4 7 9 13 18 13 14 15
    4 5 7 8
```
then the output files would be

```
C:  1 2 3 4 6 8 9 9 10 2 4 4 7 9 11 12 13 15
    18 4 5 7 8
D:  2 3 7 7 9 10 1 7 8 9 13 14 15 19 21
```

(b) Modify your program so that after having produced the output files, it uses them as the input files in a second pass through the data. Your program should continue in this way using the output of one pass as the input for the next until only 1 run remains.

(c) Write a program which reads N records from a file sorts them out into ascending order and outputs the sorted group to a second file.

(d) Modify your answer to (c) so that having processed one group of N records, the program reads, sorts and outputs further groups until the input file is exhausted. Arrange that the output runs are distributed alternately on 2 output files.

(e) Combine your answers to (b) and (d) so that you have a program which will take an arbitrarily large file of unsorted integers and, holding no more than N integers in main memory at any time, will produce a file containing the integers in ascending order.

29 Write a program which takes a file (T) containing a text, a file (D) containing a dictionary of words and produces a file (W) of the words which are in T but not in D. The program should deal sensibly with hyphenated words and with upper and lower case characters.

30 A relational database "relation" may be represented by
    (i) a list of field names

(ii) a file of records

Certain operations may be performed on relations. PROJECTION and JOIN are two of these and are defined below. Write a program which allows a user to

(a) input a relation
(b) output a relation
(c) apply the PROJECTION and JOIN operators to existing relations creating new ones.

PROJECTION
  relation1 = PROJECTION (relation2, name1,...nameN)

The result of the PROJECTION operator is relation1 having the selected attributes of relation2. There are no duplicate records in relation1.

JOIN
  relation1 = JOIN (relation2, nameA, relation3,
                    nameB, op)

The result of the JOIN operation is relation1. An instance of recordI in relation2 is concatenated with each recordK in relation3 wherever

  (nameA of recordI) op (nameB of recordK)

is true. Typical instances of op are =,<,>,etc. There are no duplicate records in relation1.

31 A macroprocessor is a program which reads a file containing text and macro definitions and outputs an expanded version of the text. In its simplest form a macro definition consists of a macro name and a replacement text. The macroprocessor replaces all occurrences of the name with the corresponding text.
  Implement a simple macroprocessor as described above. Extend it to allow macros to take parameters and also to support nested macro calls. Demonstrate that your program works by, for example, generating tailored form letters of some kind.

32 Create a file containing records of the performances

of race horses. An updating program should read from a file containing the details of a race and amend the records of those horses taking part. A query program should read a file containing a list of names of horses and output the information held about each one. It should be possible to retrieve details of an arbitrary race. Carefully test and document your system.

33 Write a program which takes

    (i) a file containing the text of a book
    (ii) a file containing a list of words and phrases
   (iii) an integer N

and produces an index for the book. The index entries are the words and phrases in (ii) ordered alphabetically. Each entry is followed by the number(s) of the page(s) on which it appears. Assume that the first N lines of file (i) appear on page 1, the next N lines on page 2 and so on.

34 A testing centre scores multiple choice tests and produces useful statistics for the examiners. A mechanical form scanner generates a file containing

N	(number of questions)
C1 ..CN	(correct answers, each 'a', 'b', 'c', 'd', 'e')
id1 A11..A1N	(id and answers of first student)
id2 A21..A2N	(id and answers of second student)
....	(id and........................)

A space character for a student answer indicates that the question was not attempted.

Write a program which processes this file and outputs the required report which contains:

    (i) each student id-number together with the number of questions the student answered correctly. This list is ordered by id-number.
   (ii) a cumulative distribution showing, for each different total score obtained, the

percentage of students getting that score or better.
(iii) for each question
 (a) percentage of students giving the correct answer
 (b) table showing, for each possible answer (including no answer), for each quartile of the students, the percentage of students in the quartile giving the correct answer. That is what percentage of the top quarter of the class, what percentage of the next quarter and so on.
 (c) a measure of how well the question discriminated between good and weaker students - based on (b).

35 Write a program which inputs a filled crossword diagram (the output perhaps from the program of exercise 42 and selects a clue for each word from a file of word-clue pairs (see for example exercise 14 of this set). In order that puzzles of varying difficulty may be created arrange that each word-clue record contains an estimated solving time. Apart from the diagram, input a range of times and ensure that the total times of the selected clues falls within this range.

36 Modify the file of clues so that an additional field of each record contains the type of clue (definitional, anagram, quotation and so on). Modify the program so that it is possible to specify, in the input, sets of clues (for example anagrams and quotations only) from which the selection is to be made.

37 A multi-access computer system writes to a log file records of events. The events recorded are:
 (a) log on
 (b) log off
 (c) a program K bytes in size is loaded
 (d) program ceases execution and is deleted from main memory having used C milliseconds of processor time.
Each record is tagged with the appropriate user

account number and the time (in minutes after midnight) at which it occurred.

The computer manager needs a report on each day's activities listing, for each of the following resources,

    (i) connect time (measured in minutes)
    (ii) processor time (measured in seconds)
    (iii) memory space measured in millisecond * kilobytes.

an ordered list of the 10 heaviest consumers of the resource each with the percentage of total consumption that they were responsible for.

Write a program which reads the log file for a 24 hour period and produces a suitably annotated report.

38 Write a program which reads 2 files and reports on the differences between them. Aim to produce the smallest set of differences. One possible form of output is a series of editing commands which, when applied to the first file, produces the second file.

39 Write a program which inputs a file of text and outputs to a file a neatly formatted version. For generality it should be possible for a user to include directives to the formatting program in the input file. Directives will determine page size and numbering, line spacing, headings and so on. Ensure that your program is adequately documented.

40 A published scientific paper may be represented by five or more 80-character records in the following way. The first character of a record (key-character) indicates its type and the remaining characters contain appropriate information. Valid key-characters are:

    Y = year of publication
    T = title
    A = author
    J = journal

Each paper has only "Y" record and one "J" record, there may be one or more of each of the other types.
Write
(a) a program which takes a serial file (REFERENCES) containing a large number of document representations and creates appropriate files to support a query program. In REFERENCES the "Y" record of a representation comes first with the remainder following immediately in any order.
(b) a program which takes a serial file of queries about the papers and answers them as efficiently as possible. A valid query is a boolean expression in which the operators are AND, NOT, OR (usual precedence). The operands are of the form
        ⟨key-character⟩ = ⟨value⟩
        e.g. Y=1956
            T=A FAST SORTING METHOD
Parentheses may be used. Thus the query
  Y=1974 AND (A=JONES OR A=BROWN) AND NOT J=CACM
should result in a listing of the details (as they appear in REFERENCES) of all papers published in 1974 by either JONES or BROWN except for those published in CACM.

41 Set up a file of records of the form

    { Town A,
      Town B,
      Length (in minutes) of the fastest plane
        service from A to B}

(a) Write a program which inputs a file of pairs of town names and outputs, for each pair, information about the sequence of flights between the first and second town which minimises time in the air. The names of towns, if any, where it is necessary to change planes and the total time spent in the air should be output.
(b) Modify the file so that the third component of each record, rather than being the length of the fastest journey, is a list of the arrival and departure times of all the planes from the first to the second town. For example a record might

be

```
{ Los Angeles, Las Vegas,
  ((9.00,9.46), (11.05,12.10), (13.00,13.30)
  (15.05,17.15), (17.00,17.40))
}
```

(c) Modify your program so that for each pair input it now prints the information (i) and (ii) above for the journey with the shortest elapsed time.

(d) Modify your program so that it is possible to delete plane services from the file (cancellations) and add them (e.g. holiday specials).

42 Write a program which inputs a representation of a crossword grid and, by making use of an on-line dictionary, outputs the grid filled with words in the normal fashion. If the dictionary is inadequate to enable the grid to be filled then a message to this effect should be output.

By including a random factor, arrange that your program can output different filled grids of the same form.

43 A particular chess game may be represented by

   (i) a list of move descriptions
   (ii) match details - names of players, winner (white or black), date and location etc.

Set up a data base of chess games and write one or more programs which permit the following operations to be performed:

(a) addition of a new game to the data base. Your program should check the legality of the list of moves. Note that two games may differ only in the match details.

(b) interrogation of the data base. It should be possible for a user to specify

   (1) a sequence of opening moves in a game
   (2) a positive integer N

and receive, from each game which started with the specified sequence, the next N moves together with the match details. (If two or more games have the same continuation then the match details of those games should be output after a single instance of the continuation).

A more useful alternative to (1) would be to allow a user to specify a board position (e.g. in Forsyth notation).

10 | Interactive programming

Most people involved with computers are familiar with the idea of an interactive program. They may not be aware of this but playing games is a very common method of interaction. In such a situation a person sitting at a computer terminal responds to prompts from a program running within the computer. The input to that program takes the form of information typed by the player. Output takes the form of a response by the computer. In this kind of way progress is made.

In this chapter we shall be concerned mainly with interactive programming. However we shall relegate the topic of game playing until the last section basically because of the greater importance of the other application of computers to computer-assisted learning and simulation.

There is a large class of interactive problems which we just mention in passing; serious consideration of these is beyond the scope of this book. Computers, often in the form of microprocessors, can be used to control other devices. These devices may be complex machinery such as aircraft or they might be pacemakers used to stimulate the heart. We shall omit consideration of these and other similar applications.

10.1 Simple interaction

In an interactive programming environment the progress of the program is determined by directions or just the input given by a user. To make the prospect of using such a program attractive it is vital that the interface between the program and the computer be inviting.

The nature of man-machine interface design is a complex but important business. Briefly, it is important that computer responses are polite and restrained, helpful and complete yet not verbose and irritating, and so on. It is often important that the dialogue that is designed should be set out in a manner which is attractive and clearly differentiates between the text produced by the computer and that produced by the user. Further, it should be abundantly clear when a user is required to type text; where possible that text should be kept to a minimum.

One way of achieving clarity is to employ a menu type of system. If a list of possible answers or options can be displayed, a user can be asked to select one of these. In this way it is not necessary for the programmer to deal with a large variety of possible inputs from a user.

In the interactive situation reliability takes on an added importance. Interactive programs should not be seen to collapse in the event of a user making a typing error; the specification of the program should take this into account.

Exercises 10.1

1 Prepare an interactive program which, given the initial state of a bank account together with a list of deposits or withdrawals, indicates the new state of the account. Ensure that the program prints some initial explanatory text to indicate how the user should proceed.

2 The timetable of computer science classes in a university is stored in a particular file. Design an interactive program which will produce the times of any class on request.

3 Consider the assumption of the previous question. Assume also the existence of a file containing a list of classes offered by other departments, e.g. mathematics, electronics, together with their times. Design an interactive program which will produce a list of the subsidiary or supplementary classes that can be taken by a student who takes specified computer science courses.

10.2 Computer-assisted learning

Envisage a situation where a student is sitting at a terminal connected to a computer. A lesson is in progress. The computer asks the student a question. He responds. The computer indicates that the answer is wrong and asks the student to type again. On this occasion the answer is correct and another question appears for the student to answer. And so on.

In a situation such as this there is a dialogue between the computer and the student. Interaction is occurring. Within the computer, there is a program the progress of which is determined by the answers it receives from the student. Its output takes the form of questions to the student; its data takes the form of the student's replies.

The situation described above is one of the more common aspects of a wider topic known as computer-assisted learning, CAL for short. Other aspects include the simulation of various situations so permitting a student to obtain some feeling for the influences at work. Others include designing packages for student use. These and other aspects of the subject are included elsewhere in this book. For the moment we shall concentrate on the particular topic discussed above. There are two different ways in which the situation described above can be programmed.

In the first case the method is quite independent of the particular topic being taught. In a file there are questions and answers. The questions are asked and the student is expected to type the correct answer, or one of several possibly correct answers that might be held. The questions and answers may be about computing, mathematics, a foreign language, etc. In all cases the one control program is all that is required. Let us illustrate the typical contents of this file:

```
qu    Simple arithmetic
qu    Lesson one
qu    What is the value of 4 + 7?
ca    11
ty    Very good
wa    47
```

ty No. You must add, not place side by side!
....

The two letter codes have special significance: qu means that the contents of the line should just be printed; ca indicates the correct answer; wa indicates an expected wrong answer - unexpected wrong answers are processed in a standard way; ty holds the text printed when an anticipated response appears.

The ideas given above can be extended to allow several attempts, to skip some questions if the student seems to be good, and so on. However, a criticism of this kind of approach is that it is terribly static and inflexible. It cannot readily be adjusted so that it moulds itself to the real needs of the individual student.

A more flexible system makes use of random number generators. Assume the existence of some function

      RANDOM_INTEGER (M,N)

which produces a random integer which lies between M and N inclusive. If such a function is not provided within a given programming language it is usually a simple matter to introduce it; see the examples in chapter seven on the design of random number generators.

Example 10.2.1   Simple arithmetic

A simple program which provides exercises in simple arithmetic is illustrated by the following:

```
Print preliminary text.
Let COUNT be RANDOM_INTEGER (4,7).
Perform COUNT times the following task:
  let N be RANDOM_INTEGER (1,9);
  print - "What is the value of 1+", X;
  read ANSWER
    if ANSWER = 1+X then
      print "correct"
    otherwise
      print "wrong"
    end if;
  end of task.
```

This simple example can be made more sophisticated in several respects

(a) in the event of an error several attempts can be given; attempts can also be made to analyse the error and deduce what aspect of the material is not understood

(b) the number of questions can be altered and even based on some measure of the ability of a student which can be remembered from lesson to lesson in a file

(c) the number of items to be added (or subtracted) can be made variable; individual students will also appear to get different lessons.

The ideas outlined here have particular application in the areas of arithmetic or mathematics, basically wherever numbers are involved. However, random numbers can be used to access different positions in a table holding, for instance, French words and their English counterparts. The preparation of high quality CAL material is far from easy. In this book we only scratch the surface of a very difficult area.

Exercises 10.2

1 Design and test a program which implements the program outlined in example 10.2.1.

2 Make the program of example 10.2.1 more sophisticated by

(a) ensuring that the same question is not repeated

(b) arranging that simple examples occur early and more difficult examples occur later

(c) writing the question in such a way that the sum of 1+4 or 4+1 may be requested randomly.

3 Design a program that produces exercises on a variety of questions on simple arithmetic all involving the addition of two quantities but of increasing difficulty.

4 Design a program that tests vocabulary of a foreign language.

10.3 Simulation

Simulation and modelling can be viewed as part of the wider topic of computer-assisted learning. In using a computer for simulation there will usually be a program that simulates some particular situation, e.g. the spread of some infection, the effects of dangerous physical particles such as X-rays. By interaction a student can then gain experience of situations that would be difficult, dangerous or prohibitively expensive to reproduce in reality.

In more sophisticated environments the computer can help in teaching pilots how to land aircraft perhaps in poor visibility or in a variety of weather conditions; more generally it is possible to teach pilots to cope with situations that could not be reproduced with safety. Simulation can also be used to model flights of spacecraft, the performance of large computers, the performance of a country's economy, etc. The topic is very important and complex and is one on which we shall manage to touch only briefly in this book.

A fine distinction can be made between simulation and modelling. Simulation permits a user to control the input to the program and to observe the output that results. Modelling is something more. Briefly a user can alter the program, i.e. the model, as well as witness the results of his actions in the form of witnessing a simulation of a particular model.

The topic of simulation does not demand an interactive environment. However there are substantial advantages in having the ability to interact since then a participant can more easily investigate the properties of a particular model.

Let us look at some examples.

Example 10.3.1 Population control

Assume the existence of an island which supports only foxes and pheasants and assume that the foxes prey on the pheasants. We wish to investigate the ways in which the two populations might interact by simulating the events that can occur.

Let there be P pheasants initially. If these are allowed to breed unhindered then after one time period (e.g. 1 month or 1 year) the number of pheasants in existence will be

$$P + aP - bP$$

the aP term indicating new births and the bP term indicating deaths. It is a straightforward matter now to predict the number of pheasants in existence after several time periods.

Let us now introduce foxes into the scene and assume that the number of pheasants killed is related both to the number of foxes and the rate with which pheasants can be found. After one time period the new pheasant population might be

$$P + aP - bP^2 - cPF$$

where F is now the number of foxes in existence initially. Further we could assume that the more pheasants in existence the more food there is for foxes and so the greater the number of baby foxes born. Hence after one time period the new number of foxes will be

$$F + dFP - eF$$

where the eF term takes care of the situation in which P=0.

With these two equations we can predict the manner in which the populations will change with time. We can calculate the sizes of these populations after one time period and, using the new information, the population sizes after two, three, etc. time units. It is even possible to predict the effect of killing foxes or pheasants, introducing new animals, and so on.

Example 10.3.2 Simulation of computers

Simulate the actions of some computer C, say, by means of a program written in some high-level language.

  Given a machine-code program for C each instruction can be taken, inspected and decoded in turn. When the decoding has occurred, appropriate alterations can be made to the simulated store and registers of C; the latter can be represented by variables and arrays of an appropriate kind. A simulator should allow a programmer the option of executing machine code instructions one at a time or several at a time. Further it ought to be possible to see the effects of instructions on the various locations in store.

Exercises 10.3

1 Simulate the population control problem discussed in example 10.3.1. By writing programs to draw suitable graphs show how the population of the foxes and pheasants change.

2 A rumour spreads through a group of N friends in the following way. When one person hears the rumour he chooses one of the remaining N-1 people at random and and phones that person to pass on the rumour; he then takes no further interest in spreading the rumour. On hearing the rumour the second person again chooses one of the remaining N-1 at random and passes it only to that person. In this way the rumour spreads.
  Simulate the spread of the rumour by means of a suitable program.
  Write a program which estimates the likelihood of

everyone hearing the rumour.

3 Patients arrive in a doctor's waiting room randomly for one-hour surgery which lasts from 5pm until 6pm. Assume that 12 patients arrive in the hour and that the doctor takes 5 minutes to deal with each patient.
   Simulate the situation by showing when each patient arrives, when he sees the doctor and when he leaves.
   Calculate the average waiting time per patient and the total waiting time, if any, of the doctor. How might the doctor's waiting time alter if he started 5 minutes late?
   Note: use a random number generator to generate 12 integers in the range 0-60, these representing the time when each patient arrives.

4 How might the simulation of the previous example alter if the doctor took a random time (between 1 and 9 minutes inclusive) to deal with each patient?

10.4 Game playing

Most aspects of the way in which computers play games require little description. Most computer personnel will have seen ample evidence of the range of possibilities. One side of the programming of games does merit special attention.

Assume a situation in which a programmer (in the form of his program) plays some player. If the programmer wishes his program to appear clever then he will rarely allow the program to indulge in random moves. Before deciding on some move it will be necessary to perform an analysis of the current situation in the game.

When only a small number of possibilities exist the programmer can do this analysis in advance. The flows of control within the program can then be viewed as a tree structure or graph - the precise route is determined by the responses of the player.

In more complex situations the program can, in effect, make all the possible moves and examine the consequences of each one. Indeed it can look ahead by several moves. As a result of this, some best move can be selected;

what is meant by 'best' will vary from situation to situation.

Exercises 10.4

1 Design a program that will play snakes-and-ladders with a willing player.

2 Design a program to play tic-tac-toe (noughts and crosses) and never lose.

3 Design a program to play dominoes. Try to make your program 'intelligent'.

10.5 Miscellaneous exercises

1 A grassy island supports a population of rabbits and foxes. In one month the change in the rabbit population R and the fox population F can be represented as

$$0.5R - 0.014RF$$
and
$$-0.5F + 0.014RF$$

respectively. Simulate the changes with time in the rabbit and fox population.

2 Write a program which generates a random number in range 1-100. The user then has to guess what it is. The program should respond HIGH or LOW or CORRECT.

3 A user thinks of a number in the range 1-100. Write a program which tries to guess what it is. The user should respond to guesses by typing HIGH, LOW or

CORRECT. Ensure that your program deals sensibly with erroneous responses.

4 Read and store a list of names of towns and the distances between them (as a triangle of distances). Design a program that reads pairs of names of towns and outputs the distance between them.

5 Devise an interactive program which, when given a polynominal with integer coefficients, will find any integer roots.

6 Prepare a simple desk calculator facility which permits a user to perform calculations involving integers. State clearly the limitations of your system.

7 Prepare a desk calculator facility which allows a user to perform real arithmetic involving the addition, subtraction, multiplication and division of reals.

8 A hare starts from the point $(0,0)$ and runs due north at some speed P. A fox initially at the point (X,Y) where $X>0$ and $Y>0$ gives chase at some speed Q, running directly towards the present position of the hare. What is the 'curve of pursuit' of the fox?

9 Write, test and carefully document a very simple text formatter which operates as follows.
   In an initial dialogue a user is able to specify whether input is from a file or the terminal. Similarly output can be directed to a file or the terminal. In the case of keyboard input, a user is prompted for page length and width parameters. If input is from the keyboard a user should be able to type text without worrying about line breaks.
   The program collects words into lines (as many words in a line as possible subject to width limit). When a line is complete it is output 'right justified', i.e. spaces are inserted to ensure that the final character appears at the right margin.
   The only event that can interrupt this state of affairs is the presence in the source text of a line

which starts with a space. Then

(a) if the line is completely blank any text that has not yet been printed will be forced out

(b) if there are N spaces at the start of the line any unprinted text is again forced out and a new line indented by N spaces is produced.

10 A certain road has two lanes, one running in each direction. When repairs are required one lane at a time is closed and temporary traffic lights are installed to control the flow of traffic; of course, at peak hours the flow of traffic in the two directions may vary. Simulate this situation and thereby determine how the lights should be regulated to provide the best possible traffic flow?

11 Two drunken helicopter pilots flying their machines are 20 metres apart on a line due North-South. At each second they each independently decide either to remain stationary or to move ten metres in one of 6 possible directions (up, down, N, S, E, W). They choose each of the 7 possible actions with equal probability and they start off high enough for the risk of hitting the ground to be ignored.

Write a procedure which simulates their behaviour for one minute or until they crash (i.e. try to fly to the same point or to swap positions). Run your procedure repeatedly to try and estimate the probability of a crash within one minute.

12 Design a suite of facilities which allows a programmer to make certain enquiries about files. For example

what is the number of lines in the file?

what is the number of characters in the file?

what is the frequency of occurrence of individual characters?

Similar questions can be asked about words, sentences

and paragraphs occurring in files of text.

13 Design a simple CAL system for testing the vocabulary of a student wishing to learn, say, French.

14 Design a program which will list all or selected parts of a given file. Provide documentation which explains clearly how your program works.

15 Design a simple CAL system for testing a student's knowledge of, say, French regular verbs.
Indicate how you might deal with irregular verbs.

16 A roulette wheel 'generates' a random sequence of numbers in the range 1-35. Bets may be placed in two ways:

   (i) a straight bet with odds 30:1. To win one has to predict precisely the next number generated.

   (ii) a black/white bet with odds of 'evens'. To win one has to predict whether or not the next number is odd/even.

   Write a program to simulate such a game of roulette. You start with $500 and the input to the program is a series of triples - one per spin of the wheel - the numbers represent:

   (a) the type of bet ((i) or (ii))
   (b) in case 1 the number to bet on, in case 2 a number ((i) or (ii)) indicating odd/even
   (c) the amount staked.

   After each spin print out details of the bet, the result of the spin and your resulting financial position. Your program should halt if your stake reaches zero or a zero bet is encountered.

17 Design an interactive program which helps a user in the layout and preparation of a letter.

18 Prepare a desk calculator facility which allows real

arithmetic together with the inclusion of, at least, the mathematical functions SIN, COS, TAN, SQRT and LOG.

19 Simulate traffic control at a T-junction with traffic lights and suggest how the timing of the traffic lights should alter with the traffic flow in different directions. State clearly any assumptions you make.

20 Simulate traffic control at a cross-roads with traffic lights and suggest how the timing of the lights should alter with traffic flow. State clearly any assumptions you make.

21 Devise a suite of lessons for giving children exercises in the addition of two or more integer quantities.

22 Devise a lesson for testing a student's ability to factorise simple quadratic expressions (with integer roots). Generate the answers first and then formulate the questions.

23 Write a program which generates a 4-digit random integer (H) and responds to a user's attempts to guess it as follows.

    (i) for every digit in the user's guess which matches the corresponding digit in H the users scores 1 bull.

    (ii) for every digit in the users guess which does not match the corresponding digit but which matches some otherwise unmatched digit in H, the user scores 1 cow. Thus for example

H	Guess	Bulls	Cows
1234	6284	2	0
1234	4321	0	4
1234	1212	2	0

The program should stop when the user guesses H correctly.

24 Devise a control program to accommodate lessons prepared using the qu,ca,ty,etc. notation described in section 10.2.

25 The timetable for each teacher in a school is stored in a file the name of which is related to that of the teacher. Design an interactive system which will permit an interested party to discover the location of any teacher at any time of the day.

26 Implement an interactive editor for the Basic programming language. Your editor should operate in such a way that

(a) only complete lines can be altered

(b) lines are numbered in the usual fashion and the numbering implies the order of the lines

(c) renumbering of lines is permitted.

The editor should hold a Basic program as a list of lines.

27 Write a program which processes requests for seats on an aircraft. The aircraft has 40 rows of seats each of the form

          W S S A S S S S A S S W

where W=window, S=seat and A=aisle.

The first 10 rows are first class (F), the next 20 rows are ordinary class (O) and the final 10 rows are economy class (E). A request will be of the form – number of seats, class – for example 3,E or 1,F. Your program should allocate seats if possible and report the numbers of the seats allocated or report that no seats are available of the type requested.

When allocating seats your program should
    (i) attempt to seat a group of N people in the same row, preferably with no aisle intervening
   (ii) given a choice of two sets of seats to allocate, choose that which includes a window

seat.

28 Write a program which acts as an air traffic controller. In the initial dialogue the program should request the minimum distance between planes. Further input is a series of flight requests

   starting point, course, speed, time of entry

A request for entry into the controlled zone will either be granted or denied (with reasons). Attempt the program first on the assumption that all planes fly at the same height, then extend it so that the height of the plane is another item of input information.

29 A program has to be designed in such a way that it helps with spelling. It works as follows. There is a file which acts like a dictionary. When some text has to be checked all the words in the text are sorted into alphabetical order. Then each in turn is sought in the dictionary. If it is present no significant action occurs. If it is not, the programmer is asked to check that the spelling is indeed correct. If it is, the word is added to the dictionary. If not, a corrected word is requested and the new word is checked as before.
   Implement the above idea.

30 Assume the existence of a file of names and addresses of all the members of a tennis and squash club. Associated with each name is a code which is also present in the file: the code contains a set of indicators which imply an interest in tennis, membership of a tennis team, an interest in national competitions, and likewise for squash.
   Design a program which gives a manager or coach the ability to send standard letters to all members of tennis teams interested in national competitions, and so on.

31 Design a system which will give an interested party the ability to send a standard letter to all the people whose names and addresses are in some file.

32 Design a package (for use with CAL programs) that allows a user to keep records of student progress and performance.

33 Design a program which will produce the graph of a function supplied by a user. State clearly the limitations of your program.

34 Devise a lesson for testing ability to differentiate polynominals with integer coefficients.

35 Prepare a set of carefully graded exercises to testing a student's ability in integration.

36 Write a program which simulates a simple landing on the moon. At each time interval the program should report current height and speed and request a throttle setting. Estimate impact crater size.

37 Write a program which enables different users of a computer system to send mail to one another.

38 (a) Write a program which maintains an appointment diary for an unlimited time period. The program should be capable of
   (1) entering an appointment in a given time slot
   (2) removing an entry from a given time slot
   (3) enquiring about a given time slot
   (4) enquiring about appointments of a particular type.

   (b) Extend the program so that it is possible to use "templates" to identify one or more time slots. This would enable a user for example

   *to reserve Thursday evenings for volleyball until the end of March
   *to remind himself to vote on the first Tuesday in November
   *to list all appointments on June 17th.

39 Write three programs as follows:

296   GRADED PROBLEMS

(1) This reads N followed by details of N second-hand cars, for example, for each car its licence number, colour, mileage, date of manufacture, model and price. It then writes to a file CARFILE a record for each of the cars.

(2) (a) This is an interactive program which requests details of the car that the user would like to buy, for example, preferred colour, mileage range, price range, model and so on. The program reads CARFILE and outputs all details of any car which matches the user's specification.
   (b) Since reading the file is relatively slow compared with processing, modify your program to input a number of customer requests (each identified by a unique customer number) before scanning the file. Details of any car matching any of the requests should be output and tagged with the number(s) of the request(s) they satisfy.

(3) This should add/delete cars to/from CARFILE.

40 (a) Write a simple stock control program for a shop selling for example shoes or car accessories or groceries or stationery etc. Your program should maintain:
  (i) a file containing one record for each different type of item sold. This record should include:

   (1) item number
   (2) item description
   (3) quantity currently in stock
   (4) re-order level - quantity at which an order is placed
   (5) re-order quantity
   (6) supplier details
   (7) expected delivery times on reorder
   (8) flag indicating if an order is outstanding.

  (ii) a file containing one record for each outstanding order. In this file a record should include:

(1) order number (unique)
(2) item number
(3) date ordered
(4) date by which order is expected to be satisfied.

Your program should

(1) allow on-line entry of sales
(2) allow on-line receipt of goods ordered
(3) print suitable re-order forms
(4) enable interrogation of the two files, for example to find overdue orders or items completely out of stock.

(b) Extend
(1) the file structure to include information about wholesale and retail prices
(2) the program to record on a third file, sales figures for each day
(3) the program to output on request, total value of stock, total amount payable on outstanding orders.

41 Design and create files which support an interactive library query system. The following specification assumes that it is a library of books, it could be modified for a library of records or paintings, etc.

Each book has an ISBN; all copies of the same book have the same ISBN which is different from that in any copy of any other book. Assume that a particular volume may be identified by specifying an ISBN and if necessary a copy number. Assume that a borrower may be identified by name and if necessary an address.

Write a program which enables a user to perform the following operations:
   (a) enquire about the status of a book. If the book is currently on loan, the program should give the name and address of the borrower.
   (b) enquire about the books currently on loan to a specified borrower. For each book borrowed the program should print the title, author, ISBN (and copy number, if appropriate).
   (c) record the borrowing of a book by specifying

the book and the borrower.
- (d) record the return of a book by specifying the book.
- (e) record an addition to the library. The title, author, ISBN (and copy number if appropriate) are input.
- (f) record a permanent removal of a book.

42 A project to maintain a hierarchy of "pages" of information for example cinema listings, recipes, FORTRAN error messages. In addition to the text, each page should contain (a) a title and (b) pointers to its immediate successors.

   A user of the interactive access program should be able to
- (i) display the title or contents of the current page
- (ii) display a "menu" of the titles of the successor pages
- (iii) move to either the parent of the current page or a selected successor.

In addition there should be password protected facilities for adding and deleting pages.

   An extension would be the addition of a "death date" to each page and the automatic deletion of the page on that date.

43 Modify the query answering problem of exercise 40(b) in chapter nine. Rather than process a serial file of queries the program should allow a user to enter boolean expressions from a terminal.

   In response to a query the program reports the number of documents satisfying the expression, forms a set of pointers to the representations of these documents and allocates a number to the set. Set numbers may be used as operands in an expression with their natural meaning.

   For example

```
FIND A=JONES AND J=CACM
25 documents.........(1)

FIND (1) AND Y=1978
2 documents..........(2)
```

Users should be able to print, in a variety of formats, the document representations pointed to by the contents of an arbitrary set.

44 If you have visual display units (VDUs) on your computer system, write a screen editor program.

A screen editor displays on the VDU a portion of the file being edited. Changes to the displayed part of the screen should be possible using a simple set of commands. As well as updating the file the editor also updates the screen display reflecting the changes made.

It should be possible for a user to move freely backwards and forwards through the file. The display should be 'scrolled' appropriately.

45 This project is concerned with a telephone directory and its objectives are to
- (i) enable queries about the directory to be answered rapidly
- (ii) permit subscribers to redirect incoming calls to another number temporarily
- (iii) enable directory entries to be deleted
- (iv) enable new entries to be inserted
- (v) perform (i) to (iv) with a reasonable degree of security.

(a) By writing a program to generate random records or by some other means, create a file in which each record is of the form

{last name, first initial, address, telephone number}

(b) Write a program to set up appropriate index files so that queries in any of the following forms may be answered without extensive searching:

- (1) what is the name and address of the person with number X?
- (2) what is the number of the person living at address Z?
- (3) what are the names and numbers of people at address Z?

(c) Modify your answer to (b) so that it requests and verifies a password before processing any queries or updates.

(d) Modify your program further so that the additions to and deletions from the file (and appropriate indexes) can be accomplished.

(e) Modify your program so that temporary redirection of calls can be effected without altering the main file or indexes.

46 Write a program which, by
    (1) maintaining a file containing a binary tree
and
    (2) querying a user

"learns" about the characteristics of animals. The internal nodes of the tree contain characteristics, the leaf nodes contain the names of the animals. For example

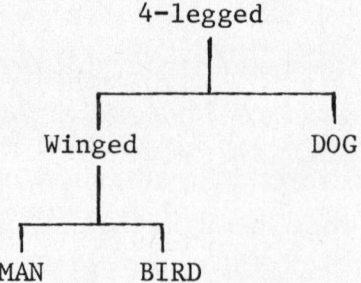

A user of the program should be able to add to its knowledge by thinking of a new animal and responding appropriately to questions posed. For example if the user thinks of SNAKE, the dialogue might run as follows (user responses underlined).
  4-legged? NO
  Winged? NO
  Is it a MAN? NO
  What is it? SNAKE
  Give me a characteristic which MAN has but SNAKE does not: 2-legged

The tree now becomes

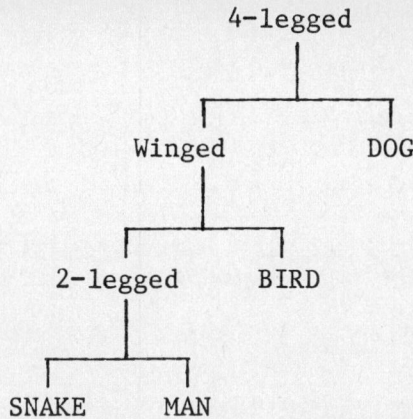

47 Given a serial file containing a dictionary of words (in no particular order) create files which enable all words fitting a given template to be retrieved as quickly as possible. Write a query program which accepts a template in the form of a string such as

    * E * A * *

and outputs the matching words, in this case those 6-letter words with second letter E and fourth letter A. The program would be useful in solving crossword puzzles.

48 Devise a suite of CAL programs for testing ability in simple algebraic manipulation, i.e. the addition, subtraction and multiplication of simple algebraic quantities such as 2x, 4x+5, 3x.

49 Prepare a desk calculator facility which allows a user to perform integer arithmetic to an arbitrary precision.

50 Devise a lesson for testing a student's knowledge of arithmetic by providing sets of arbitrary arithmetic expressions, of reasonable but increasing difficulty, to evaluate.

51 Design a simple interpreter for a programming

language such as Basic. Include in your system:

    immediate mode parsing and evaluation
    stored program mode
    LIST RUN line editing
    run-time profiling as part of your system.

52 Prepare an information management system to help with the syntactic definition of a grammar expressed in BNF notation. It should be possible for a user to ask such questions as:

    how many terminals or nonterminals are in the grammar?

    what is the syntactic rule defining a particular nonterminal?

    what terminals (or nonterminals) can follow or come before an occurrence of a particular nonterminal?

    which subset of the grammar defines, say, <expression>?

and to include facilities for arranging nonterminals alphabetically. Ideally the system should include cross-referencing information which would provide references to sections in the original formal definition.

53 Design an interactive program for playing draughts or checkers. Try to give your program as much 'intelligence' as possible - try to look ahead and determine the consequences of moves.

54 Prepare a desk calculator facility for performing real arithmetic to a specified precision. Deal only with addition, subtraction, multiplication, division and exponentiation involving reals and integers. Provide proper documentation to accompany your system.

55 Prepare a desk calculator facility which allows a

user to perform real arithmetic to an arbitrary precision. Include facilities for finding SIN, COS, TAN and SQRT, at least. Provide clear documentation to accompany your system.

56 Design a simulator for some computer of your choice. Permit a user to proceed an instruction at a time through the program and to inspect locations and view them as integers, characters, instructions, etc.

57 Design a debugging facility for use with some high-level language with which you are familiar. It should be possible to include breakpoints at which execution will be stopped and then program variables, etc. can be examined.

58 Design a context editor for Basic. The editor should permit the usual kinds of editing to be performed but there is an added restriction. By means of an edit it should not be possible to produce a syntactically illegal program.

59 Design an interactive program for playing chess with a computer. Try to make the computer seem as 'intelligent' as possible.

60 Design a set of carefully graded exercises in teaching integration by change of variables. Make sure the student is aware of any limitations of your system.

61 Write a program which attempts to determine a 4-digit number (H) thought of by a user as follows. In response to a 'guess' (G) by the program the user will input the number of 'bulls' and 'cows' scored by the guess.

   (i) 1 bull is scored for every digit in G that is the same as the corresponding digit in H. Thus when the program scores 4 bulls it has guessed the number correctly.

   (ii) 1 cow is scored for every digit in G which does not match the corresponding guess in H but which matches some otherwise unmatched digit.

Your program should check that the user responses are consistent.

62 Given a suitable grammar describing a programming language, write a program which allows a compiler writer to describe certain features that he wishes included (or not included) and then generates test programs for the compiler.

63 Keep a database of family relations and write a program which answers simple questions like "who is the aunt of", or more complicated questions like "what is the relationship between" ?

64 Show how one could design a model of, e.g. the economy of a car factory, so that a manager could make better decisions on how many of each model to make, whether to commission market surveys, hire or fire, and so on. The program should produce sales figures and take into account economic measures such as interest rates.

65 A game called 'closing the curve' is played between two players called A and B using a rectangular grid of dots of any size.
   The players make alternate moves. Player A moves by drawing a solid vertical or horizontal line between two adjacent dots on the grid. Player B then moves by drawing dotted vertical or horizontal lines between adjacent points. Once two adjacent points are linked, they may not be reconnected in any subsequent move.
   Player A wins if he can form a completely closed curve. Player B always goes second and he wins if he can prevent player A from winning.
   Write a program which takes the role of player B and always wins.

References and suggestions for further reading

Aho, A.V., Hopcroft, J.E. and Ullman, J.D. 1983. 'Data Structures and Algorithms'. Reading, Mass: Addison-Wesley.

Aho, A.V. and Ullman, J.D. 1977. 'Principles of Compiler Design'. Reading, Mass: Addison-Wesley.

Alagic, S. and Arbib, M.A. 1978. 'The Design of Well-Structured and Correct Programs'. New York: Springer-Verlag.

Anderson, T. and Lee, P.A. 1981. 'Fault Tolerance: Principles and Practice'. Englewood Cliffs, New Jersey: Prentice-Hall.

Anderson, T. and Randell, B. (Editors) 1979. 'Computing Systems Reliability'. Cambridge, England: Cambridge University Press.

Barnes, J.G.P. 1981. 'Programming in Ada'. London: Addison-Wesley.

Bradley, J. 1982. 'File and Data Base Techniques'. Eastbourne: Holt, Rinehart and Winston.

Brown, P.J. (Editor) 1979. 'Software Portability'. Cambridge, England: Cambridge University Press.

Calingaert, P. 1982. 'Operating System Elements: A User Perspective'. Englewood Cliffs, New Jersey: Prentice-Hall.

Dahl, O.J., Dijkstra, E.W. and Hoare, C.A.R. 1975. 'Structured Programming'. London: Academic Press.

Date, C.J. 1981. 'An Introduction to Database Systems', 3rd edition. Reading, Mass: Addison-Wesley.

De Bono, E. 1968. 'New Think: The Use of Lateral Thinking in the Generation of New Ideas'. New-York: Basic Books.

Denning, D.E. 1982. 'Cryptography and Data Security'. Reading, Mass: Addison-Wesley.

Dijkstra, E.W. 1976. 'A Discipline of Programming'. Englewood Cliffs, New Jersey: Prentice-Hall.

Foley, J.D. and van Dam, A. 1982. 'Fundamentals of Interactive Computer Graphics'. Reading, Mass: Addison-Wesley.

Gries, D. 1981. 'The Science of Programming'. New York: Springer Verlag.
Hunter, R.B. 1981. 'The Design and Construction of Compilers'. London: John Wiley & Sons.
Jackson, M.A. 1975. 'Principles of Program Design'. London: Academic Press.
Jones, C.B. 1980. 'Software Development: A Rigorous Approach'. Englewood Cliffs, New Jersey: Prentice-Hall.
Kernighan, B.W. and Plauger, P.J. 1976. 'Software Tools'. Reading, Mass: Addison-Wesley.
Kernighan, B.W. and Plauger, P.J. 1978. 'The Elements of Programming Style', 2nd edition. New York: McGraw-Hill.
Knuth, D.E. 1974. 'The Art of Computer Programming: Vol 1, Fundamental Algorithms', 2nd edition. Reading, Mass: Addison-Wesley.
Knuth, D.E. 1981. 'The Art of Computer Programming: Vol 2, Seminumerical Algorithms', 2nd edition. Reading, Mass: Addison-Wesley.
Knuth, D.E. 1973. 'The Art of Computer Programming: Vol 3, Sorting and Searching'. Reading, Mass: Addison-Wesley.
Lewis, P.M., Rosenkrantz, D.J. and Stearns, R.E. 1976. 'Compiler Design Theory'. Reading, Mass: Addison-Wesley.
Lister, A.M. 1979. 'Fundamentals of Operating Systems', 2nd edition. London: Macmillan.
McGettrick, A.D. 1982. 'Program Verification using Ada'. Cambridge, England: Cambridge University Press.
Martin, J. 1977. 'Computer Data-Base Organization', 2nd edition. Englewood Cliffs, New Jersey: Prentice-Hall.
Maryanski, F.J. 1980. 'Digital Computer Simulation'. London: Hayden Press.
Newman, W. and Sproull, R. 1979. 'Principles of Interactive Computer Graphics', 2nd edition. New York: McGraw-Hill.
Polya, G. 1971. 'How to Solve It'. Princeton, New York: Princeton University Press.
Rohl, J.S. 1975. 'An Introduction to Compiler Writing'. Amsterdam: Elsevier (Computer Monograph Series, number 22).

Rohl, J.S. and Barrett, H.J. 1980. 'Programming via Pascal'. Cambridge, England: Cambridge University Press.

Sommerville, I. 1982. 'Software Engineering'. London: Addison-Wesley.

Standish, T.A. 1980. 'Data Structure Techniques'. Reading, Mass: Addison-Wesley.

Warnier, J.D. 1974. 'Logical Construction of Programs'. Ontario: Van Nostrand Reinhold.

Wetherell, C. 1978. 'Etudes for Programmers'. Englewood Cliffs, New Jersey: Prentice-Hall.

Wirth, N. 1973. 'Systematic Programming: an Introduction'. Englewood Cliffs, New Jersey: Prentice-Hall.

Wirth, N. 1976. 'Algorithms + Data Structures = Programs'. Englewood Cliffs, New Jersey: Prentice-Hall.

Index

absolute value, 16
abstract data type design, 196-200
abstraction, 3, 77, 115, 162, 170
Ackermann's function, 91, 183, 198
actual parameter, 75, 76, 79, 80
adjacency matrix, 116
air traffic control, 20, 21, 24, 56, 292
airline reservations, 176, 293
algebraic manipulation, 301
amicable numbers, 93
animals, 300
arbitrary magnitude, 196, 204, 301-2
Aristosthenes, 132
arithmetic lesson, 281-4, 292
array declaration, 96
array index, 96
array initialisation, 97
array subscript, 96
array,
   jagged, 117
   ordered, 101
   space requirements, 95
   when to use, 95
arrays and iteration, 98
assembly code translation, 191
average, 30, 244

B-trees, 258
backtracking, 212-15, 219, 224
Backus-Naur-Form (see BNF), 216
bag, 200
balanced string, 125, 159, 226
balancing, 85, 239
bank account, 253, 280
bank statement, 263, 265
bar chart, 157

base transformation, 52, 71
Basic, 27, 96, 231, 232, 302, 303
bill calculation, 19-22, 31
binary chop search, 111, 134, 209, 210, 226, 254, 258
binary tree, 175, 184
bingo, 141
bit pattern, 201
block exchange, 156
block printing, 89
BNF, 216, 217, 225, 229-31, 234
book records, 261
book sales, 266
boolean expression, 15
bottom-up approach, 88
bracket checking, 41, 125, 178, 201
bridge, 133, 142
bulls and cows, 292, 303
buzz-phrase, 182

calendar, 37, 62, 138, 202
cancelling fractions, 63
card dealing, 142
card shuffling, 133
card trickery, 120
case statement, 17, 18
census, 123, 164
change maker, 12
character testing, 38, 78
Chebyshev polynomials, 157
checkers, 302
   one-dimensional, 229, 236
cheque processing, 48, 150-2
chess, 212-15, 228, 229, 234, 235, 277, 303
clock display, 152
clock patience, 144
closing the curve, 304
clue selection, 274
coincident birthdays, 38

concordance, 185
combinations, 49, 205
comma-free code, 230
compiler, 215, 218
complex number, 166, 196
component, 162
computer dating, 270
concordance, 185
conjunctive normal form, 188
constant, 1, 5, 190, 191
continued fraction, 205
control constant, 31
control program, 281, 293
control variable, 32
cribbage, 140
cricket scores, 58
cross reference program, 205, 206
crossword puzzle, 265, 274, 277, 301
cube root, 50
cummulative sum, 48
currency exchange, 146
curve of pursuit, 289
cyclic decimal, 138

dartboard, 91
data count, 29
data format, 7
data terminator, 39
date-time conversion, 203
day-date calculation, 12, 23, 24, 37, 90
debugger, 303
declaration, 2
density plot, 59
design methodology, 245
designer-user comparison, 73, 199
desk calculator, 289, 291, 301, 302
determinant of a matrix, 146, 238
dialogue, 281
diary, 295
dictionary, 255, 256, 271, 301
  bilingual, 185
differentiation, 295
Diophantine equation, 48, 239
direct access file,

properties, 255
directory file, 242, 247, 257, 270
disjunctive normal form, 188
distance calculation, 13
distance enquiry, 289
divide-and-conquer, 84-6, 208-12, 239
divisibility test, 61
document retrieval, 247, 257, 276, 299
dominance, 208-11, 227
dominoes, 288
draughts, 302
  one-dimensional, 229, 236
driver program, 87
driver record, 265
Dultea, Jacques, 181

e approximation, 205
Easter Day, 23
editor, 138
  Basic, 293, 303
  screen, 299
eight queens problem, 212-15
eight rooks problem, 228
elimination, 132, 178
encryption/decryption, 49, 121, 263
end-of-file detection, 243
environment, 189, 197, 198
equation solving, 13, 21, 22, 28, 40, 48, 54, 70, 145, 150, 160, 239
error analysis, 283
error file, 254
escape character, 138, 225
Eudoxus' numbers, 50
examination score, 21, 50, 55, 117, 121, 245, 251, 262
examination timetable, 186
execution profile, 231, 302
exponential evaluation, 88, 227
expression evaluation, 23, 187, 289, 301
expression generation, 238
expression simplification, 228
external sorting, 251, 270, 271

extra-sensory perception, 158
factorial, 31, 62, 76, 78, 202
factorisation, 68, 231, 292
family relationships, 304
Fibonacci number, 40, 41, 50,
    55, 57, 78, 84, 89, 132
field, 162
fifteen-puzzle, 240
file amendment, 243
file copy, 245
file difference, 275
file enquiries, 290
file format check, 250
file of questions, 281
file organisations, 242
file pointer, 243, 252
file rewinding, 243
file searching, 224, 225
file update, 177, 252-4, 270
file, properties of, 242
finite precision number, 43
fixture list, 154
flight simulation, 290
formal parameter, 75
formatter, 150, 204, 275, 289
forward differences, 143
fraction expansion, 89, 179
frequencies of ranges, 103, 104
frequency distribution, 102, 145
fuel consumption, 8

games, 279, 287, 288
Gaussian integer, 201, 205
Gaussian prime, 205
generic module/package, 200, 201
Goldbach's conjecture, 55
golf scores, 149
grade report, 268
grammar checking, 228, 229
grammar cleaning, 228, 233
grammar display, 234
grammar enquiries, 302
grammar transformation, 231
graph, 114-17, 175, 287, 295
    paths through, 116
    weighted, 115, 116
graph isomorphism, 237

graph plotting, 60
gravity, 10
Gray code, 154
guarded command, 17

Hamming distance, 154
harvest, 11
hashing, 254, 255
helicopter flights, 290
hexagons, 136
highest common factor, 46, 84, 89, 184, 192
histogram, 118, 122
hotel reservation, 157
Huffman codes, 185

ice skating, 50
identifier, 1
    choice of, 2
if..then, 15
if.. then..otherwise, 16
illumination, 59
incidence matrix, 116
index, 96, 252, 258-61, 273
index generation, 182, 184
induction, 31
information retrieval, 261, 298
input/output, 1, 2
insipid integers, 126
integration, 13, 66, 69, 92, 295, 303
interchange, 81
interface, 208
interface design, 279
interpolation search, 134
interpreter, 301
ISBN, 266
island area, 238
iteration, 29

Jackson notation, 246-50
Jackson, Michael, 245
join, 272

key, 252, 255, 258
    non-unique, 259
    primary, 252, 255, 258
knight moves, 235
knight's tour, 145, 228

KWIC index, 184

lambda expression, 230
language generation, 238, 241
language lesson, 283, 284, 291
large print, 128
latin square, 129
league table, 176, 268
learning program, 300
least common multiple, 53, 58, 84, 89, 184
least squares fit, 53
left recursion, 220, 221
lesson,
 arithmetic, 281-4, 292
 individual, 281
 language, 281, 284, 291
letter generation, 294
letter preparation, 291
lexical analyser, 218
libraries of routines, 189, 191-201, 230
library queries, 297
life game, 160
limits to precision, 43
linear regression, 53
linked storage, 168-175
LISP, 227
list, 168-74
 circular, 172
 compared to array, 169, 170
 deletion from, 171
 doubly-linked, 173, 174
 insertion into, 170
 loops in, 174, 183
 recursive aspects, 171
list flattening, 183
list of lists, 173
list processing primitive, 171, 172, 178, 179, 183
loan repayment, 10
log analysis, 274
logarithmic search, 111, 134, 209, 210, 226, 254, 258
logical expression, 15, 187
look-ahead, 287
loop body, 27
loop counter, 32
loop index, 32
loop termination, 42, 43

lowest common multiple, 53, 58, 84, 89
Lucas test, 180
lucky numbers, 147
lunar lander, 295

machine characteristics, 191
machine independence, 6
macroprocessor, 272
magic square, 129
magnetic tape, 11
mail, 295
man-machine interface, 279
map making, 118, 155
Mastermind, 292, 303
mate-in-N problem, 237
matrix determinant, 146, 238
matrix manipulation, 123, 129, 166, 196
matrix, sparse, 204
maximum, 13, 17, 29, 100, 211, 227
maze solving, 235
measurement conversion, 8, 9, 11, 37, 78, 81, 192
measurement manipulation, 167
median calculation, 146
meeting scheduling, 182
memo function, 178, 179, 183, 202
memory dump, 137
menu, 280
mergesort, 112
merging, 111, 251, 257, 270
Mersenne primes, 180
minimum (see also maximum), 100
Mobius function, 94
model, economic, 304
modelling, 284, 285
module bond, 195
module design, 190
modules, separation of, 195
money breakdown, 124
moon landing, 295
move analysis, 287
moving average, 123
multi-length arithmetic, 179, 180
multinomial coefficients, 120

312 INDEX

multiple-choice test, 273
multiplication decode, 61, 65

N queens problem, 234
nested loop, 44, 45, 114
nested multiplication, 35, 36
nonterminal symbol, 216, 226
noughts and crosses, 288
number conversion, 107, 125, 134, 144
number guessing, 288
number printing/writing, 82, 85, 86, 153, 154
number properties, 180
number reading, 80, 82
number spiral, 14, 65

one-armed bandit, 22
operators, user-defined, 165

palindrome, 101, 121
parameter checking, 75, 76
parameter type, 75
parameter,
   actual, 75, 76, 79, 80
   formal, 75
partition, 86, 92, 110, 215, 226
Pascal's triangle, 60
pattern description, 222-3
pattern matching, 139, 221-5, 301
pattern representation, 224
paving, 239
payroll, 264
pension, 20
people matching, 270
perfect number, 54
permutation, 53, 136, 146, 148, 149, 205, 215
personnel file, 168, 175, 262, 266, 294
phrase finding, 257
pi approximation, 58, 181, 205
plane geometry, 12, 20, 23-5, 136, 137, 155, 156, 167, 175
pointer, 168-75, 252, 259
   null, 169, 172
poker, 133, 150

polynomial manipulation, 13, 184, 204-206
polynomial root, 289
portability, 6
postal order, 21
powers, 88, 227
precision, 43, 196, 204, 301-2
preprocessing, 218
primary key, 252, 255, 258
prime factor, 89, 91
prime number, 34, 35, 41, 51, 55, 56, 60, 61, 132, 180, 192, 205, 245
primitive operation, 246-50, 256
principal and interest, 9
problem decomposition, 87
problem description, 6
problem specification, 6-7
procedure characteristics, 79
procedure generality, 81
program analysis, 230
program decommenting, 138
program formatter, 232
program generation, 229, 233, 304
program output, 5
program portability, 6
program resequencing, 265
program specification, 6, 7
program structure, 208, 248
program testing, 7, 85
program-data relationship, 95, 171, 210, 218, 248
programming contest, 139
project allocation, 235
projection, 272
proofs of correctness, 8
pseudo-random numbers, 57, 203, 204
pursuit curve, 289
Pythagorean triangle, 59

queen attack, 229
question and answer file, 281
queue, 200
queue simulation, 287
quicksort, 110

race horses, 273

INDEX 313

railway lines, 149
rainfall, 59
random numbers, 57, 144, 203, 204, 282, 287, 288
range frequencies, 103, 104, 118
range of variable, 4, 77
rank, 208-11, 227
rank correlation, 130
rational number, 8, 51, 163, 166, 192-5, 205
recogniser, 215, 217, 218, 221, 231
recogniser generation, 231
record(s),
  characteristics, 162
  compared to array, 163
  component access, 163
  components of, 162
  fields of, 162
  variant, 166-8
  linked, 168-75
recursion, 82-9, 184, 207, 210
  inefficiencies, 83
recursive descent, 215-21
relational database, 271
reliability, 280
report generation, 65, 262, 270
resistors, 56
result of function, 75
reverse Polish, 182, 187
Rhine test, 158
river crossing, 235
river detection, 238
roman numeral, 69
root of function, 52, 289
roulette simulation, 291
route finding, 232, 276
Rubic cube, 241
rumour spreading, 286

s-expression, 227
sale prices, 31
screen editor, 299
search, self-organising, 134
sentence symbol, 216
sequence production, 252
serial accessing, 243-5
series summation, 33, 34, 43-5, 48, 52, 59
set, 200
set generation, 142, 188
set operation, 132, 135, 179
side-effects, 198
sieve of Aristosthenes, 132
sign insertion, 148
sign of number, 18
simulation, 64, 67, 68, 71, 93, 130, 279, 284-7, 292, 303, 304
simulation of computer, 206, 286, 303
simulation of population, 285-7
snakes and ladders, 147, 288
sorting, 108-13, 123, 130, 131, 251
sorting by interchanging, 108
sorting by merging, 112
sorting,
  bubble, 109, 110
  linear selection, 109
sparse matrix, 204
specification, 6, 7, 77, 79, 199
speedometer calibration, 63
spelling aid, 294
spelling checker, 267, 271, 294
spirals, 14, 65
square root, 39, 47, 50, 181
squares, 51, 71
stable pairings, 159
stack, 196-9
STAIRS, 247, 258
stamp selection, 233, 240
standard deviation, 66, 269
standard environment, 189
standard function, 2, 73
  characteristics of, 74-5
standard representation, 194
stepwise refinement, 86, 87, 207, 208
stock control, 296
straight line fitting, 53
string editing, 107
string generation, 227
string manipulation, 203
string ordering, 107

314 INDEX

string processing, 105-7, 125, 128, 170, 221-4
string, well-formed, 153
strings as arrays, 105

structure (see also record), 162
student grades, 268, 269
student records, 185, 270
subsets, 130
surveying, 161
syntactic category, 216, 217

table search, 124, 132, 134
tabulation, 46, 47, 53, 55, 61-4, 70
tape library, 269
tax checking, 268
tax computation, 9, 37, 124
telephone directory, 164, 299
telephone numbers, 119
ten-pin bowling, 127
terminal, 279
terminal symbol, 216, 219, 225
test data, 7, 19
testing, 6-8, 19, 77, 85
text compression, 41, 156
text expansion, 56
text formatting, 150, 204, 279, 289
text generation, 145
text processing, 38, 52, 55, 64, 66, 89, 121, 123, 125, 137
tic-tac-toe, 288
time, 166
time difference, 164
timetable enquiry, 51, 276, 280, 293
timetable of examinations, 186
top-down approach, 87
topic independence, 281
towers of Hanoi, 90, 92
traffic simulation, 290, 292

travelling salesman, 231
tree, 174, 175, 187, 210
tree drawing, 187
tree sort, 184
trigonometric function, 191, 192, 202, 206
trigraph, 267
trimming, 124
twin primes, 51, 65
two-dimensional array, 113-17, 130
type conversion, 193
type, user-defined, 164-6, 192-5
typographical error, 267

union, 166-8
user-defined operator, 165, 166, 193, 194
user-defined type, 165, 193
user-designer comparison, 73, 199

validation, 19, 262
variable, 1
variable type, 2, 4
  choice of, 3
variance, 32, 269
variant record, 166-8
vector, 202
vehicle enquiries, 296
vehicle records, 263, 265, 296
visibility, 197, 207, 210
voltage measurements, 118

wallpapering, 10
well-formed string, 153
while loop, 38
windowing, 25
wine cellar, 159
word finding, 257
word stem, 261

Zeller's congruence, 12

K